Resistance, Freedom and Empowerment

About the Author

Gennet Zewide is a Ph.D. from School of International Studies, Jawaharlal Nehru University, New Delhi (India). She has teaching experience of about two decades with Addis Ababa University in the Faculty of Education. She is at present Ambassador Extraordinary and Plenipotentiary of the Federal Democratic Republic of Ethiopia in India. A Member of the Ethiopian People's Revolutionary Democratic Front and twice Member of Parliament, she has been responsible for formulation and implementation of the education policy in her country. Among other important assignments she has been Chairperson of the Forum for African Women Educationists (FAWE). She was a Member of UNESCO Executive Board and also a Member of the Board of Capacity Building Institute for Africa of UNESCO both for two terms.

Resistance, Freedom and Empowerment

The Ethiopian Women's Struggle

Gennet Zewide

CONCEPT PUBLISHING COMPANY PVT. LTD.
NEW DELHI-110059

ISBN-13: 978-93-5125-028-9

First Published 2014

Published and Printed by

Concept
Since 1974

Concept Publishing Company Pvt. Ltd.
A/15-16, Commercial Block, Mohan Garden
New Delhi-110059 (India)
T: 25351460, 25351794, *F*: 091-11-25357109
E: publishing@conceptpub.com, W: www.conceptpub.com
Editorial Office: H-13, Bali Nagar, New Delhi-110 015, India.

Cataloging in Publication Data--*Courtesy:* D.K. Agencies (P) Ltd. <docinfo@dkagencies.com>

Gennet Zewide.

Resistance, freedom and empowerment : the Ethiopian women's struggle / Gennet Zewide.

p. cm.

Includes bibliographical references (p.) and index.

ISBN 9789351250289

1. Women--Political activity--Ethiopia. 2. Women--Ethiopia--Social conditions. 3. Women in development--Ethiopia. 4. Women in development--Government policy--Ethiopia. I. Title.

DDC 305.420963 23

DEDICATION

Without the prolonged struggle and sacrifice of women and men for democracy, and development, the present Ethiopia where the equality of women and men is legally acknowledged would not have been possible. Thus this book is dedicated:

To our patriotic mothers and grandmothers who have fought in different ways to keep foreign aggressors at bay; to Emma Senedus of the time who paved the way for women's public participation; to those mothers who courageously stood the agonizing sufferings inflicted on them and their children during the red terror; to the Martas and Tariques, who lost their lives heroically in the armed struggle; to Azebs and Nigests, who were brutally tortured, languished in prison and lost their lives during the red terror; to Amans and Hakkis who grew in prison born of imprisoned mothers; to the children of prisoners who grew up deprived of the love and affection of their mothers at their tender ages; to the democratic men and the present generation who should draw to close the unfinished struggle of women's equality and empowerment.

Foreword

Gennet Zewide has written a remarkable book. I say so for many reasons. This book gives a synoptic yet wide and painstakingly accurate view of Ethiopian women's movement for freedom and empowerment. It locates this struggle in the historical moments of relevance to Ethiopia. It frames all the issues within the structures of patriarchy that envelope an almost universal structure for women worldwide. It relates the specificities of women in traditional African and especially Ethiopian traditions. Gennet is brutally frank about the social, economic and gender biased conditions that women faced within these structures. She examines the roots of violence against women that are manifest in the brutality of practices like female genital mutilation as well as the use of force in everyday relations. Gennet contextualizes her text in the framework of feminist understanding and braids this with a very clear understanding of Ethiopian the state.

I believe the sections of this book that deal with the oppressive Derg Regime and the resistance against it, especially the underground revolutionary women's movement are particularly valuable as they record the voices of many women like Nigist Teffera, Azeb Girma and others whose memories should not be lost. Gennet's own involvement, her experience of jails, and the resistance is not only moving but a record for the younger generations of Ethiopians, Africans and women because it gives a first hand account of how women struggled for the cause of their gender, their rights, their nation holistically. This book is thus an important primary document for those who want to understand women's multiple roles and their relation to liberation movements as well as with the state and society.

Gennet deals with great expertise on the issue of women's empowerment and what it means. She links the local with the international in a dialectical way, to show how women intersect the local, regional, national and international and how women need to collectively deconstruct patriarchal structures at all these multiple levels.

Gennet's book is also one of hope, as her own work, success and never ending endeavors show. Gennet's book shows that women's freedom and women's empowerment can only come with women's resistance. Resistance not only against patriarchy but all forms of exclusisons and discriminations. The Title of Gennet's book is her message. I also believe this book is also an embodiment of her own life – that struggle and change is the essence of life. All in all, this is both a foundational book as well as an inspirational one.

Professor Anuradha M. Chenoy
School of International Studies
Jawaharlal Nehru University

Preface

As is the case in many underdeveloped countries, the majority of women in Ethiopia are the poorest of the poor. Though many studies and experiences have indicated that it is important to make women participate in the political process and economic endeavours of countries, Ethiopian women were denied such opportunities.

The subordinate position of women in every aspect of their private and public lives was the results of repressive government policies and a patriarchal ideology which governs the relationship of the sexes. Patriarchy as an ideology propagates division of labour by gender and ascribes behavioural norms associated with males and females in a given social group.

Government institutions sanctioned the subordinate role of women through laws that relegate women to the power of men. For instance the 1960 Civil Code of Ethiopia dictates that a husband is the head of the family and a wife needs the permission of her husband to decide her domicile, and change jobs; moreover a women needs a man to represent her in any legal matters. Tradition as reflected in the family lives, the popular medium of poems, songs, and the media depicted women as feeble minded and weak whose usefulness does not transcend beyond the household. Often times when people are confronted about women's place in society, they resort to the common saying that "Women are our mothers, sisters … so, we don't hurt them". The fact that women are human beings whose rights should be respected regardless of their relation to others is mostly unrecognized. Even worse, the capability of women in contributing to society in the production process in addition to their "natural" roles of motherhood is seldom accepted. Thus, women in Ethiopia lacked opportunities, status and dignity which limited their meaningful participation in the social, economic and political process of the country.

However, Ethiopian women have challenged the ideological basis of patriarchy and have struggled for their rightful place in society. Women stood up and fought against colonialism, national oppression and undemocratic rule. During the February Uprising of the Ethiopian people against the Monarchy, thousands of women from all walks of life both in urban and rural areas joined the movements demanding "land to the tiller", "equal pay for equal work" "paid maternity leave" "women's and religious equalities". Women factory workers, students, teachers and Moslem women, took to the streets demanding their rights. Similarly, women waged relentless resistance and struggle against the Military Dictatorship using both peaceful and armed struggles. During the armed struggle that took about 17 years, women organized themselves and took up arms to fight for gender equality along with the struggle for democracy, peace and prosperity of the Ethiopian people; and in the process, they developed self-esteem and self-confidence that enabled them to challenge the patriarchal ideology.

As a result of the relentless struggle of the Ethiopian people for democracy, equality and prosperity in which women participated, political power was transferred from the military dictatorship to a democratic government. Since 1995, Ethiopian women have gained constitutional rights to own property, have access to social services as well as entitlement of affirmative action to redress the historical legacy of inequality and discrimination suffered by them. The harmful customs, laws and practices that oppress women are rendered unconstitutional. However, the negative values and practices of patriarchy that are prevalent in the minds of men and women continue to be the stumbling blocks that affect the equality of women.

This is a book based mainly on reflections of how women of my generation lived, resisted, fought and to a certain extent contributed to the struggle that changed the condition of women in Ethiopia today. In writing this book, pertinent policy and strategy documents and primary data of the Government of Ethiopia on issues relevant to women has been reviewed. I have also used the information that has been gathered from a small number of female graduate students and graduate programme and gender unit coordinators of Addis Ababa University through focus group discussions and interviews. Furthermore, women who were in prison, those who participated in the various forms of struggle including in the armed ones has also been interviewed. The book discusses how women have struggled beyond survival to change the statutes and in the process they have been humiliated, impriosned, tortured, and summarily executed. Of course in these struggles, women joined hands with men who like them were determined to bring about a democratic order where women and men attain their true equality. Being neither a gender expert nor a historian, this book is not based on a theoretical analysis of history and gender rather mostly on my reflections.

The book is organized in four parts with three to four chapters each.

Part I, introduces the reader to Ethiopia, its people, culture and society. The place of women in Ethiopian society is discussed along with the global situation of women, their achievement and challenges.

Part II discusses the participation of Ethiopian women in the resistance war against the brief occupation by Italy and their involvement in the Ethiopian student movements of the 60s and early 70s. Women's Underground Struggle against the Military dictatorship and their sufferings in prisons are discussed illustrated by the stories of the women who participated in the struggle. The heroic deeds of women in the armed struggle and the sacrifices they made for human and democratic rights as well as the prosperity of the Ethiopian people is recounted along with the implications of the struggle to the empowerment of women.

Part III, the entitlement of Ethiopian women as expressed in the Constitution and their legal rights and the role of the Ethiopian government in empowering women and safeguarding their citizenship rights is dealt with here.

In Part IV, the participation of women in social, economic and political arenas as well as in the household is elaborated. The opportunities and challenges of the Ethiopian women under the new Federal Democratic Ethiopia, their efforts to access social services and participate in the political and economic activities of the country is discussed at length. A chapter is also added to show how the unchanged roles of women in the household affect their public lives. Finally a few suggestions are included for the younger generation of women so that they may complete the unfinished business of Ethiopian women's empowerment.

It is my privilege to contribute all the proceeds from this book to The Ethiopian Women's Federation.

Acknowledgements

In the process of writing this book many colleagues, friends and family members, have contributed to its finalization through providing comments, suggestions as well as collecting documents and books pertinent to the subject. Some also shared their experiences and information which they have acquired while working with women in one way or another. In this regard, I would, particularly like to express my gratitude to Mrs. Zenebu Taddesse, Minister of Women and Youth; Dr. Kesete Birhane, Minister of Health; Honourable Mrs. Roman Gebreselassie, Minister of State and the Whip of TPLF in the House of Representatives, Mrs. Shitaye Minale, Deputy Speaker of the House of Representatives, Honourable Mrs. Moferiate Kamile to Haile Melekote Mewale; and Miss Taitu Ali. My gratitude also goes to Ato Sebsebe Kebede, General Manager of Ethiopian Press for granting me permission to use the archives of the press; Ato Dagne Abera, Press Photographer, Mrs. Felekech Agaffare and Mrs. Workenesh Bechu of the Document Department of the Press who helped me secure important photographs and news paper clippings that I used in the book.

Many thanks also go to H.E. Teffera Walewa, former Minister of Capacity Building, Dr. Gudaye Immeru, Assistant Dean of The Graduate Programme of Addis Abeba University, Dr. Tekaglege Wolde Mariam of the History Department of Addis Abeba University, Honourable Dr. Adhana Haile, member of the Ethiopian Peoples Council for spending their precious time to read the manuscript and give me valuable comments and suggestions towards bettering the content of the book.

I had the privilege of having conversation with family members and friends of those I referred to in the book: thus, my appreciation goes to all of them including but not only, to Dr. Sammuel Assefa and Miss Yewebedar Yilma, Dr. Mekuria Teffera, Mrs. Nahu Senaye Girma and Ato Anteneh Girma.

Some of the materials used in the paper are collected through focus group discussion and interviews with the graduate female students of Addis Abeba University while I was doing my Ph.D. dissertation on Empowerment of Women through Ethiopia's New Education Policy, I, therefore, would like to thank those who participated in the study.

My sincere gratitude goes to Professor Anuradha M. Chenoy, of JNU who went through the whole manuscript, gave me suggestions and wrote the Foreword.

I am also grateful to both Mrs. Uma Wadhwa and Mr. Gagan Malhotra of the Ethiopian Embassy in India, who gave me their unreserved assistance when I was preparing the manuscript.

I owe a debt of gratitude to my two daughters Mefthe and Teyent Tadesse who gave me their unconditional love and understanding though I could not give them adequate time and attention that they deserved due to the circumstances surrounding my life. If it were not for their continuous encouragement in all my works, this book would not have been completed.

Contents

List of Tables

List of Graphs

List of Acronyms

AAU	Addis Ababa University
ADLI	Agricultural Development Led Industrialization
ANDM	Amhara National Democratic Movement
CBSP	Capacity Building Sector Program
CEDAW	Convention on the Elimination of All forms of Discrimination Against Women
CERTWD	Center for Research Training and Information for Women Development
CSO	Central Statistics Office
EC	European Commission
EC	Ethiopian Calendar
ELF	Eriterian Liberation Front
EPDM	Ethiopian People's Democratic Movement
EPLF	Eritrean People's Liberatoin Front
EPRDF	Ethiopian People's Revolutionary Democratic Front
EPRP	Ethiopian Peoples' Revolutionary Party
EMIS	Educational Management Information System
ESDP	Education Sector Development Program
ESDPRP	Ethiopian Sustainable Development and Poverty Reduction Program
ESM	Ethiopian Students Movement
ESUE	Ethiopian Students Union of Europe
ESUNA	Ethiopian Students Union of North America
EWCC	Ethiopian Women Coordinating Committee
ETPS	Education and Training Policy and Strategy
EWVSA	Ethiopian Women Volunteers Service Association
EWWA	Ethiopian Women's Welfare Association

FDRE	Federal Democratic Republic of Ethiopia
FGM	Female Genital Mutilation
GFR	Gross Enrollment Ratio
GWESA	Gender and Work in East and South Africa
HSIU	Haile Sellasie I, University
ICT	Information and Communication Technology
MoE	Ministry of Education
MOFED	Ministry of Finance and Economic Development
MoWA	Ministry of Womens' Affairs
NCTPE	National Committee for Traditional Practices in Ethiopia
NETP	New Education and Training Policy
NGO	Non Governmental Organization
NER	Net Enrollment Ratio
NEPAD	New Partnership for African Development
OLF	Oromo Liberation Front
OPDO	Oromo People's Democratic Organization
PASDEP	Plan for Accelerated and Sustained Development to End Poverty
PDRE	Peoples' Democratic Republic of Ethiopia
PRSP	Poverty Eradication Strategy Program
PSR	People Section Ratio
PTR	People Teacher Ratio
REWA	Revolutionary Ethiopian Women's Association
SADC	Southern African Development Community
SSA	Sub-Saharna Africa
TPLF	Tigraye Peoples' Liberation Front
TTI	Teacher Training Institute
TVET	Technical Vocational Education and Training
UCAA	University College of Addis Ababa
UNESCO	United Nations Educational, Scientific and Cultural Organization
UNICEF	United Nations International Children's Emergency Fund
UN	United Nations
UNHR	Universal Declaration of Human Rights
USAID	United States Agency for International Development
USUAA	University Students Union of Addis Ababa
WPE	Workers Party of Ethiopia
WHO	World Health Organization

Part One

There are three chapters in Part One that briefly introduce the readers to the Ethiopian people, the society in general and the place of women within the society in particular. The situation of women globally, their struggles, achievements and challenges are also introduced in this unit.

CHAPTER I

The Background

Economic, Social, Political and Cultural Settings of Ethiopia

Ethiopia is a country situated in the Horn of Africa, at the crossroads of the Middle East and Africa. It borders Djibouti in the East, Eritrea in the North, the two Sudans in the West and North West, Kenya in the South and Somalia in the South East. The population of Ethiopia is about 82 million. The country has a land mass of 1.1 million sq.km. It was during the reign of Emperor Menelik II (1889-1913) that the country attained its present configuration through a process of military expansion.

Ethiopia is home to a mosaic of nations, nationalities and peoples whose population sizes vary from more than 18 million to less than 100. There are over 80 different ethnic groups, each with its own language, culture and traditions. According to the 2007 Census, the country is among the least urbanized in the world with 83.6 per cent living in rural areas. The largest city in the country is Addis Ababa, the capital, with 2.7 million people accounting for nearly 4 per cent of the total population. The average size of a household is 4.7.

The country is the origin of some of the earliest hominid populations where *Homo erectus* evolved and expanded out of Africa. The most notable pale anthropological find in the country was "Lucy" a female *Australopithecus aphaeresis* discovered in 1974 and referred to as *Dinqnesh* (you are marvelous) by Ethiopians. The country is also one of the oldest civilizations in the world with a rich diversity of people and cultures which includes the unique letters of the alphabet that has existed for about 3,000 years.

In March 1896, Italian troops attempted to enter Ethiopia forcibly and were defeated by Emperor Menelik II and his army at the battle of Adwa. The battle of Adwa was the only victory of an African army over a European army that has not been reversed during the partitioning of Africa. Ethiopia is the only African country never to have been colonized, although the Italians briefly occupied the country from 1936 to 1941. The independence that emerged from that battle has contributed greatly to the Ethiopian sense of nationalistic pride in self-rule, and many perceive Adwa as a victory for all of Africa.

Ethiopia became one of the two African countries to be a member of the League of Nations back in 1923 and subsequently became member of the United Nations. The country is also the seat of the Organization of African Unity, which is now evolved into the African Union.

For almost sixteen hundred years, the nation was ruled by a monarchy with close ties to the Orthodox Church. Emperor Haile Selassie, the last monarch ruled from 1930 to 1974 and was overthrown by a military junta known as the Derg. Ethiopia then became a totalitarian state in between. In 1991, the Derg was overthrown by the Ethiopian People's Democratic Front (EPRDF) and a transitional government was established.

The Ethiopian people had been subjected to famine and civil war because of undemocratic rule that could not fairly accommodate the diversity and plurality of the Ethiopian society.

In 1995, Ethiopia became a Federal Democratic Republic by the ratification of a new Constitution. The Constitution established a federal political system along with parliamentary democracy. It divides state power not only between the Federal Government and the regional governments, but also among the three branches of government at both federal and regional levels.

The Federal Democratic Republic has three branches of government and administration. The executive branch includes the Prime Minister, Council of Ministers and Council of Regional States. The legislative branch has a bicameral Parliament consisting of the House of Federation or upper chamber and the

House of People's Representatives or lower chamber, the latter being elected by popular vote from single-member districts to serve five-year terms. The judicial branch comprises federal and regional courts.

There are nine regional states: Tigray, Afar, Amhara, Oromia, Somali, Southern Nation Nationalities and Peoples' Region (SNNPR), Benishangul-Gumuz, Gambella, and Harari; and two city Administration councils of Dire Dawa and Addis Ababa. The regional states and city administrations are subdivided into administrative Woredas (districts). A Woreda/District is a basic decentralized administrative unit and has an administrative council comprised of elected members. The Woredas are further divided into Kebeles, the smallest administrative unit in the government.

There are regional and national political parties as well as civil society and the private media. National legislative elections are held every five years since 1995.

Society, Cultures and Traditions

Ethiopia adopted Christianity in the fourth century A.D. and the Ethiopian Orthodox Church is the oldest sub-Saharan African church, just as the first mosque in Africa was built in Ethiopia. Christianity and Islam have coexisted peacefully for hundreds of years. There are also traditional religions that are followed in some parts of the country.

Religion associated celebrations and festivals play an important part in the people's lives. While Church ceremonies are major features of Ethiopian society, Islamic traditions are also strong and offer a colourful contrast particularly in the eastern and south-eastern parts of the country.

The vast majority of the languages spoken in the country can be classified into three families of the Afro-Asiatic super family of languages: the Semitic, Cushitic, and Omotic. Semitic language speakers mostly live in the highlands of the north and center. Cushitic language speakers live in the highlands and lowlands of the south-central region as well as in the north-central area. Omotic speakers live predominantly in the south. The

Nilo-Saharan super language family accounts for about 2 per cent of the population, and these languages are spoken along the Ethio-Sudanese border.

Amharic has been used as a working language for the last 150 years or so and English is the most widely spoken foreign language as well as the language of instruction in secondary schools and universities.

The economy is based on agriculture, which is the occupation of 85 per cent of the population. Most people in the highlands live on subsistence farming (the situation is a changing one) and those in the lowlands, on cattle rearing. The monarchy, the aristocracy and the Orthodox Church traditionally controlled and owned most of the land until the overthrow of the monarchy in 1974.

The main staple crops include a variety of cereals, such as *teff*, wheat, barley, corn, sorghum, and millet; and coffee as well as pulses and oilseeds. Grains are the primary staple of the diet and are thus the most important field crops. Pulses are a principal source of protein in the diet.

Men do physically taxing activities like plowing on the farm, and they often spend their free time socializing outside the home, while women are restricted from leaving home to engage in social activities. Women take care of the household chores. If a man participates in domestic activities such as cooking and child rearing, he is looked down upon and may even become a social outcast. Men are encouraged to develop traits that translate into leadership, political and economic supremacy, and women into dependency and domesticity (NCTPE, 2003). For instance, priority is given for education of boys over girls as it is believed that women's roles in the household do not need much of education. Depending on their sex, of course, young children get involved in the household and farm labour at an early age. Girls usually have a greater amount of work to do than boys as they also work on the farm in addition to the household chores.

The traditional values of Ethiopian society encourage traditional marriage customs that vary from one ethnic group to other, although many customs are transethnic. Arranged marriages are the norm, although this practice is becoming much less common, especially in urban areas. The presentation of a dowry from the male's family to the female's family is common. The dowry may include livestock, money, or other socially valued items. The amount is not fixed and varies with the wealth of the families.

The basic family unit is much larger than the typical western nuclear family. The man is the head *'Abawerra'* of the family. A woman would never be recognized as one unless she was a widow or divorcee. The oldest male is usually the head of the household and is in charge of decision making. Men, due to their control over income, control the family economically. It is the primary duty of the mother to care for the children as part of her domestic duties. Children are socially required to care for their parents. Descent is traced through both the mother's and father's families in most ethnic groups, but the male line is more valued than the female. In most ethnic groups, it is customary for a child to take the father's first name as his or her last name. Elders are respected, especially men, and are regarded as the source of lineage. In general, an elder or groups of elders are responsible for settling disputes within a kin group or clan. Age is a factor in social behaviour, and the elderly are treated with the utmost respect. The number of cattle and amount of grain that a person possesses signifies a high social status in the rural areas while wealth, high paying jobs as well as level of education signify status in the urban areas.

While diversity in culture, language and religion are the mosaic that forms the Ethiopian society, patriarchal structure determines the relationship between the sexes is reflected as the stress put on the different roles that are assigned to men and women. Thus democratic order and institutions are required to safeguard both the plurality and multiculturalism of the society and ensure gender equality.

CHAPTER II

The Global Setting

The Erosion of Patriarchy

The economic, political and social oppression of women is universal as is their struggle to liberate themselves from gender discrimination. As the Ethiopian women's quest for equality is part of the global struggle, this chapter is added to discuss the global situation of women, their achievements and challenges worldwide.

Literature attributes the cause of the inequality between men and women to patriarchal traditions, beliefs and practices which depict men as the perfect norm against which women are measured. In her essay "Woman and Others" Simon de Beauvoir wrote that a woman, "is defined and differentiated with reference to man and not with reference to her; thus, she is the incidental, the inessential as opposed to the essential, and he is the Subject, the Absolute and she is the Other" (www.got.net/elained/patriarchy.html).

Patriarchy as an ideology propagates division of labour by gender and ascribes behavioural norms associated with males and females in a given social group or system. Patriarchal thinking about work enhances the belief that men are superior while women are inferior.

Patriarchy applies various forms of interpretations and explanations to justify the position of women in society. Thus biological explanation is forwarded in support of the belief that women are weaker than men; and its economic justification characterizes women as providers of domestic support for the working male and/or cheap army of reservc labour. Likewise the cultural interpretation of patriarchy places greater value on the skill of men than of women. The unfortunate fact about patriarchy is that women themselves have accepted its domination for so long. The exploitative relationship between the sexes could not have been perpetuated without the consent of the victims as well as of the dominant sex. Patriarchy is very well strengthened by factors such as culture, religion, tradition etc. For instance, male-supremacist theology is a big factor in keeping women "in their place".

Patriarchy has been the oldest form of forced and exploitative division of social activities the feature of which has been accepted as natural. History tells us that women have always worked under highly exploitative arrangements in virtually all societies where sex has been an important basis for societal organization. Some sources locate the origins of the sexual division of labour in the fact that women historically have had primary responsibilities such as the care of children (Wharton, 2006). Hence, children's dependence on their mothers' care shapes the type of labour women can perform. Others attribute to hunting and gathering societies where women were likely to be gatherers and men to be hunters thus working according to their physical strength (Collins *et al.* 1993). However, in these societies, where each set of tasks contributed to the group's survival by providing food that supplied necessary calories, women's labour provided most of it (Lenski *et al.* 1995; Tanner and Zelman 1976).

The role of providing more food to the community shifted to men as an agricultural system based on the plough was adopted. Here, men became the providers of more calories of food than women; and when women's labour became less vital to family survival than men's, their relative social status diminished. This line of argument suggests that the relative contributions of women's and men's labour for survival influence the degree to which each sex is socially valued, implying that women and men are more equal in societies where the value of their labour is more similar. But, this argument does not provide an explanation for the division of labour that exists today.

Engels, in *The Origin of the Family, Private Property and the State* (1984), states that in primitive society the relation between the sexes was based on equality though there was division of labour whereby women were responsible for domestic work and men for agriculture and animal husbandry. According to Engels, even in the pairing family, descent was calculated through the female line, which he referred to as Mother's right. However, with the development of domestication of animals and breeding of herds, men gained property and power over others which attributed to the change of the egalitarian situation; which in turn prompted men to pass on their property to their children. Hence, the traditional order of inheritance through mothers was overthrown and to ensure strict paternity, monogamy was enforced on women who eventually became the property of the men. As the men took command in the home, the women were degraded and reduced to servitude. This historical development relegated women to an inferior position in society as they became dominated by men. And Engels referred to the overthrow of the mother's right as "the world's historical defeat of the female sex" (1884). Hence, patriarchy came to reign supreme, and became universal in human history and soiety.

The Doctrine of Separate Sphere

In the pre-Industrial period, work and family were closely intertwined with no distinction between them since work to provide food for the family was performed close to the homestead. Though, the task was still divided on the bases of gender and age in these societies, all members of the family that is, husbands, wives and children contributed to the household and produced goods for the market too. Neither women nor men experienced a separation between the world of work and family (Wharton 2006). In fact the word "housework" was not introduced in the written English language until 1841 (Hudson and Sullivan, 1990).

In the course of time, industrialization changed this arrangement. The most important aspect of the change was the geographic separation of work and family life. With the establishment of factories and industries, production moved out of the home which forced members of families to work in factories that were placed in different locations. In the process, the interdependence of work and family was affected. The new phenomenon of industrial urbanization intensified the process of the separation of work and family.

A. Kantar (1977) states that, workers (men) who could afford to move their residences to locations far from places of employment often did so; and, in the process, the points of contact between the rest of the family and the organization were removed. Since work became the place of middle class men, their roles were organized around the status of "work", "bread winning" and that of the middle class women "mothering" and "homemaking". However, being employed in blue- collar, clerical and service jobs, working class men could not afford to relocate themselves to the suburbs of the emerging urban centers, therefore, they lived close to their work place. This situation created an opportunity for the wives of working class men to work for wages in the nearby factories in addition to their domestic responsibilities. But, despite the fact that many working class women were working for wages, the experience of the middle class became the basis for the norms of employers' practices which still identifies work and work place as "male". To this effect, Reskin and Padavic (1994) observe: "The sexual division of labour that assigned men to the labour force and women to the home encouraged employers to structure jobs on the assumptions that all workers were men and that all men had stay-at-home wives" (p. 24). Having stay at home wives, of course, created a perception that male workers were free from domestic responsibility and that they could work 12 to 14 hours a day in their work places.

This line of thinking which historians and sociologists call as "the Doctrine of Separate Spheres" not only determined a relationship of the separation of home and work but also the qualities deemed desirable in women and men. Paid workplace was seen as a place that requires qualities such as competition, rationality and achievement that became attributed to men. Canian (1989), also elaborated that "the ideology of separate spheres" reinforced the new division of labour and by so doing portrayed the family as a harmonious, stable nuclear household with an economically successful, independent, father but dependent, angelic and loving mother. This doctrine provided cultural justification for the gender division of labour as revealed in the treatment of those who deviated from its prescriptions. Men who were not working or whose work was too minimal to support their families were denigrated not merely in their roles as workers, but as men as well. Therefore, for men not working means not being whole persons. However, a completely different obligation was put in place for women. According to Canian, an ideal woman centered her life on love of husband and children, a love expressed mainly through emotions and piety, rather than practical action (1989). As the doctrine of separate spheres penalizes men who do not provide for the family, it also stigmatized women who are not full-time family caretakers.

The doctrine of separate spheres governs the relationship between the sexes in many parts of Ethiopian society where men are perceived as breadwinners and, heads of households who represent the family outside of the home whereas women are relegated to domestic work looking after the children and the social wellbeing of the family. Hence women are assigned the roles of a wife, mother and house-keeper while men are bread winners, protectors and supporters (Allasebu 1988). This separation of different spheres led to role enforcement and control of women's autonomous choices that characterized patriarchy.

Global Struggle for Equality

Despite the doctrine of "separate sphere", women's work and participation in activities outside the home has tremendously increased. A gradual transformation of the world economy from production of goods to that of services has created a great opportunity for women to join the work force. As most of the service jobs were traditionally women's tasks such as cooking, caring for children and the elderly, it became very easy for them to participate in paid jobs. The status of women also moved from homemakers to workers as their jobs were transformed from unpaid to paid ones. At the same time, the availability of these services in the market freed families from depending upon women's unpaid work in the home.

Ironically, the Second World War had also contributed to the transformation of women's participation in the labour force. While on the one hand, military conscription of men reduced the availability of the work force; on the other hand, war production generated rapid economic expansion which required more labour. Thus the shortage in the labour force created opportunities for women to enter jobs that were traditionally reserved for men. With conversion to war production, many entirely new occupations emerged with no clear sex labels. Wharton (2006) observed that people could not be certain where to draw the boundaries between "men's" and "women's" work. War is often viewed as a period where job segregation by sex broke down, albeit temporarily. Once the war was over, women were sent back to domestic chores.

As capitalism developed, patriarchal domination also loosened to some extent. However, the success of gaining economic and political rights was achieved because of the women's movements that challenged patriarchy. As marginalized groups, communities have always organized themselves to advance their causes. Likewise women in Europe and the United States of America and later on all over the world have organized themselves legally or otherwise in order to gain political, social and economic rights.

The most notable movements that deserve credit in advancing the causes of women are the feminist movements. Unfortunately feminism has been given wrong meanings, shades and colors, and as such to be a feminist is considered to be against family, marriage, even men by those who politically oppose what the movement stands for. Influenced by such views many women do not want to be associated with feminism, hence they go out of their way to demonstrate that they were not feminist even when they stand for the rights of women. Some men also label women who challenge their chauvinistic attitudes, values and practices as feminists to discourage the challenge.

For the sake of clarity and understanding of the meaning of feminism, I would like to quote Faludi' (1991):

> "Feminism asks the world to recognize at long last that women aren't decorative ornaments, worthy vessels, members of a "special-interest group." They are half (in

> fact, now more than half) of the national population, and just as deserving of rights and opportunities, just as capable of participating in the world's events, as the other half. Feminism's agenda is basic. It asks that women not be forced to "choose" between public justice and private happiness. It asks that women be free to define themselves—instead of their identity defined for them, time and again, by their culture and their men (p xxiii)."

Until such time that feminist movements started challenging patriarchy, women remained trapped in sexism without a clear identification of the real enemy. Feminist movements challenged patriarchy and characterized it as a social system that uncritically accepted male physical strength as the ultimate means for settling social conflicts due to millennia of human experience. Feminist movements were buttressed by feminist theory that developed in a variety of disciplines such as anthropology, economics, women's studies etc.

Initially, feminism was primarily concerned with establishing the fact that women were nothing but human beings who should not be treated as property. Thus, they fought for equal property rights and against ownership of married women by their husbands. Later on, the feminists campaigned for the women's vote which was followed by the struggle to gain the same social, political, economic and legal rights as that of men. Though feminism as a movement started in the industrialized countries, it later took a global perspective as the third world women joined the struggle in order to gain equality within their own cultural context.

There are differences in articulating the types of equality and forms of struggle to achievement. However, despite the differences in their approach to the issues of women, they all agree that gender roles are socially constructed. Thus liberal feminism advocates for the equality of rights of women through political and legal reforms without changing the existing structure, ignoring the fact that the real differences between men and women lies in the existing social structure (Jaggar and Young 1998.)

Contrarily, radical feminism believes that women can liberate themselves only when they have done away with oppressive and dominant patriarchal system. According to them, society will not be reformed as long as such a system and its values exist (Echols and Alice 1989). For radical feminism, family is a major institution with a role of fostering gender inequality through the socialization of children and the forcing of women to conform to feminine stereotypes. While some radical feminists advocate for the total uprooting and reconstruction of society, others call for only a cultural change.

Socialist and Marxist feminism connect the oppression of women to Marxist ideas about exploitation, oppression and labour. Despite minor differences, both groups attach women's discrimination to the capitalist exploitation and the system of private property (Jaggar and Young 1998). Socialist feminists see women as being held down as a result of their unequal standing in both the workplace and the domestic sphere (Wilding 2007). Since they see the oppression of women as part of the oppression of the whole society, socialist feminists advocate the cooperation of all oppressed groups in order to change the *status quo*.

Contemporary Marxist feminists have attempted to explain the relative lower pay of women than that of men to the sexual division of labour that assigns women's primary responsibilities to take care of the family as well as their economic dependence on the income of their husbands. Therefore, the wage of the female worker need not be equal to the male worker's since it is assumed that she is partially supported by her husband.

Marxist and socialist feminists have a wide range of proposals as to the solutions for women's inequality, such as the compensation of reproductive and household labour, to the socialization of domestic work, and to the abolition of capitalism.

Feminists were criticized on the ground that they were ethnocentric and that they did not take into account the unique experiences of women from the third world. Nevertheless, third world feminism was developed by women who acquired their views in taking part in the struggle for equality in their respective societies. Women's participation in revolutionary struggles for independence against colonialism and foreign domination in the third world has been linked with the development of feminist consciousness. Studies of women involved in revolutionary movements such as in China, Cuba, Mexico and Nicaragua document the origins of feminist movements in these countries within the context of male dominated national struggles that contributed to understanding the patriarchal dynamics within their societies. The struggle of women in South Africa against apartheid and those of Algerian, Kenyan and Zimbabwean women against colonialism are also few of such examples.

The parts that follow discuss the progress women have made the world over in attaining their equalities and participation in the public arena. The women's participation in education, political and economic participation are used here as these three areas are usually used as a measure to gage women's empowerment.

Participation in Education

Education is both a human right and a means to realize rights. As an empowerment tool, education is the primary vehicle by which economically and socially marginalized people can liberate themselves from poverty as well as obtain the means to participate fully in their societies (UNESCO 2005). According to Article 13 of the International Covenant on Economic, Social and Cultural Rights, education has a vital role to play in empowering women, safeguarding children from exploitative and hazardous forms of labour and sexual exploitation (2005, p. 7). Thus the most important factor that contributes to women's participation in expanding job opportunities is education. As the exclusion of girls by way of sex discrimination was challenged legally, opportunities have to be made available for women to participate in education. Education is the main gate and the ladder on which it is possible to walk up and reach higher positions as it is believed to play an important role, if not a key role in economic, social and political empowerment (Thakur, 2000). Education develops the personality of individuals, qualifies them to participate meaningfully in certain political and economic functions. The social mobility of individuals and equalizing among citizens coming from different social, ethnical and class backgrounds is facilitated through education. Realities in the industrialized countries today demonstrate that they would not have been able to reach the present level without research and development, and technological transformation all of which require educated people.

Education has a tremendous contribution to the empowerment of women economically as well as politically. Peasle (1965) studied the relationship between growth in primary education and GNP per capita between 1850 and 1960 for 34 industrialized countries and found that none achieved significant economic growth without first achieving universal primary education. Another study by Benavot (1985) which covered 110 developed and developing countries concluded that there is a positive correlation between primary education and economic growth.

Furthermore, studies reveal that girls' education has multidimensional effect. Since skills acquired enable girls to learn new methods of operation which lead to higher output and greater productivity, they can earn higher wages. Even for those who are self employed or are in the informal sector, education can increase their opportunities of access to vocational training and credit schemes. Educating women means educating the whole family.

Emphasizing the importance of education in changing values and perceptions, Thakur (2000) states that:

> "The education system is the only institution which can counteract the deep foundations of the inequality of the sexes that are built in the minds of men and women through the socialization process. It must make a deliberate, planned and sustained effort to replace the traditional value system, based in inequality, by the new value system which accepts equalization of the sexes".

Apart from economic benefits, girls' education has significant social contribution as well. Given the fact that women are the main actors in domestic activities, educating girls leads to improved childrearing practices, better family health and lower fertility.

There are a number of factors that are identified as the causes for poor participation of women in education. Coombs (1988) attributes the underlying causes for disparities between boys and girls in education to cultural values of a given society.

The role of women in a society and the organization of the school system were also cited as major causes for low participation of women (Debele 1980). Women are generally regarded as intellectually inferior in many societies. Such views also have an impact on the self image of girls. Duncan (1989) states:

> "Images of women reflect the values and pressures of society but at the same time they permeate mental attitudes and underpin societal conventions...they fashion habits of thought, and together with the family and economic structures peculiar to each society, help to determine the status of women".

The labour markets of many developing societies which are characterized by low participation of women have a bearing on their education (Gennet, 1991). The knowledge that there are a limited number of job opportunities reserved for women, affects the occupational aspirations and expectations of female students. The selection of field of specialization by parents and teachers will also be influenced by the knowledge of which job is available for women.

The societal values that are reflected in the structure of the school, its administration, the "hidden" curriculum, teachers' behaviour and attitude, as well as the school textbooks work as influencing agents on women's education. In this regard, Duncan (1989) observes the following:

> "While women form the majority of the teachers in primary schools in the Western countries, this is not true in many African countries. The proportions decline even further at the secondary and tertiary levels. Less information is available concerning women in administrative positions. Nevertheless, it is clear that in most African countries few are appointed as principals, administrators etc. thus segregating women into the lowest states of jobs."

In many developing countries, particularly in sub-Saharan Africa, women's participation in education is characterized by low enrollment, especially at the secondary and tertiary levels. A large percentage of female students also drop out or repeat classes. Lack of women's participation in education has an adverse effect not only on their personal, professional and political empowerment but also on the development of the society as a whole (Thakur 2000). As women constitute half of the society, no country can attain economic, social and political development without their participation.

In many African countries girls are expected to contribute to childcare or domestic work at an early age (Psachoropoulos, 1985). Education of girls is a low priority in many poor families while that of boys is taken seriously by way of security for old age. Poverty and unwillingness to bear the educational cost of books, uniforms and other expenses could adversely affect girls' education. However, the cause for not sending girls to school is not solely economic but also social. Psachoropoulos (1985) states that in the Middle East and in North Africa, religious and socio-cultural traditions such as early marriage and child bearing, even unwillingness to allow girls to travel long distances are factors for the low participation of women in education.

Table 2.1: Gross Enrollment Rate at Primary Level (1995, 2000, 2007)

Region	*Primary GER (Females) %*		
	1995	*2000*	*2007*
Arab States	79.2	83.5	90.8
Central and Eastern Europe	104.1	100.0	97.0
Central Asia	85.8	98.1	98.7
East Asia and the Pacific	M	M	112.0
Latin America and the Caribbean	140.7	119.0	115.0
North America and Western Europe	103.3	101.5	101.3
South and West Asia	80.7	83.0	106.1
Sub-Saharan Africa	68.3	75.3	93.3

Note: M=Missing value.

Source: UNESCO institute for statistics database, 2010.

Between 1995 and 2007, progress towards gender parity in primary education has occurred in most countries where disparity traditionally existed. Since 1995, many countries in all regions have moved from a position of disparity in favour of boys to achieving or almost achieving gender parity by 2007. As shown in the Table 2.1 above, gender parity in education has generally been achieved in Central and Eastern Europe, Central Asia, Latin America and the Caribbean, and North America and Western Europe.

In many countries, women are found at the lower level of the educational hierarchy; mostly, as primary school teachers. The percentage of women at the highest echelon of educational administrations, (department chairs, deans and presidents of universities) is very low. The form and scope of women's educational work varies from one level to another because of the familial and educational demands made on women. Acker (1982) calls these dual institutions as 'greedy institutions'. These institutions require from women a high degree of loyalty, commitment and productivity on equal level. For many women teachers and academics, success in one institutional setting might carry penalties in the other which poses a domestic problem. The involvement in two 'greedy institutions' means that these women have to demonstrate unequivocally that they have indeed come to terms with this dilemma; that the successful performance in one of these institutions is not being achieved at the expense of the other. It might be argued that modern men also experience a tension created by involvement in familial and waged work. But the difference between women's and men's involvement is defined through an ideology which propagates sexual division of labour in the home. According to this ideology, the man's commitment is to relatively fixed operations and that of the woman is constantly extendable. The cultural and state acceptance of the ideology of sexual division of labour makes it even difficult for women to choose between work and family.

Economic Participation

Whether they are working for paid jobs or are self employed, women contribute to the household income and expenditure. The Global Monitoring Report of 2007 indicates that the contributions of women in poor households are crucial for maintaining the families. In emphasizing the importance of women's economic contribution, a World Bank Gender Action Plan, quoted in the *Economist* (2006) states that "forget China, India and the internet:

economic growth is driven by women". Despite the importance of women's contribution to the world economy, they have been largely invisible in the international political economy

Because of the domestic chores that take up much of their time, women face many constraints when they decide to seek paid employment. In a study undertaken in the Kyrgyz Republic, 24.8 per cent of the women who participated reported that housekeeping, taking care of children and of sick persons or the elderly kept them away from working outside the household (Morrison and Lamana 2006). Chores, specially fetching water, collecting firewood and cooking for the family not only take up their time but also sap their energy. In sub-Saharan African countries like Burkina Faso, Uganda and Zambia, a woman in the rural areas spends on an average 125 hours a year to fetch potable water (Barwell 1996). Thus women spend most of their time in routine household activities that could have been put to good use in paid jobs.

In sub-Saharan Africa where agriculture is the main occupation of the majority of the people, women are the predominant workforce, making substantial contributions to the production, processing and distribution of food crops (African Women's Report 2009). However, many of them neither own the land on which they work nor get cash payment for their work. Most of the women who work on the farm are unpaid family members and the land belongs mostly to a male owner. Land is not only a vital means of production but also serves as security and collateral for accessing credit and agricultural inputs; and, needless to say access to inputs such as land, credit, capital and technology is very essential for self-employment. Though limited, evidence indicates that the distribution of land to women is non existant in many countries. In Latin American countries, 70-90 per cent of the land owners are men (Deere and Leon 2003). The same is also true in sub- Saharan Africa. Even when women own land, their holdings are smaller than those of men. In fact, in many African countries, permanent land rights are held by men under customary law. Land distribution and land registration programmes exclude women thus maintaining the *status quo* that favours male household heads (Jacobs 2002). In regard access to credit, there is no problem that is peculiar to women as they neither get rejected when applying for loans nor are they charged more interest than men. But women are less likely to apply for loans than men since they don't have property or land to offer as collateral. However, wherever micro credit schemes are available, women become beneficiaries of these schemes though they are constrained by credit limits as shown in studies done in Bangladesh and Malawi (Diagne and others 2000). This is regardless of the fact that the positive impact on the household is greater when women rather than men become beneficiaries of credit.

Programmes such as structural adjustment, economic liberalization and privatization that are designed to boost economic growth often compel governments to cut down their expenditures on social services like education and health. This has grave consequences for vulnerable groups especially women (Adeleye-Fayemi 2004). A study undertaken by the Kenya Human Rights Commission has documented the injustices experienced by workers in Export Processing Zones. Most of the injustices were related to lack of prospects for skill acquisition and career advancement as well as low pay. Health and safety measures such as sexual harassment and denial of maternity and other benefits are injustices inflicted on women (Gwaunza *et al.* 2000). This is also the case in Ethiopia where many women in the urban areas work as maids, baby sitters and cooks without any such benefits. These women work 10 to 15 hours a day, take rest only once a month. Those who are not in support of promulgating a law to regulate the working conditions of such domestic workers insist that it would backfire on the employees as it is difficult to enforce such laws at household level.

Since 2001, a series of studies on Gender and Work in Eastern and Southern Africa (GWESA) was undertaken regarding domestic workers who are mostly women (Namara 2001; Lung'aho 2001). These studies highlighted the reality that domestic work was beyond the purview of labour regulations and unions. Similar work that focuses on women workers who make up the majority of the work force in the informal economy also indicated the inability of these workers to benefit from health and safety regulations like workmen's compensation and minimum wage (Dwasi 1999; Manuh 1998). Those who work in commercial (plantation) agriculture face similar problems compounded by the fact that they are seasonal workers and therefore not fully employed (Manuh 1998; Mbilinyi 1991; Auret and Barrientos 2004)

In those cases where women are employed either in the civil service or the private sector, their income is not equivalent to men. After a hard won struggle for equal pay for equal work, men and women tend to be on the same salary levels for doing the same category of work within the civil services. However, in civil service organizations of many countries particularly in Africa, women constitute the majority within low paying clerical areas that require low qualifications. Often, women are also found in the social sectors rather than in the economic one. Promotion to a higher position is more difficult for women as they are viewed as incompetent and not reliable enough to take up responsible positions.

Political Participation of Women

In a situation where the public sphere is reserved for men, women were not expected, and in fact, not allowed to engage in any form of politics; they were thus denied rights of voting and standing for elections when parliament was first established in the early twenties.

However through women's organizations, they struggled for women's suffrage. The most known struggles are the ones fought for the right to vote. Many women activists, notably the "suffragettes" in Britain demanded and mobilized people to fight for women's right to vote; hence, American and British women won the right to vote in 1920 and 1928 respectively, marking the beginning of women entering political activities. Though, New Zealand was the first country that gave right to women to vote in 1893, it was Finland that allowed women to be elected in 1906. By the turn of the twentieth century, women especially in Britain and America acquired a certain level of legal independence such as a married woman's ability to own property, custody right of their children and protection from physical abuse by their husbands (Bryson 1992). In Asia, women's voting rights were acknowledged at different times starting from 1924 when Mongolia first allowed women to vote.

Subsequently, women have struggled to secure a whole lot of social, economic and political rights such as the right to education, property, and equal pay for equal work, constitutional rights etc., through their relentless struggles. Of course, these rights were not recognized easily but fought for by many national, regional and international women's organizations.

As recognizing rights was not enough, their implementations requires that structural and institutional barriers/laws, norms/ values that curtailed women from political, social and economic participation in their respective societies needed to be challenged as well. To this end, a number of international forums that were held at different times and their resolutions have emphasized the point that women should participate in decision-making and political affairs. For instance Article 21 of the Universal Declaration of Human Rights (UNHR) affirms the right of every woman and man to participate in the governments of their respective countries. Article 7 of the Convention on the Elimination of All Forms of Discrimination Against Women (CEDAW) requires that states take all appropriate measures to eliminate discrimination against women in their respective country's political and public life. Article 7(1) affirms the equal right of women to hold public office and to participate in the formulation and implementations of government policies.

Ever since the UN World Conference on Women held in Mexico City in 1975, different organizations have been working for the elimination of discrimination against women. These organizations advocate that women should make meaningful contribution in shaping the political and economic landscapes of their respective societies by participating in all institutions in which important decisions are made. Twenty years after first UN Conference on Women, a plan of action known as The Beijing Plan of Action was published in 1995 stressing the importance of women's participation in decision making and leadership positions, and called upon governments to increase their numbers.

Moreover, the UN in 2000 declared women's participation in parliament to be one of the criteria in measuring the Millennium Development Goals (MDG). Though membership of parliament is not any more off limit for women as it used to be in many countries at the turn of the twentieth century, the progress is still slow. Since the Beijing Platform of Action, women's participation has increased from 15.9 per cent in 1995 to 18.5 per cent in 2009 with an increment of only 3 per cent (IPU, 2010). In a conference entitled "Is Parliament Open to Women?" in 2009 it was stated that despite incremental progress over the past 15 years, the average that of 18 per cent remains well below the 30 per cent target established in 1995. Progress with an average increase of less than one percentage point per year means that the 30 per cent target would not be reached before another 15 years (IPU, 2010, p. 5).

One might ask as to why 30 per cent was set as a minimum percentage that is required for women to be in parliament. Parliamentarians have a crucial role to play in ensuring that those policies and programmes as well as their implementation are gender sensitive. Unfortunately, there are only few women participating in parliament today and they have not been able to effectively use the platform to enhance women's empowerment. Thus, to make women participate in various parliamentary committees where different policies and strategies are tabled and their implementations are monitored in the parliament deliberations, the 30 per cent minimum target is needed.

Even though there are challenges for both men and women in relation to participation in parliament, there are problems that are faced by women only. For instance when women seek election, they are scrutinized far more than men for not only their compenticies and integrity but for their personal character, behaviour, etc. Such acts might appear to be necessary to have a better candidates, however, over scrutiny can discourage women from running for parliament. Since politics is considered the preview of men only, it is one of the factors that hinder women's nomination and election to parliament. The attitude towards the roles of men and women in society affects the electorate as well as the political parties which in many countries approve nominations. Lack of women candidates (especially in countries where candidates had to pay for election related expenses) and balancing the public and domestic responsibilities of women as well are additional factors that restrain them from participating in elections.

In order to surmount these challenges of women, some countries have established measures such as quotas for women's participation. For instance, out of the 25 countries that have achieved 30 per cent in 2009, 22 have implemented the quota in their electoral systems. As shown in Table 2.1, in countries where these measures have been adopted (Uganda, Rwanda, South Africa) there is a sharp increase in women members of parliament. Political parties also set up their own quota in some countries where the electoral system does not allow a gender quota. The Labour Party of Britain deployed party based quota to increase the participation of the number of women in Westminster (Judith Squimer, 2004). Countries have identified the quota system as a simple answer to redress the historical marginalization of women, though it should not be taken as a lasting solution but rather as

Table 2.2: Countries with Women Representing 30% or More in the Lower or Single House of Parliament (1st July, 2013)

Countries	*Percentage*	*Countries*	*Percentage*
Rwanda	56.3	Mozambique	39.2
Sweden	44.7	Belgium	38.0
Norway	39.6	Andorra	50.0
Finland	42.5	Iceland	39.7
Denmark	39.1	South Africa	42.3
Netherlands	38.7	New Zealand	32.2
Argentina	37.4	Germany	32.9
Cuba	48.9	Guyana	31.3
Spain	36.0	Burundi	30.5
Costa Rica	38.6	United Rep. of Tanzania	36.0
Seychelles	43.8	Ecuador	38.7
Senegal	42.7	Timor-Leste	38.5
Nicaragua	40.2	Mexico	36.8
Uganda	35.0	Angola	34.1
The F.Y.R. of Macedonia	34.1	Grenada	33.3
Nepal	33.2	Serbia	33.2
Slovenia	32.2	Algeria	31.6
Italy	31.4		

Source: Inter-parliamentary union, see http//www.ipu.org/ Wmn-e/classif.htm

Table 2.3: Trends in Women's Participation in Parliament (Selected sub-Saharan African Countries)

Country	*Percentage of seats held by women (1987)*	*Percentage of seats held by women (2000)*	*Percentage of seats held by women (2011)*
Angola	15.0	15.5	38.6
Benin	4.0	6.0	8.4
Botswana	5.0	8.5	7.7
Congo (Brazzaville)	10.0	12.0	7.3
Cote d'-Ivoire	6.0	8.0	8.9
Kenya	2.0	3.6	9.8
Mali	4.0	12.2	10.2
Mozambique	16.0	25.2	39.2
Rwanda	13.0	17.1	56.3
Senegal	11.0	14.0	22.7
South Africa	1.0	30.0	44.5
Uganda	1.0	17.9	34.9
Zambia	3.0	10.1	11.0
Zimbabwe	11.0	14.0	15.0

Source: Inter-parliamentary Union. See www.ipu.org/wmn-e/classif.htm

stop gap measure to fast track women's participation in Parliament.

Recently, many African countries have recognized the importance of women's political participation through constitutional frameworks. Examples include Ethiopia, Ghana, Malawi, South Africa and Uganda. Constitutions are only commitments of countries to gender equality in principle that serve as a sign post towards the kind of social relations to which they aspire. Substantive laws that guarantee gender justice in specific areas like family and property, along with fair procedures had to be put in place since constitutional frameworks alone will not facilitate access to entitlements.

The African Union (AU) also stipulates that 50 per cent of the AU commissioners should be women. As a result, five out of the ten commissioners are women today. A Gender Promotion Directorate in the office of the Chairperson has also been established to advance women's issues in the continent (Schoeman 2004).

One of the indicators set by UNDP to measure gender equality and women's empowerment is their participation in national parliaments. Studies reveal that despite the efforts of UN and other governmental organizations the percentage of women in national parliaments is still low. Various forms of bias in the institutions of civil society and the political sphere, along with conscious discrimination, exclude women from participating in national and regional assemblies (Spencer 2003).

The way the quotas are applied makes a difference in the way women's representation is perceived, that is, whether it is mere "token" or not. For instance in countries where parties in power fill women's seats, the women simply become additional vote banks of the ruling party (Spencer 2003). Moreover in some places, women who enter parliaments through such measures are not usually drawn from the ranks of the poor and thus they are less responsive to the needs and priorities of poor women.

Spencer (2003) argues that greater participation and influence in local government structures, where decisions that directly affect the lives of the poor are made, is more relevant for poor women than increasing their seats in national parliaments. This is what emerges after reviewing a study done in Madhya Pradesh, Kerala and West Bengal in India.

While the increase in the number of women participating in parliament and other decision making posts is a big stride in the struggle for women's equality, it is not an end in itself; rather it should be taken as an instrument in further advancing women's concerns. In some countries where women are elected through party tickets, loyalties to the party rather than the issue rains supreme in their interaction in the parliament; specially if the party program is not gender sensitive, and pro poor etc. In these kinds of settings one may ask how effective the women are to push a gender friendly agenda if it was against the interests of the party or government. The increase of women in parliamentary membership in the British House of Commons in the 1997 Election of the Labour Party for instance did not result in advancing women's issues. The impact made by women because of their participation in these institutions is not conclusive as to whether or not major changes in transforming women's lives have been effected. The reason for relatively little or no effectiveness of these women is the lack of access to institutional rules and values as well as networking and influence of structure. The situations become even more difficult when women do not belong to a party leadership where most political agendas are set and articulated. Similarly, the specific socio-economic and political climate, women's level of education, economic independence, all play roles in curtailing or advancing women's political participation. Despite these problems, the increasing presence of women in politics has provided an additional voice in propagating women's rights. Women's visibility in politics has its own contribution to the enactment of laws that deter the abuse of women.

Political parties shape the economic and political landscape of a country thereby affecting the lives of people as well as of individuals in their respective societies. This is intensified further in parliamentary politics. Political parties have the power not only to influence political systems of nations but also major decisions in governments. Owing to this important role, in the lives of people, the Beijing Platform for Action (1996-1999) urged political parties to remove discriminatory practices and incorporate gender perspectives into party platforms as well as ensure women's access to executive bodies.

As not all political parties may be gender friendly; and parties whose organizational values, structures and culture do not render them fit for women's participation, women members may have to challenge the situation in order to pursue the agendas of women's equality.

Conclusion

Progress in the lives of women has been attained in many places though it varies from region to region. While some countries in the west such as Scandinavians have much advanced in women's empowerment, others such as sub-Saharan Africa and South Asia lag behind. The progress that has been recorded in women's attainment of certain rights and degree of freedom in leading their own lives was the result of women's rights movements at the beginning of the nineteenth century that took place in many parts of the world especially in the west, in the form of political activism, demonstration, lobbying and collective mobilization. These movements called for women's education as education is an empowering tool, and true enough it is in those countries where women have access to all levels of education that they are able to meaningfully participate in the politics, attain economic power and social status. However, the hurdles and bearers that curtail women from achieving their rightful places in the public arena are not totally eliminated yet. Thus, it will be the role of women's organization to constantly put demands on governments and regional and international organizations such as the United Nations, African Union (AU), and the European Union (EU) to the effect they apply themselves to the task of surmounting challenges that are still faced by women.

CHAPTER III

The Place of Women in Traditional Ethiopian Society

The World of Women

The people of Ethiopia belong to many different ethnic groups each with its own language, tradition and culture; yet many share a culture and tradition of patriarchal norms and values. However, the traditions and the culture discussed below are from Amhara and Tigray regions with which I am familiar.

The doctrine of separate spheres governs the relationship between the sexes in many parts of Ethiopian society where men are perceived as breadwinners and heads of households who represent the family outside of the home, whereas women are relegated to domestic work looking after the children and the social well-being of the family.

If a woman is found to be brave, competitive or courageous etc., she would be referred to, admiringly, as "**ወንድ ናት**" meaning "She is [like] a man" as if such traits are alien to the nature of women. There are many lyrics and sayings that assert that the place of women in Ethiopia is in the home with clear subordination to their husbands.

Men and women in the society have clearly defined roles that are dictated by the dominant ideology which is patriarchy. In all cultures of Ethiopia, women are generally considered inferior to men. In this regard, Levine (1974) states that in some ethnic groups for instance in the Gurage, women are viewed as inherently immoral creatures who contaminate men unless they perform cleansing rituals after childbirth and menstruation. Among the Kafficho (a people in southern Ethiopia) men regard women as weak, lazy and highly dangerous. The Amharas and Tigraians characterize women as unreliable and treacherous. As breadwinners, men are heads of households with authority to represent the family outside of the home.

Since house work is solely the responsibility of women, a man hardly ever cooks.* Paula (1987) identified the following tasks that are performed by women in rural areas as part of their domestic chores:

(a) Budgeting the household's resources, they have to see that not only is there enough food for the family any particular day but also that there is enough food stored until the next harvest;
(b) Processing of the raw material that is, storing cleaning, grinding, pounding, cooking, etc.
(c) Cultivating vegetables and spice gardens; only soil preparation is done by men;
(d) Assisting men in soil preparation, applying manure, weeding and harvesting. Weeding and harvesting of some crops such as peas and lentils is done by women;
(e) Milking of cows and cleaning of the sheds.
(f) Weaving baskets and spinning cotton for household needs.

Despite all these responsibilities and work, women who are not employed outside the house are not considered to be working; and, national statistics do not capture the true picture of women's lives; and, fail to count women's work as contribution to the national economy. For instance, in most surveys conducted by the Central Statistical Office (CSO) of Ethiopia only women who are employed outside of their houses, earning income/wages are considered as economically active disregarding the fact that millions of women toil over long hours in agricultural work and the household.

* This situation is beginning to change as a few men have started to share household chores.

Marriage Practices

In the absence of compelling reasons such as severe disease, a woman is expected to have been married between eighteen and twenty five.

In many Ethiopian cultures; marriages are arranged by the couple's parents and/or relatives. Marriage was not only based on the mutual consent of the spouses, it also established unequal relationship that bestowed authority on the husband over the wife. Tradition and religions in Ethiopia insist that a wife must be faithful and obedient to the husband while the same is not required of the husband. Wife beating and mistreatment are believed to be necessary to shape the character of 'unruly' women.

Marriage is valued not as a process that unites the two marrying partners, but also the two families of the marrying partners. The bride to be had no say in matters regarding her marriage. However, we also find a very different practice in Kunama (ethnic group in a Tigray Region), who unlike the practice in many of the other groups, a girl can choose her future partner; and virginity which is cherished in most ethnic groups of Ethiopia is disregarded here. Thus a girl may or may not be a virgin at the time of marriage. In the same manner the Kunama do not treat children born out of wedlock any differently from other children.

Marriages which are sanctified by religious rites and ethnic culture in many parts of Ethiopia were recognized by the civil code. Different marriage ages for men and women were also set. In Fetha Negaste "the law of the kings" (a code used before the civil law was enacted) the marriage age set for men and women was 20 and 12 years respectively. And the Sharia sets the marriage age at 9 and 12 years for women and men respectively (Lishan 1974). When the civil code was enacted in 1960, the marriage age for women was raised from 12 to 15 and remained so until it was changed to the age of 18 in the new Civil Code of 2000.

To insure the sexual chastity of women and safeguard the power of their husbands over them, women are circumcised at different ages depending on the custom and/or religious practices of their families. Female genital mutilation by circumcision and excision are the most common forms of FGM used in Ethiopia. Circumcision is believed to subdue the sexual urges of women and make them totally obedient to the man.

The 1960 civil law denied women the right to seek divorce except under a few circumstances no matter how unhappy and stifling the marriage is for the women. There are three very stringent issues that can be accepted as cause for divorce in a court of law. These are, to be mentally unfit for marriage; when one of the parties has been found red handed having sexual intercourse with a person other than the wife or husband; and abandoning the family for a period of two years. In fact divorce is always looked upon as an act that is the result of the woman's fault. But a husband can divorce his wife if she does not bear a child, uses contraceptives without his permission or has an abortion or is disobedient to him.

Types of Marriage

Early Marriage: In most highland societies of Ethiopia, particularly among the Amhara, Tigray, and Oromo marriage was usually arranged by parents or relatives. Once the parents, essentially the fathers, have consented, the day of marriage is fixed. Girls and sometimes boys enter marriage outside their own choices especially in the rural areas. Some girls were forced into marriage at a very tender age. In areas where early marriage is frequent, the child particularly the girl, was in no position to understand what was going on, let alone to participate in any decision. Early marriage was prevalent in the northern part of Ethiopia where little girls as young as seven were married to teenage boys and grew up together in the boys' parents' houses until it was believed that the marriage could be consummated, usually when she was ready to have sex or after her first menstruation (Helen, 1992). Though parents anticipate that a girl is ready to have sex, she may not be so biologically; hence the problem of fistula ensues. Fistula is one of the health problems of women in Ethiopia particularly in the north where early marriage is prevalent. Fistula has medical, physical and psychological consequences that cripple young women affected by it. Because of the constant leaking of urine, feces, the women are unable to perform household chores and childrearing which lead to divorce and abandonment by the husbands. Since women with fistula are often forced to live in isolation because of the odor intensity of the stigma as well as the isolation, loneliness and the shame lead them to depression.

In early marriage, the marrying partners do not understand the implication of marriage itself. My mother, who was subject to marriage at the age of seven, informed me that she had thought that her mother-in-law to whom she was given was one of her family members. She was not aware that she was married until she was rescued by another family member who opposed the marriage and took her away to put her in a newly opened girls' school. It is also assumed that once a girl is married, she has become an adult regardless of her age. Marriage of a young girl to an elderly man where the man is typically between the ages of 40 and 50, at times even 60 is also practiced. This is to provide care in the husbands' old age.

Promissory Marriage: There are marriages in which oral promises are exchanged between two families to give each other's children in marriage in order to create bondage between the marrying families. The promise could be made right after or even before the birth of the children.

Since not being married is a disgrace, there is a fear of being stigmatized by some community. "*Kumoker*" is a derogatory term used by the community to refer to a girl who is not married. It literally means one who 'remained standing'.

A girl who is not a virgin at her first marriage is considered unfit for family life and a disgrace to her family; moreover, in some cases, the husband and the in-laws could send her back to her family, which is the worst disgrace that can happen to a girl. In fact virginity is so important that a girl's family becomes nervous if they are not approached for their daughter's hand. Sometimes this concern is also shared by the girls themselves as suggested by the traditional Amharic poetic expression by means of which they are believed to warn their parents of the consequences of not giving them in marriage. It runs as follows:

ጡ ቴ አጎጠጎጠ አበባ ሊያወጣ
ተው አባቴ ዳረኝ አመል ሳላወጣ

"My breast is growing,
Please marry me off my father
Before I misbehave"

Unable to run the household and shoulder responsibility, child brides have difficulty in getting along with their in-laws, they run away from their homes and become subjected to commercial sex work.

Factors that justify early marriage are interconnected and mutually reinforcing. It is a reflection of the gender bias in traditional society where the status of women in general is low. The girl or the woman is thought of as a chattel by her own family, to be controlled and disposed of as they see fit. She is disposed of as early as possible to limit the threats (loss of virginity, premarital pregnancy, and loss of face) and maximizing the advantage. Because of the high value accorded to virginity, she is guarded closely after a certain age, continuously warned and made insecure in her relationships with any male. Early marriage is one of the most effective ways of ensuring control over a woman's productive labour, by inculcating the norm of obedience and subservience to the older "father-figure" husband at an early age (NCTPE 2006:153). As a child bride she is subdued by the older husband and the whole new environment of the in-laws. These are difficult transitions making any girl insecure for life. Poverty has also exacerbated this problem, with some parents marrying off their daughters to wealthy men at an early age because of the bride price. Though the causes of early marriage vary from region to region, the most common reasons are poverty, parents' desire to protect their daughters' chastity, and more importantly the low status of women.

Forced Marriage: Forced marriage is prevalent in Southern Ethiopia, particularly in Oromia and in the SNNP Region, where girls are often forced to marry relatively better-off men against their will and through pressure from elders. Forced marriage also includes widow inheritance, in a situation where a husband dies the widow is forced to marry one of his brothers or close relatives. In some parts of Oromia, a younger sister of a widower would be forced to marry her brother-in-law regardless of the age difference. In both regions, the existence of polygamy contributes to the prevalence of forced marriage. In the case of widow inheritance, it is justified in terms of ensuring the welfare of the children of the deceased and providing protection as well as assistance to the widow. In actual fact, however, the underlying cause of the practice is to prevent loss of family property in case the widow decides to marry a man outside the family.

Abduction: Abduction is considered as one form of marriage. Marriage by abduction, also called marriage by kidnapping or by capture, occurs to a varying degree all over Ethiopia (NCTPE 2003:145). Marriage by abduction is more widely used in Oromia and SNNP than in any other part of Ethiopia. The reasons for such a practice are avoidance of payment of bride-price, anticipation of rejection by the family of the girl and avoidance of wedding expenses which sometimes are very costly.

In each of these types of marriage, the arrangement (or final endorsement) is made through negotiation between two families and the requirement of the bride (who has no idea who her husband would be) to be a virgin.

In line with the patriarchal ideology, the family in Ethiopia is male dominated, as also sanctioned by the Ethiopian civil law of 1960. Family is an important social unit and the relationship between the nucleuses and extended family members is very crucial where the father plays a dominant role over the entire family (Yeshimebrat 2007). Both mobile and immobile properties like land, houses, cars, businesses, and the like are registered under the name of the husband. As women's role is restricted to the household chores, she is worthy only as the self sacrificing mother and wife (Yeshimebrat 2007). The best wife is one who abides by the rules and regulations set by the husband, and is willing to take orders from him. A mother has little say in the affairs of her children, marriage or divorce. A woman's place in Ethiopian society was determined by her reproductive rather than productive role. Hence, according to Lishan (1974) a woman is important to her husband only as a mother of his children.

Talking about gender based discriminations that are prevalent in Ethiopia, Allasebu (1988) states that while there is discrimination against women in all spheres of life it is marriage that bundles it. Until a new family law was enacted in 2000 and the Civil Code of 1960 revised, married women were considered as almost as property by their husbands even by the law.

Hence, it is clear that the patriarchal ideology sanctioned by the law of the land demanded complete subordination or submission of the wife to the husband denying her human and democratic rights. However in 2000, Ethiopia enacted laws that amended the former family law where most of the gender inequalities were abolished; but, marriage through Sheria law is still recognized provided that the couples prefer their marriage to be governed by the Sheria over the civil one.

FGM in Ethiopia

There are about 140 traditional practices that adversely affect the lives of people in Ethiopia. Some of these are, the massaging of the abdomen of pregnant women, tattooing, incest, domestic violence, encouraging excessive fertility, bloodletting, Female Genital Mutilation, feeding a new born baby fresh butter, rape, sexual harassment and forced prostitution (NCTPE in 2003).

One of the most widely practiced harmful traditions in most African countries including Ethiopia is Female Genital Mutilation (FGM). Though the type and the degree vary from place to place, FGM is practiced across sub-Saharan Africa from Somalia in the East to Senegal in the West.

FGM is practiced in both rural and urban areas in all regional states of Ethiopia with the exception of Gambia and some ethnic groups in SNNP. Educated and uneducated families alike practice FGM though its prevalence is decreasing as a result of the big campaigning that is underway, and since it was prohibited by the criminal law of 2006. According to WHO (1990), though there are several types of FGM, only four of them apply to Ethiopia.

(a) Type I is Clitrodoctomy, removing the clitoral hood, sometimes along with part or the entire clitoris. It is the simplest type of FGM and it is also referred to as Sunna.

(b) Type II (Excision) here both the clitoris and a part or all of the labia minora is cut. Both types I and II are commonly practiced in Ethiopia.

(c) Type III (infibulations or 'pharonoiac circumcision'. In this type of circumcision, the clitoris is removed, some part or the entire labia minora is amputated, and incisions are made on the labia majora to create a new surface. A small opening is created to allow the flow of urine and menstrual blood. This is the most severe form of FGM which is practiced in Somali, Afar, Harar, Dire Dawa (eastern Ethiopia) and Benshangul Gumuz (western Ethiopia).

(d) Type IV is the operation performed on the external genitalia including intercession.

Regardless of the form applied, FGM has the following lasting effects on the girl on whom it is practiced according to IIRR (2003):

(1) Done without anaesthetic, it is very painful,
(2) The risk of bleeding to death is high,
(3) Wounds resulting from cut can be infected.
(4) The scars can be reopened during sexual intercourse,
(5) Because of complications, death of the child and/or the mother can happen during childbirth,
(6) As the operation scars the girl physically and emotionally, she will be deprived of sexual pleasure for life.

The age at which FGM is performed, varies depending on the ethnic group and the type of operation. In Amhara, Tigray and among the Argoba, types I and II are performed as early as the seventh or eighth day after delivery. On the other hand in Somali, Harare and SNNP, the practice is done at a later age ranging from four to over 20 years. In some areas like Oromo, Benshangul Gumuz and Goffa, FGM is considered as a prerequisite and preparation for marriage. Thus, in this areas it takes place just a few days before marriage (IIRR, 2003).

Custom and tradition are by far the most frequently cited

reasons for FGM. It is regarded as a norm so much so that the society cannot imagine a woman who has not been circumcised (Hannah, 1997).

In many Ethiopian societies, it is believed that FGM reduces a woman's desire for sex, thereby reducing the chance of a girl losing her virginity as a result of premarital sex and also to curtail women's sexual activity outside marriage. In addition, FGM is performed to avoid difficulty of penetration as well as to enhance the man's sexual pleasure in some areas. (NCTPE, 2003, Hanna, 1997). Followers of different religions including Muslims and Christians prescribe FGM as religious significance; however, it has no basis either in the *Koran* or the *Bible* (NCTPE, 2003; Hanna 1997; Robinson, 2006).

More importantly FGM prepares women for marriage since a man will not marry a girl unless she is circumcised. In this respect cultural expectations encourage women to undergo FGM since it is often associated with positive attributes such as gaining respect within the community and becoming a woman. Girls who have not undergone FGM are considered more likely to be promiscuous and, therefore, unworthy of marriage.Though FGM causes many kinds of psychological, physical and medical complications for women, all of these have been ignored until recently. In short the socio-cultural justifications for practicing FGM are related to the low status of women in a society (Guday 2004, 2007).

Ironically, it is the women who insist that their daughters have to undergo FGM; and it is also the women who perform the incision. However women carry out this practice within the context of traditions where men do not accept wives who have not been circumcised leaving them women with little choice. I once had a fierce argument with a woman acquaintance who was preparing to have her daughter circumcised. According to the lady, circumcision has to be practiced on girls so that they will not be promiscuous, disobedient to their husbands etc. I challenged her with scientific evidence about its harmfulness ; however, sensitized with patriarchal values that her education (she is a college graduate)could not sweep away, she gave a deaf ear to my appeal and went ahead with circumcision of her daughter. In a culture where women do not have much of a choice than being housewives, the mothers can do nothing but prepare their daughters for marriage. Women socialized in patriarchal ideology which is presented as universal traditions like FGM were practiced by them.

Domestic Violence

Domestic violence is a common phenomenon in Ethiopia. In a recent study, 81 per cent of Ethiopian women believe that wife beating is an acceptable (justifiable) form of punishment for arguing with the husband, neglect of children, going out of the house without informing the husband, refusing to have sex or not preparing food well. A man does not need a plausible reason to beat his wife; merely answering back is enough to instigate beating, after all she is his property.

In a study done in one of the regional states (Amhara), sixty percent of women reported that they had experienced some forms of physical violence by their intimate partners in their lives and 74.45 per cent of married men reported that they practiced some forms of physical violence on their wives in their lifetime. Slapping or punching with fist, pushing, shoving or pulling of hair and hitting with stick or any other object etc. are among the common practices of physical violence that women experience at the hands of their intimate partners.

Wife beating is acceptable in the culture. In the same study cited above a significant proportion of women responded that wife beating was acceptable under some circumstances (70%). It can even happen in public as a means of shaping the character of the wife. In fact a popular saying such as "A donkey and a woman need the stick"is invoked to justify wife beating.

Property Ownership

Being an agrarian economy, 83 per cent of the Ethiopian population live in rural areas. Of these 49.8 per cent are women (CSA 2001). Women perform both agricultural work in the fields and household chores at home. As domestic work is solely the responsibility of women, they work fifteen to eighteen hours a day both at home and in the field/s. According to a time use study done by Almaz (1991), seventeen different tasks are undertaken by women. These tasks include fetching water, grinding, fuel collecting, food preparation, milking cows, cleaning stables among others. As most women neither own nor control land, they are economically dependent on the income of their husbands regardless of the amount of work they do both in the household and in the fields. In most areas especially in the south, where a husband was a tenant farmer, the wife was also obliged to work in the household of the landlords.

As an agrarian economy, land in Ethiopia is not only an important element of production but also a source of power. During the monarchy, land belonged to the royal family, the Orthodox Church, and the landlords.

During this period, there were different land tenure arrangements in Ethiopia known as *'semon'* , *'gult'* , *'Maderia'* , *'mengist land'*, *'rest'* and *'rest gult'*, almost of all of which exclude women's ownership. H. Mariam (1994) describes land granting arrangements as follows: (a) *'Semon'* land is granted to those men who serve the Coptic Church but women are not allowed to serve in the church; (b) *'gult'* land is granted to the nobility who are mostly men providing service to the crown; (c) *'maderia'* land is given for meritorious service rendered by men in the army; and (d) '*Mengsit*' land is land owned by the State. Due to these land granting criteria, women were not entitled to possess it. It is only in the *'rist'* and *'rist gult'* arrangements, which were practiced in the northern part of Ethiopia that women could be entitled to some degree of land ownership. The 'rist' system is kinship-based or village based, therefore, women who were descendents of the previous owners would be entitled for inheritance of land; however, even though women could theoretically "own" land under this system, it is the men who control it. In many ethnic groups of the south, women don't inherit land under any circumstance (H. Mariam 1994). Exceptionally, women in Kembatta could inherit their parent's property as equals with their brothers (IIRR, 2003).

In the pastoralist areas such as Afar, Somali and Borana women may own livestock which is the backbone of the economy in the area but it is their husbands who control them. Regardless of the burden of heavier workloads than men, women in the pastoralist areas have very little decision-making powers about their produce.

The situation of women in the urban areas was not much different than the situation of women in the rural areas in terms of property ownership. Though women migrate to towns and cities in search of employment, they find it impossible to get any productive engagement because of the absence of industries or businesses that generate employment. Most women were found in the informal sector, in '*gulit*' or temporary street vending sites where they sell small quantities of food and vegetables. But despite the unavailability of work, women migrated to urban areas. As housework is considered part of women's responsibilities, most women become domestic workers like cooks, and babysitters in a condition where they are not treated humanely. Apart from toiling from dawn to midnight every day (the only break most have is once a month where the labour law does not govern the domestic workers) for a meager amount of money, maids are subjected to sexual violence, rape and unwanted pregnancy by their employers. The other "option" women have is to be commercial sex workers which is regarded as immoral, or antisocial though promiscuity by men is considered normal. However, in the face of abject poverty and absence of choices or options, women put themselves in such degrading situations.

As industries like textiles, food processing etc. began to emerge in the country, they started hiring women with little education or were semi-literate (Tsehai 1984). Here again women were paid less than the men for the same kind of work. They were not even entitled to take maternity leave with pay which meant that they had to take the traditional 40 days' stay in bed without payment. In addition to working long hours a day for a small amount of money, they had to work at home preparing food, taking care of children etc., since they couldn't afford to hire help.

Though opportunities were scarce in wage labour for both sexes, it was more so for women. In 1986, out of the total workers employed in public and private sectors, 82.1 per cent were men and only 17.9 per cent women. Of those women employed in the wage labour force, two-thirds of them were in the manufacturing sector (mainly textiles) and social services of a clerical nature (Allassebu 1988) Women had little opportunity for education (especially in skill training) and access to credit; therefore, the chances of starting their own businesses was very bleak.

Conclusion

The patriarchal structure of the Ethiopian society has curtailed women from having education, gainful employment or access to property as well as access to political participation and in the process they have been subjected to despicable dependence on their fathers, husbands, and sons. In return, the country also loses the contributions of women for development. Acknowledging women's right to property, to education, to health, to political participation not only empowers them but also the whole family and society as well. That is why, patriarchy has to be challenged not only by women but also by everyone else as it is one of the impediments that slow the country's progress.

Part Two

This part discusses the dawn of change in the lives of Ethiopian women: their attendance at school, their participation in the anti-colonial war, their involvement in the students' movement which spearheaded the Ethiopian Revolution of 1974. It also discusses women's role in the Ethiopian people's struggle for democracy and prosperity, the sacrifices they made for democracy in the underground movements and the armed struggle.

CHAPTER IV

The Dawn of Change

Introduction

Ethiopian women registered notable achievements in public life through active involvement in anti-colonial struggles of the Ethiopian people as well as in the struggles to advance democracy and bring about equality. Women played a significant role in the fight against Italian colonial ventures on two occasions, first during 1895-96 and later during the invasion and occupation of 1935-41. Early in the second half of the twentieth century, Ethiopian women played a key role in the student activism that was influenced by the global struggle of women for liberation. Both in its timing and in substance, the activism of Ethiopian women closely paralleled the activism of women all over the world.

Involvement in Anti Colonial Wars

The involvement of Ethiopian women in activities outside the domestic domain is yet to be recorded and published. I am not aware of any such writings save a few that have appeared in the last two or three years' publications.

In most history books written about Ethiopia, the stories of women are under-reported; notwithstanding the stories of wives of kings, queens and princesses or the few women who were close to politically powerful men. This could be attributed to the widespread view of the time that "women do not make history".

Thus in writing this section, I am forced to use information from a few published and unpublished works, and my own experiences, observations and encounters.

Ethiopian women had stood up and fought against colonialism, national oppression, undemocratic rules etc. During the Italian invasion of 1895-96, women fought for freedom and sovereignty in the Battle of Adawa. However, when historians write about Ethiopia's victory in the battle, they tend to glorify only the King and the Queen as well as the nobility who were the military leaders with little or no emphasis on the gallant deeds of ordinary men and women. True, the Emperor Minilik II and the Empress Taitu had effectively played their leadership roles. Empress Taitu, had indeed demonstrated her insightfulness both in politics and military matters; and the latter is demonstrated in her successful strategy to force the Italian submission at the Battle of Inda-Iyesus, near Mekelle (Minale Adugna, 2001). But the victory could not have been achieved without the heroic deeds of thousands of men and women. The fact is that tradition did not deter thousands of women from joining their menfolk at the war front. Women participated in the preparation of food for the combatants, caring for the sick and the wounded, supplying water which was very essential at the war front, etc. Indeed, victory in the battle of Adawa by a country with no modern weapons against the well equipped army of the Italians would not have been possible without the participation of women.

In addition to their contribution in support of families, thousands of Ethiopian women joined the men folk as soldiers, intelligence workers, nurses etc., during the battle of Adawa where Ethiopia demonstrated to the rest of the world that a black nation could defeat a European colonizer.

During the second invasion of Ethiopia by Italy in 1935, women again joined the resistance by marching to the battle fields against the colonial forces, taking up arms along with their husbands, fathers and brothers. Beyond and above the usual task of feeding the fighters and nursing the sick and the wounded, many women actually took up arms and engaged in combat operations. Following the defeat of the Ethiopian army and the fall of Addis, women kept up the momentum of resistance through provision of intelligence and the running of errands between patriots as well as through involvement in acual guerrilla operation (Seltene, 1994). In various fronts and areas, women laid down their lives to fight for liberation of their country. There were women like Shewareged Geddle, Kebedech Seoyoum and many others who have been justly recognized for their patriotic participation in the resistance all the way from the fall of Addis to the liberation in 1941. Weyzero Shewareged, along with Weyzero Marta Newaye was, instrumental in organizing and leading the resistance efforts of many women (Seltene, 1994). But there were also many others who have not been so recognized and celebrated (Combat 1977).

The women prepared dry rations such as *dabo quollo* (roasted bread rolled and cut into pieces), *dirqosh* (a baked bread cut into slices), *besso* (a roasted barley ground into flour), and *quanta* (dried and flavored meat). The list also included some salt, *dilih* (moistened ground pepper), *Shiro* (a roasted and ground peas made into flour), butter and coffee. These supplies were secretly sent to the patriots fighting the Italians in many areas. With the fund the organization collected from different sources, the members of EWWA bought beds for wounded people, iron tables for minor operations and tents under which the Red Cross personnel operated.

To solicit moral and political support from women outside Ethiopia, an appeal to the Women's Association of the League of Nations was sent by Princess Tshehaye the daughter of Emperor Hailesellasie in March 1936. As quoted by Seltene Seyoum, the princess told the Association that:

> "For seven days without break the enemy have been bombing the armies and people of my country including women and children with terrible gases....Against this cruel gas we have no protection, no gas masks—nothing. This suffering and torture is beyond description...."
>
> (p. 30).

As it happened to the appeal of the Emperor earlier, this one also fell on deaf ears.

During the five years of war against Italy, two women's associations, the Ethiopian Women's Welfare Association (EWWA) and Ethiopian Women's Volunteer Service Association (EWVSA) were formed. Both associations' deployed members devoted to the war effort by preparing gas masks, bandages, rations as well as medical services for the war victims (Meaza, 2007). At the end of the war, the two organizations merged into one under the aegis of EWWA, and transformed themselves into a welfare association raising funds to uplift the lives of poor urban women.

The EWWA charter states the objective of the Association as being to help:

> "...the sick, the physically impaired, the widowed women, the orphans, as well as find ways of improving childcare and provoke women's advancement in home economics (Kenewena Seket 1993 EC).

A similar organization was also formed by wives of the armed forces in the early sixties which looked into the welfare of orphaned children and widows of the army. Though these organizations did not pursue any political agenda they nevertheless were the precursors of women's movements in the country.

After testing the fruits of working for a cause outside their homes, the members of the EWWA resolved to continue their activities with a different intent. The Association undertook many income-generating activities such as bazaars, lotteries etc. to raise funds. Some say that the concept of *tambola* was introduced to the Ethiopian society by the organization (Kewane and Raye, 1993 E.C.).

Orphanages, adult education centers, primary schools, mother and child clinics, and programmes for traditional birth attendants were run by the organization until it was banned by the military government.

As almost all the members of EWWA were from the ruling class sharing an ideology that women's condition in Ethiopia is

God "ordained", its aim was not to raise any political issue regarding women's equality but that of providing welfare for them. However, its contribution to the war efforts and later to the welfare of women cannot be underestimated. The organization was also the first effort by women to come together and work for a common cause where the importance of getting organized was thought of.

Regarding the experience women gained during the war, Seltene Seyoum (1994) writes. "To be organized under such associations was a new experience for many Ethiopian women who for the first time had suddenly come out in to the open, leading and led by themselves". Even though what women did for the war effort was of preparing food, caring for the sick etc., which was an extension of their traditional responsibilities, the very fact of working together in an organized manner, participating in meetings and discussions to meet the objectives of the organization gave them a new experience of leadership, organizational skill, and the like (Seltene Seyoum, 1994). Furthermore, through the discussions, speeches and poems that were read in their meetings, women also became aware of international issues which was indeed a new horizon for many of them.

Attending Schools

When modern education was introduced by Emperor Minilik II, there were no female students in the school named after the Emperor himself, or in those opened subsequently. This, despite the fact that the Emperor's Educational Act of 1898 (EC) requested parents to send both their sons and daughters to school. Though a handful of enlightened families sent their daughters to mission schools operating in the country, the participation of girls in modern education became a reality only when a girls' school named after Empress Menen was opened in Addis Ababa in 1923 (EC). The relevance of women's education was perceived, at the time, from the viewpoint of preparing them to be good housewives in the fashion of the finishing schools of Europe. This is evident from the fact that the curriculum, for the first few years, was very different from that of schools opened for boys: the school was not teaching subjects like mathematics and the sciences. Rather the curriculum concentrated heavily on home economics and subjects such as cooking, grooming and needlework, etc. Tsehaye (1984), alludes to the fact that Ethiopian men who were educated in the 1940s paid fees for their fiancés in trendy boarding schools opened in Addis Ababa to train them as 'accomplished ladies' who knew 'modern' cookery, dress-making, general home-making and some music. Stories are told of eligible bachelors from the nobility who used to go to the girls schools to choose their future wives from among the students.

Despite the objective of these schools and efforts to teach home economics, the popular view regarding girls' education was still a negative one: it was believed that modern education spoils women rendering them to be bad wives. A popular couplet ridicules women who attend school by referring to their alleged incompetence in cooking. It went as follows:

> የእቴጌ ተማሪ የሰራችው ዶሮ
> አይኗ ፍጥጥ አለ እንደ ሴት ወይዘሮ

> "In chicken stew cooked by the students of Menen School,
> the chicken's eye pops up
> like the eye of a lady".

The school girls, in other words, could not even dissect the chicken properly. When comprehensive high schools were introduced in Ethiopia, girls were not admitted in the industrial and academic streams. Their options were limited either to home economics or secretarial courses. Since it was believed that women should be nothing else but secretaries, female students were denied access to the accounting department of the Commercial Schools of Addis Ababa by a directive given to the school by the Ministry of Planning of the Military Government. A counter directive to allow women join all departments of the Commercial School had to be written by the then Deputy Minister of Higher Education Commission in 1992. The struggle for women's equality in education however kept on going.

Constraints against girls' education can fall under four important factors that are economics-related, family-related, school-related and culture-related (Emebet, 2003) with each influencing the other. Culture related barriers can be observed in both the schools and the family. A good example is the view that education for boys and girls should be different because of the social division of labour a view which is shared by teachers, parents and the larger community alike.

The economic problem which is closely associated with the poverty of the country applies equally as a problem in the education of both boys and girls. In a poor country like Ethiopia where governments do not have the requisite budget to open and run schools, parents are constrained to cover educational costs such as school fees and school materials, etc. Furthermore, in poor households, parents look at the opportunity cost of sending children to school since many of them bring in family incomes by working in the informal or formal market. But poverty has an additional negative impact on girls' education too. In a society like Ethiopia where girls' education is viewed as a waste of money, time etc., preference is always given to boys when parents have to make a choice of who to send to school. Moreover, girls' labour is also required more than the boys' since they work both within and outside the household. Not only girls in poor households, but also those in relatively better off families are overworked. This is because of the general belief that women's primary role is to be housewives and mothers; hence they have to learn the basics of housekeeping, cooking, child rearing, etc. at an early age.

Apart from poverty and housework loads, there are traditional practices and beliefs such as early marriage, abduction and rape, etc. that hinder families from sending their daughters to school. As noted earlier, girls used to get married as young as 10 years or 11 years of age. This almost always meant dropping out of school before they complete a level of education. Abduction and rape occur widely and until recently were not even considered as crimes. Parents would discourage their daughters from studying with their friends, or walking long distances to school because of fear of abduction or rape that might result in pregnancy or loss of virginity, both viewed as disgraceful to the family. The distance of schools from home, lack of teaching–learning materials, gender unfriendly school environment are also factors that affect girls' education. In regard to the latter, discrimination of girls in the classroom, harassment by both teachers and male students and lack of supportive structure are problems that are commonly faced by girls. School authorities and the staffing structure reinforce the view that women occupy a subordinate position in the work place. The low number of female teachers, school administrators, deans and department heads of colleges/universities confirm this fact. Women are also depicted, including in school textbooks, as weak and inferior and hence should be confined to house work. A study undertaken by the Curriculum Department of the Ministry of Education revealed that no female-focused topics were used in science subjects and the majority of the proper names in the text books were men's. The adjectives used to describe women were fertile, pregnant, breast feeder, pretty while those used to describe men were revolutionary leader, freedom fighter, general, etc. If women were depicted in the textbooks it was in relation to the household chores for instance, "Almaze (a female name) and her broom". I was once challenged by my third grade daughter, whose social studies text book has described the role of a mother as one who stay at home to cook and take care of the family, while I was working outside of the home. The third grader was disturbed that her mother did not stay at home to take care of her and her sister. It is hoped that the my grand daughter will not receive such stereotyped education to confront her working mother (my daughter) with a similar question.

In regard to higher education, the participation of women was painfully slow and gradual. There were actually no women students when the first public institute of higher learning, the UCAA opened its doors. The first woman entered the university college in 1952 and by the year 1960, there were 40 female students (Balsvik, 1985). Female students not only lived in separate quarters under special dormitory supervision but also had to be in their rooms by a certain time; moreover, first and second year female students were not allowed to study in the library after 7 p.m. This was done apparently to appease the parents who were concerned as well as reluctant to send their daughters to college where they were being educated with men.

Women in higher education were also seen with disapproval since their 'emancipation', 'westernization' was regarded as lack of respect for their traditions. Partly for this reason, men including those who were educated, were ambivalent about marrying educated women. They tended to prefer less educated women for marriage. There were also issues about educated women's intellectual capacity. Balsivic (1985) cites topics that were debated such as "Is emancipation of women beneficial to society"? "Who has contributed more to the making of civilization, men or women?" and "Educating women is a mistake" which were discussed in the university. Women in the university also felt uncertain of their new positions as they were confronted with opposition and suspicion by the community (Balsivic, 1985). Openly questioning the value of higher education for women was over by the middle of the 1960s although female students continued to be regarded neither as active participant in extracurricular fields nor in the intellectual sphere where male students began urging them to be so.

Despite obvious signs of male approval of female participation, the relationship between the sexes in the university remained problematic. Male and female attitudes were determined to a large extent by the ingrained norms of traditional society concerning marriage and the nature of male friendship. Parents chose spouses and arranged marriages; brides were supposed to be shy and virgins, which again presupposed segregation of sexes.

The 1960s and 1970s were a period where very rapid changes were experienced by the students in HSIU. As such, it was only to be expected that a mixture of seemingly opposing attitudes, values, and ideals coexisted. Although there were exceptions, the prevailing tendency among male students appeared to have been accepting that of university education for women and consciously fighting male prejudices against this new role hence female students seemed to gain personal assurance and integrity.

SENEDU GEBRU: A Woman with a Mission

One key person who contributed to the changed educational landscape of women in Ethiopia was Senedu Gebru. Senedu worked as an assistant directress first and then as directress of the Itege Menen girls' school in Addis Ababa. This promoter of women's education was appointed as the first Ethiopian directress to the post in 1949, and headed the school for eight years. Senedu believed that women's education was a means of their empowerment through skills and knowledge. In the words of Rita Pankhurst (1991),

> "Perhaps Senedu's main goal throughout her career as an educator was to see more Ethiopian women entering into professions and public life, to become 'somebody'. As a first step in this direction she was instrumental in introducing secondary grades at the school. At the beginning of every school year, she puts a notice outside the school gates inviting girls to register, telling them that if they went to school they would become leaders in their country.

Senedu applied different strategies to encourage girls' education, some of which are still used today. She protected the bright girls from marrying before completing their schools against the wish of their families, arranged extra tuition and nutritious food during exam times, and invited successful women to share their experiences. Moreover, she counseled girls specially the promising ones, so that they did not choose the stereotypical "women's" fields of nursing or secretarial jobs. Rita Pankhurst (1991) who interviewed some of Senedu's students such as Metasebia Dmissie, Kibkab Tafesse, indicated that the students were counseled, in some cases even forced to join academic streams rather than vocational training which helped them to join the university and change their lives. On another occasion, when Senedu heard that four girls decided to become telephone operators, she went to the Ministry of Post, Telephones and Telegraphs and persuaded the minister to release the girls so that they could complete their studies before rejoining the ministry.

When students revealed that they were leaving school to get married against their wishes, Senedu would come to their rescue; however, such occasions were rare since students would not normally report about marriage arrangements because it was a taboo subject. In most cases students who were betrothed felt ashamed if others knew about it. Nevertheless, Senedu used to be angry when she discovered that a student had left school to be married. According to Rita Pankhurst (1991), Senedu once introduced a very controversial rule demanding that parents sign a contract with the school declaring that they would pay back to the government the expenses incurred on account of their daughters if they withdrew their daughters from school for the purpose of marriage (Rita Pankhurst, 1991). The rule met with fierce opposition from the parents as the latter thought that marriage was a destiny for women and that it had to be consummated at a young age. However, Senedu never gave up on her struggle but changed her approach from confrontation to dialogue; hence she would continually and positively talk to the families about the importance of education and the benefit it would bring to a girl, her families and her country.

In the conversation I had with Dr. Samuel Assefa, a son and Yewebdar Yilma, a niece of Senedu, in December 2011, I asked them about the motivations or the reasons behind the unusual (for her time) conviction of Senedu regarding women's education. Dr. Samuel attributed Senedu's education abroad, her involvement in the war and her life in exile as well as imprisonment in Italy in shaping her personality, conviction and beliefs that the visibility of women can be enhanced through education. Her father, Kentiba Gebru, a remarkable man for his age who encouraged all his daughters to be educated abroad, had a big influence in her life. The friendship and solidarity of Senedu with the well-known member of the Suffragette Movement, Silvia Pankhurst, had also sharpened her view on the equality of women as both believed that they could change the men's' world (Dr. Samuel 2011).

Having realized that Senedu's life looms larger in public unlike women of her generation, I wanted to know how she managed to balance her public and her private life; therefore, I had an interesting discussion with her son and niece. According to

Dr. Samuel (2011), his mother was a very strong headed person who firmly believed that women should not be limited to domestic life but be involved in public life as well. She believed that every aspect of life, be it politics, social or economic concerns women. Hence they must not be pigeonholed to what are commonly considered "women's" affairs only. Being the only woman member of Black Lion, a resistant movement during the Italian occupation, she was told by the leader to withdraw her membership and go abroad as fighting would be very difficult for her. Well, her response was a very firm "no" challenging him that she could not be denied of her civic responsibility on account of her sex. Hence she continued to work in the war front, recruited more women to join the movement and established Ethiopian Red Cross Association. Later on, she was elected as Vice President of the National Red Cross and Vice Chairperson of the International Red Cross and Red Crescent Board. While she was the vice chairperson of the board, she wrote an article for nuclear disarmament in line with the non-aligned movement (Dr. Samuel 2011).

Senedu struggled to balance her public and private life, however, her inclination tilted to the public. Though Senedu admired and acknowledged the native intelligence and knowledge of traditional women, Dr. Samuel said, she "hated traditional life with a vengeance and rejected it with extreme fashion; I have neither seen her wearing lip stick or eye shadow and the likes. She believed that she belonged to the public life rather to her family". Her niece, Yewebedar, thought as a child that her aunt never cared about her family and relatives as had no time to deal with them. It was only when she grew up that she understood Senedu's plight in juggling between the two aspects of her life.

Explaining her sense of public responsibility, Dr. Samuel (2011) remembers that during the military coup of Mengistu Neway in 1960, Senedu had to leave her young children at home to stay with a delegation of foreign women who came to attend a meeting in Addis Ababa, as she felt that it was her responsibility to see that the delegates are safe and comforted.

However, Senedu was a very loving mother who allotted time to shape her children into being responsible citizens. Dr. Samuel remembers the times he had spent with his mother in her office at home most afternoons, for an hour or two, discussing serious matters as she expected *kume neger* from her children.

To the credit of her husband and her matriarchal family, her attitude towards the importance of public life was accepted within them. Showing how proud and supportive his father was to his mother, Dr. Samuel remembers his father's comment, "This award should have been given to your mother not to me" when he was awarded Minilik's National Award by The Emperor. However, Senedu's behaviour was cause for concern within the larger society as it was unwomanly to assume public life at the time. Dr. Samuel believes that his mother must have been in pain because of the lonely situation that she found herself as she did not have likeminded women to share her views with.

Senedu had many preoccupations. She loved art, literature and had written many articles, poems etc. Unfortunately most of her writings, except the book entitled *"Yelebe Metsehaf"*, are unpublished. Furthermore, she had established an organization for physically impaired where they develop handicraft skills so that they become self reliant. (Yewbdar Yilma 2011).

Having a strong commitment for women's equal participation in every aspects including in politics, Senedu stood for parliamentary election. During her campaign, unlike others, she addressed a large group of the Imperial Body Guard emphasizing her role and experience as a member of "Black Lion" movement during the Italian occupation. And, the campaign played her a big role in winning the election (Dr. Samuel 2011).

Senedu became one of the first two women MPs in Ethiopia's first parliamentary elections of 1957. Subsequently, she was elected vice president of the house of deputies. Four years later she was re-elected and run for the office of Presidency in parliament. At that point she met fierce opposition from male MPs who were against the view that such a high post be held by a woman.

A proposal was tabled in the parliament recommending that women should change their names to that of their husbands in line of the practice of the west, about which Senedu argued against and became victorious (Yewbedar 2011). Subsequently, she tabled bills in parliament which sought to legislate that (a) the joint property of a married couple could not be mortgaged without the signature of both parties, (b) the principles of equal civil rights for women and men and elimination of unequal inheritance customs from Ethiopian civil law on the grounds that humanity, not sex, should be the main consideration in the law. Due to the obviously undemocratic order of the time, the bills were rejected.

Despite her intelligence, competence and the strong role Senedu played as noted earlier, she had never been appointed to a bigger government post than as educational attaché in Germany where her husband was an Ambassador. I wonder could it be because of her gender, perhaps.

Nevertheless Senedu's struggle for women's equality was not all in vain. Indeed in many ways she was a trail blazer. Today, girls' education is given paramount importance not only by the government but by parents' as well. The marriage age is set at 18, no girl child can be forced to get married without her permission as there are committees in most schools where they can report and even take parents to court. All the civil and democratic rights of women including the right to property and inheritance are acknowledged in the Constitution of 1995.

Participation in Student Movements

In the struggle for democracy and the political and economic rights of the Ethiopian people, university and high school students have played a significant role. They demanded land reform, recognition of the rights of nationalities and civil and democratic rights, education for all, and later on for women's rights. As it was true of the student movement the world over in the 60s and 70s, the movement was left oriented. With a fighting spirit, students joined hands in challenging first the monarchy and then the military dictatorship. In a book entitled *Ethiopia: The Political Economy of Transition*, Arai and Kiros observed that in a country where there was no democratic culture, students were to shoulder a mammoth historical task and advocate the cause of the masses (1995). Students demonstrated, boycotted schools, and raised their voices championing the causes of the poor. In 1965, students took to the streets of Addis Ababa under the slogan 'Land to the Tiller'; the demonstration was a historic event in the growth of the Ethiopian Student Movement since it ushered in a new era of student political consciousness and radicalism (Tesfaye Demelash, 1984).

The issue of nationalities and national rights in the multi-ethnic country came to the fore in 1969. In a student publication entitled *Tagele* (Struggle) a university student leader Wlelegn Mekonnen argued that all nations and nationalities had a right to self-determination, including secession. In spite of repression by the state, student opposition grew stronger and stronger. The focus of the protest was on a wide range of issues from concrete socioeconomic matters which had a direct bearing on the livelihood of workers and the poor in Addis Ababa to the military presence and cultural hegemony of U.S. imperialism in Ethiopia. The student agitation took various forms including organizing rallies and panel discussions, poetry reading, class boycotts, strikes and street demonstrations. In all of these female students participated actively though not from the very beginning. For instance, out of the six students who were killed and imprisoned by the monarchy for hijacking an Ethiopian Airlines plane in 1965 (EC) two were female students. While one of them by the name Tadellech Kidane Mariam was put in prison, Martha Mebrahtu was killed. Martha was a senior year medical student at Haile Sellasie University who used to organize discussion forums on the question of women in the university. She was also the president of the Ethiopian Medical Association.

Despite the participation of women in all the political activities of the student movements it took some time for the women's issue to be articulated openly. It was with the establishment of a student organization known as University Students' Union, Addis Ababa (USUAA) that the women's question was reviewed and analyzed in the light of anti-feudal and anti-imperialist lines of Marxism (Combat 1977). Thus women's subjugation was analyzed and interpreted from the Marxist viewpoint as a "dual oppression" inflicted on women by both the state and male chauvinism.

As the struggle of the students, teachers and workers intensified, so did the struggle of women. However, many women were not at the center of things though they participated in the demonstrations, class boycotts and the like. Because of the patriarchal thinking that politics was not for women, the leaders of the student movement deployed the female students to such activities as typing flyers and other political material to be distributed to the public, but efforts were not made to make them understand the content of what they were typing through political discussions until study circles were organized at later dates. In regard to discouraging female students, Netsanet Mengestu who was a student of Haile Sellasie University at the time said:

> "Struggle contributed its fair share in belittling women. Everyone knows the cartoonist Zewede Hailu. He invariably portrayed women as creatures obsessed with cosmetics, miniskirts and parties. (Some of his cartoons showed girls scaling a wall after coming late from a party). His message was: that is the sum-total of their achievements. The same period of time witnessed women being harshly condemned in verse. For all that, we took part in public demonstrations, such as those staged about Rhodesia. We, women, may have been reticent, but we did not lack commitment. Not only did we participate in demonstrations, but we were at the forefront"(Bahru, 2010).

Natsanet Mengiste was a student activist when she was in the university who later become an underground worker of EPRP leaving her two children and a well paying job behind. After working in the underground for about four years she was caught and put in prison for about six years. Netsant was a founder of two women empowerment non-government organisations known as Progynist and Meklit a micro-finance institution catering for the financial and non-financial needs of women. She has been the executive director of Progynist for the last 17 years and is currently a board member of Enat Bank, the first women's bank in Ethiopia. She was also a Deputy Minister of Trade and Commerce during the transition.

A women's fashion show was organized by the University

Administration in coordination with an American Peace Corp Volunteer, Linda. This was the first instance where the women students took opposing sides on an issue, as there were women who demonstrated against the fashion show and those who participated in it. The university students denounced the fashion show as an imperialist ploy that had an objective of making Ethiopia a dumping ground for their textiles and commodities; and for such purpose they use female students. Both men and some women disrupted the fashion show by throwing rotten eggs and tomatoes at those participants as they entered the Mekonnen Hall of the university. The incident led to the closure of the university and ouster of the male students from the dormitories. Female students against the fashion show collected money from evening students and the public going from office to office to support the male students who were denied cafeteria and dormitory services. Such acts were not taken well by the supporters of the fashion show, thus a tug of war between the two groups ensued if not openly but subtly. I had the opportunity to discuss the incident with Mrs. Tirisit Agonafer, one of the participant models a few years ago about how the participants felt about the demonstration. According to Tirsit, those who participated in the show did not realize the political implication but enjoyed the excitement of being in the show with fancy clothes, walking in the manner of showing their shapes and looking "beautiful".

Though very few, there were male students who saw the importance of women's participation in the struggle and helped establish women's study circles in the university at the latter days of the movement. As the movement was not confined to students in the country those who were studying abroad also organized themselves and joined the struggle from afar. Actually, there were two student organizations outside Ethiopia: The Ethiopian Student Association in North America (ESANA) and the Union of Ethiopian Students in Europe (ESUE). Under the umbrella of these organizations, women students abroad organized themselves and tried to advance the women's agenda. Among other things, they used to write articles about the oppression of Ethiopian women in a semi-annual paper entitled *Tenesh Ethiopiawit* (meaning *Wake up Ethiopian Woman*). The title of the journal was later changed to *Tagey Ethiopiawit* (meaning Struggle of the *Ethiopian Woman*). The articles in these journals articulated the plight of Ethiopian women and called for organized efforts to bring about qualitative change. For instance, in the 1973 issue alone, articles analyzing Ethiopian women's disempowerment by tradition, the lack of property and legal rights for women, the role of educated women in the struggle were written.

Such articles served the purpose of creating awareness among the Ethiopian elite and defined the form of struggle that had to be waged to attain equality for women. However, the awareness created was limited to a small circle of educated women.

Abebech Bekele was an example of an activist student joining the movement from outside Ethiopia. Abebech joined the movement while she was studying in New York. I had the privilege of interviewing her during her visit to Ethiopia in August 2011, after 30 years of residence abroad.

According to her in the early 60s Ethiopian students studying in the U.S.A used to have an informal association that brought them together for the celebration of Ethiopian holidays. In the course of time, the association became a formal union and began to be radicalized, when new students from Ethiopia who were already involved in the student movements joined. Some of the students started questioning the political and economic situation in Ethiopia, challenging the role of the Emperor who was ruling Ethiopia at the time. Slowly some members started taking radical positions against imperialism and feudalism, which made other members withdraw from the union since they were supporters of the Emperor. In regard to women, only Abebech and one other female student by the name of Tsehaye remained in the union. The radicalization of the union went as far as taking a position to change the Imperial state in Ethiopia. In one of the meetings of ESUNA that Abebech attended new students who came from Ethiopia to the States raised the issues of the "national question" and self determination as one of the pressing demands of the Ethiopian people. However other members did not agree that "NQ" was a primary issue for the Ethiopian people and as a result the movement split into two.

Abebech not only allied with the radical view but also realized the importance of involving women in the new radical process where important national issues were being discussed; she felt that the issues should not be left for men alone. Then she started to contact Ethiopian female students in the U.S.A. and Europe and urged them to organize women's study groups.

Abebech managed to convince some students and started a group in New York with 15 women who agreed to meet twice a year and study about the oppression of Ethiopian people in general and women in particular. Successfully organizing a study group in U.S.A., Abebech then started contacting other female students in Europe and helped to organize them so that female students in both USA and Europe could jointly fight for the cause of the Ethiopian people. She received a positive response. This led to the formation of a worldwide organization of Ethiopian women affiliated to ESUNA. The aim of the organization was to create awareness about the women's situation in Ethiopia and to wage an organized resistance against the feudal state. In order to meet its objectives, the organization held forums in European and American cities. The organization agreed to publish a sort of journal called *Labaderite* meaning female proletariat. However, there was an opposition to the title of the publication by people who believed that the Ethiopian situation at the time was not ready for a proletarian revolution. Therefore, the name was changed to *Tenesh Ethiopiawit* after the first issue.

These publications were sent to Ethiopia to women who were involved in the student struggle; however, they had a very limited distribution among educated women in the cities. After the fall of the Haile Sellasie regime, the members of the organization from Europe and North America including Abebech went back to Ethiopia and continued their work.

According to Abebech, the political climate in North America and Europe, where there were different rights movements such as civil rights, women's and black rights etc., radicalized many Ethiopian students including her. Abebech remembers how she and her university friends challenged the State University of New York's administration into incorporating Black and African history into the curriculum. The international students' movement at the time was left-oriented, which led many of the Ethiopian students into reading books on Russia, Cuba, and Vietnam etc. Abebech attributes her personal radicalization to the black movement leaders such as Angela Davis and Lenin's book on *Women's Question*. She was impressed by the way Lenin expressed and articulated the issues of women and also by his proposal for women to wage a dual struggle against the oppressor class and male chauvinism, as well as on the importance of a separate women's organization. Abebech still believes that Lenin's way is the way for women's emancipation.

The Ethiopian student movement had linked up with similar left oriented organizations of the third world and it used to exchange solidarity messages with them. An example of such interaction was a message sent by Hindustani Chadar Party (Marxist-Leninist) to the 21st Congress of ESUNA that was held in Cambridge, MA, (Combat, 1973, Vol. 2, No. 1, pp. 44-46).

When the Ethiopian students' movement in North America (ESUNA) and the one in Europe formed the Federation in 1973, Abebech became the first President of the Federation. I asked Abebech what it was like to be a woman President of the Association especially in a situation where male chauvinism was rampant among the Ethiopian male students. Her response was that because the federal structure was a new form of organization with which no one had any experience, the men were not willing to take chances of perhaps making mistakes; therefore, they convinced her to be the first president despite her appeal that she had no time and experience.

Abebech who was the only woman member of the Central Committee of EPRP went to Assemba in the North of Ethiopia to join Ethiopian People's Revolutionary Army (EPRA) after working as an underground fighter in Addis Ababa upon her return from the USA.

Abebech found that there were no separate women's organizations within the EPRP's army where women could discuss and tackle issues related to male chauvinism within the army as in the larger society. The women who were there (they were about 20-30) informed her that some of the members were discouraging and making belittling remarks on account of their gender. A seminar of women in the army was called in a place called Assefa where 20-30 women participated, vowed to fight male chauvinism in the army. Sexual harassment was also one of the issues raised by women in the seminar. Then a committee to fight against unfair treatment of women was set up to monitor the undemocratic practices of men towards women in the army.

The Influence of the Student Movement

As an offshoot of the students' movement, the Ethiopian women's struggle for equality and empowerment was shaped by the left orientation; and there are both theoretical and practical explanations:

It was the socialist theory that thoroughly articulated the emancipation of women; using historical materialism as an analytical tool, it challenged the dominant belief that women's inferiority was permanent and natural.

It also probed into the argument that women have been in such a position from time immemorial as if it would be an eternal condition (Karat 2005). As discussed in Engels' book, *The Origin of the Family, Private Property and State*; historical materialism attributes women's subjection to a particular stage of social development, thus women were not always considered 'weaker' or inferior because of their sex.

In practice, the Soviet Union legislated total equality of women with men as early as 1917. Through a new family code it recognized the right of divorce, alimony, equal rights of men and women in matrimonial property and abolished the concept of illegitimacy giving all children the right of parental support whether born in wedlock or not. The 1922 land code also granted gender equality in all community held lands (Karat 2005). To ease the workload of women and also give them time to work outside the home, crèches and kindergarten, communal laundries were opened. All this was enacted way before the women in the West challenged male oppression at home.

As East European countries adopted socialism, women became beneficiaries of the measures and legal actions taken by their governments. For instance, in 1986, about 81 per cent of the children 3-6 years old were in day care centers; and 80 per cent of women were working outside their homes in East Germany as compared to 32 per cent in West Germany. In 1987, 68 per cent of all doctors in the Soviet Union were women (Karat 2005).

These gains by women had a great impact on women's movements in Ethiopia as well as in other parts of Third World countries. Therefore, in the process of participating in the students' movement for democracy, prosperity and progress of the country, women also articulated the nature of their subordination and the content and form of the struggles that they had to wage.

To conclude, Ethiopia has had a strong tradition of local women's movements. Women have participated in struggles against national subjugation and liberation wars in keeping Ethiopia independent; have participated in the student movement that shaped the present polity of the country. But, the records and history of women barely exists. Their contributions have been silenced unlike those of their counterparts because it is men who write and take policy decisions. Ethiopian women have to write their history and weave it into the national narratives.

CHAPTER V

Women's Portrayal in the Popular Culture

Universally, women are considered inferior to men albeit that the degree might vary from society to society; and, their inferiority is often depicted in proverbs, symbolic devices, and structural arrangements. For example, in the Neurs in Gambela (south-west Ethiopia), a woman is excluded from her family and friends during maternity for weeks, put in a small hut alone for a few, weeks only an elderly lady is allowed to go into the hut to give her food. Similarly, women are not allowed to participate in the Geda system of the Oromo people (one of the Ethiopian Ethnic groups).

Men are valued for their deeds, professions and wealth and women for their appearances such as their hair, eyes, nose, shape and on so. As the women's main preoccupation is to be a wife and a mother, she has to have a desirable body, and right from birth, a girl child is socialized in being beautiful, presentable and attractive both physically and manner-wise so that she can get a suitable husband and/or a lover.

Traditionally, women in many cultures including Ethiopia were groomed with different hair styles, tatoos on different parts of their bodies such as neck, forehead, gums of their teeth, legs, hands, faces as symbols of beauty. However, traditional means of beautification have been replaced with plenty of different products for all parts of women's bodies: thus many shades of eye liners and brows for the eyes, lipsticks, gloss and liner for the lips, different colour of nails and hair. Since women should have "long straight hair" those who are not endowed with it have to buy human (that is obviously dead) or synthetic ones. Globalization has ushered in a certain "standard of beauty" based on the western model that requires man made products, diet, plastic surgery, etc. The cosmetic or beauty industries producing ever ending new products target vain women who jump on them as they feel that they have to look beautiful or else they don't feel valued. Apart from the advertisement of these huge cosmetics industries, programs like beauty contests, fashion shows, films and theaters socialize women into being commodities. Alas, due to the constant message those women receive about the high value of their bodies to attract men on whom they have to depend for their livelihoods discourage them from looking into other options to be self-reliant and independent. Therefore, they spend their time, efforts and money on cosmetic products to meet the 'standard of beauty' established by advertisement.

The stress on traditional roles of women and their physical beauty as only important aspects of their lives compel many women to give priority to enhancing their domestic roles rather than developing other important traits that lead to their independence. Such socialization also leaves an indelible mark on the minds of people as to the role of women, thus perpetuating the subordinate position of women in the society. Girls who have been subjected to the views that women's physical beauty is paramount importance to their success would give more time to beautify themselves from an earlier age rather than on their studies. Their aspiration towards their future would also be limited to being wives or dependent on men. I had come across girls who have told me that, though they go to school, their ultimate goal is to attract men, get married and satisfy their future husbands in any ways as they are trapped by the stereotyped role of women that is constantly propagated.

I remember during my student days, when western products like lipstick, face powder were introduced, we use to discourage female students who concentrate on their looks rather than their studies. Thus, Mesfine Habtu* a member of the Current Events

---

* Mesfin Habtu was one of the student movement leaders in the university where he served as Secretary General of USUAA, in 1967-68.

Club at the then Teferi Mekonnen School (Now Entoto Technical Vocational School) had a very famous song whose lyrics go like this:

ቀዩን ቀለም አጥፊው ከከንፈርሽ ላይ
ቁንጅና ውበትሽ አጉልቶ እንዲታይ

Remove the red colour from your lip
So that your beauty is enhanced

Ethiopian popular culture is no different from others as it reinforces the patriarchal ideology of women's traditional roles as mothers and wives who are not only confined to domestic domain but also are dependent and subordinate to men. Women and men are repeatedly reminded where the place of women is through the following proverbs:

ሴት በማጀት ወንድ በአደባባይ

A woman in the kitchen a man in the courts

የሴት ሀገሯ ባሏ፣ ሙያዋ ጠባዩዋ?

A woman's country is her husband and her career is her character

የሴት ሞቷ በማጀቷ

A woman dies in her kitchen

Such depictions continue even today regardless of the fact that women have started assuming many other roles apart from the domestic ones. More alarming is the fact that women are demonized and vilified when they either assume roles other than the traditional ones or demonstrate characters that is deemed "unwomanly", perpetuating their subordinate position in the society.

ከሴት መምከር ለመስከር

To consult with women is like being drunk

የሴት ወበራ ትታጠቃለች ካራ

a unruly woman takes up the sword

ሴትና ዶሮ ሳያብዱ አይውሉም

A day would not pass without a woman and a chicken going crazy.

Women's personality as wicked and one without mind is popularly affirmed as illustrated in the following proverbs; subtly influencing the society that women's nature and character are not fit for public life by further stressing the common and prevalent negative views upheld in the society.

ሴት ማገዶ ስታጣ የቤቷን ምሰሶ ትነቅላለች

A woman would pull a pillar (wooden) of her house if she was in need of firewood.

ሴት መውደድ ገሀነም መውረድ ነው

To love a woman is to go to hell.

ሴት እና ፈረስ እንደኩሬ ውሀ እያደር ያንስ

ምን ሴት ብታወክ በወንድ ያልክ

A woman and horse diminish every day like reserved (natural reservation) water.

Woman may have knowledge but the decision rests with the man.

The power of dramas, proverbs, poems, songs and theaters is no less than the media in impacting the mindset of the society in any issue. particularly when they are transmitted as entertainment.

Like in any society, songs are listened to or sung in Ethiopia to express different feelings such as love, dissatisfaction, desire, etc. Thus, on the basis of their purposes, songs transmit attitudes, perceptions and values to the society socializing it to behave or not in certain ways. For instance, the lyrics of war songs motivate soldiers to keep on fighting even under precarious situations. Being listened for recreational purposes (in most cases), the message that songs transmit are very subtle too. They sensitize people indirectly about life, society and how men and women should behave.

Most love songs in Ethiopia (Amharic) underscore the physical appearances of women rather than their character, work or achievements implying that the importance of women lies on their bodies. Parts of women's bodies such as eyes, teeth, skin, hips, lips, breast, legs and neck are highly praised and associated with femininity. Contrarily, songs written about men praise their deeds, achievements and characters. The following lyrics in a famous song played by Muluken Mellese, one of Ethiopian singers makes it evident.

አይኗ ሲያንፀባርቅ እንደ ኮኮብ ደምቆ
ሽንጧ ሲተራመስ በአካሄድ ርቆ
ከብረት አይኖቿ ብርሀን ይመነጫል
ሽንጧ ሲተራመስ ፀጉሯም ይጫወታል

The sparkle of her eyes is as bright as the star
The swinging of her hips makes her gait perfect
Light comes of her eyes
And her hair plays along as she swings

Well, there is no harm in praising the beauty of women in a love song, but the concern lies in the fact that women are desired and praised for their physical beauty only alludes to the fact that women do not have any other virtue.

In instances where songs are written about their character, women are demonized portrayed as swindlers, weak, dependent, wicked and so on. According to a study conducted to investigate the image of women in Amharic songs, it was found that even the love songs characterize women as untrustworthy, irrational, unfaithful, and incompetent to accomplish anything (Tsion, 1997). The following lyrics of songs depict how negatively women are portrayed.

ይችን ቡችላዬን እሰሩልኝ በጣም

ሴት ውሻ ናትና መልከስከስ አታጣም

"Take away this poppy and chain her,
as she is a female who roams around."

Despite the fact that women are blamed for depending on men, they are also harshly criticized if they show signs of independence. In fact the following song by Bezawork, a famous woman singer tells the pain of women who are pressed to be married or to be attached to a man.

የማነሽ ይሉኛል የማን ልበላቸው

ብቻዬን ብቆይስ ምን አስጨነቃቸው

ልቤ የፈቀደውን ስኪለግስ ቀኑ

መኖሩም ይቻላል የማንም ሳይሆኑ

People ask me to know who I belong to
Why should they worry if I am nobody's
Until I find the one my heart wishes
It is possible to live without being attached to someone

In a rare situation where women are praised or criticized in war songs, it is always in relation to the deeds of their lovers/ husbands or sons; never on the basis of their performance as shown in the following lyrics. It is not because women did not take up arms that their deeds are not sung about; but, it is despite the fact that there are heroines like Mrs. Shewaregede Gedle who took up arms during the brief Italian occupation (Kenewne and Reye, 1993 EC) and many others who joined the 17 years armed struggle. So far I have not come across any Amharic song that praises women's deeds on the war front.

የጎበዝ ወዳጅ ታስታውቃለች

እመሀል ገብታ በለው ትላለች

የፈሪ ወዳጅ ታስታውቃለች

አፋፍ ላይ ቆማ ተው ሽሽ ትላለች

One can notice a lover of a hero
Since she goes to the top of a hill and encourages him to go on fighting.
One can notice a lover of a coward
Since she goes to the top of a hill and tells him to retreat.

The emphasis on a stereotyped negative character of women as portrayed in the proverbs and songs has a very far reaching effect on the achievement of women. In the first place men and women who are sensitized through such portrayal develop negative images of women. Such portrayals also support the resistance of many organizations to hire and/or promote women to higher posts as they do not trust their competencies and abilities to execute responsible duties. Women's aspirations to achieve, grow and develop will not be sustained but curtailed. Moreover, women develop low self-esteem and become de-motivated to aspire for anything other than being wives. It is not rare to hear of young women wishing to marry someone with money, a higher education degree, in a respective profession rather than asserting that they themselves can achieve all these things.

Media has far-reaching impact on the way we live as technology enables the media to make information, news, and entertainment and/or advertisement easily accessible to every family daily influencing the society's views on any issue. Hence, media has an immense power in shaping the values of the younger generation which was once the role of the family or the community. Though there is a slight change, women are still portrayed in the traditional roles in the household as wives, taking care of children and around family lives, and characterized as emotional, unstable and unfit for public service (Netsanet A. 2009). Dramas and/or plays transmitted through the media belittle women as "trouble makers", "criminals" and "anti-family" and so on if they slightly deviate from what is considered the "norm". Abainesh (1985), once pointed out that very often dramas and songs portray women as ones who prefer prostitution to marriage, or as ones who motivate their partners to commit theft or other crimes; and, these allegations are tabled without a thorough analysis or understanding the conditions under which the acts were made.

The dramas played on the radio and television during Ethiopian holidays such as Christmas, Easter, New Year etc. are good examples of how women are denigrated. The contents of the dramas played, being more or less the same, portray women as irresponsible consumers forcing and harassing their husbands to spend extravagantly on food, clothing, and the likes in the celebration of the holidays. But men as rational beings, especially in matters of finance, always arguing about saving for the future of the family. Moreover, certain dramas like Amtataw Beketema and Yekeltew Mender denigrate women; and according to Netsanet A. (2009), they would not have been allowed for public viewing if the television leadership was gender sensitive.

In a study conducted about the portrayal of women in Ethiopian television advertisements, it was revealed that gender stereotypes are widespread and the stereotyping was manifested in the character, product, type, location and services (Kenaw, 2006). Women are mainly used to advertise products such as soap, butter, oil, beauty products while men advertise cars, auto parts and technical services. According to Kenaw (2006) housework and mothering are non-negotiable women's work in the Ethiopian Television advertisement scenes. Furthermore, the same study also indicated that apart from the association of women and men with specific products, the relation of the advertiser with the products also tells a story. While women are portrayed as consumers or users of the products men are authorities of the product that they advertise. In these instances, women are portrayed cooking or washing (obviously at home) using the product and men are seen in occupational settings (Kenaw, 2006).

The print and electronic media in Ethiopia have initiated columns and programs where women are featured as early as the 60s. While the efforts of the media in featuring women's issues are commendable, the qualities of the programmes in terms of content, timing, sustainability did not advance much, given its long period of existence, the equality of women. When an Amharic newspaper called *Yeteyoupia Demtse,* Voice of Ethiopia launched its weekly column about the lives of women, in 1959 (EC), the editor of the column Ato Merse Hazen Abebe explained that the purpose of the column was twofold: (a) to write about women's contributions to the independence of their country, and (b) to give women visibility as they were not noticeable enough despite their education and work outside the home (Abainesh, 1985 EC). However, what the editor had not realized was that the invisibility of women emanated from lack of education not despite of it. Contrary to the claim of the editor, a handful of women were fortunate enough to go to school and work in offices. Furthermore, Abainesh (1985 EC) stated that the column wrote about women from male perspective and gave an example of how one article in which a picture of an Afar woman walking in front of a camel carrying lots of merchandise was written. Showing the picture, the article stressed the beauty of the women (about her breast, skin, face, height, her attractiveness etc.) but said nothing about her work and where she was taking the merchandise to. The *Ethiopian Herald* (an English daily) launched a column for women in 1957 E.C., however, as the language was not widely spoken then very few benefited from the information disseminated.

The Ethiopian radio started programmes on women much earlier than the others. At the initial period the program, home-economics, housekeeping child-care and family planning were the main focusses of the programme and the first Ethiopian women broadcaster, Romanwork Kassahun was in charge of it. During the 1974 revolution, a weekly programme named "direb chekun, direbe tagaye" (One who is doubly oppressed, dual revolutionary) was also launched by the radio where women's aspiration for equality and empowerment as well as their calls for organized opposition against male chauvinism were featured.

Ethiopian Television also had a weekly programme called Kemajet Eske Adebabaye, (From the Kitchen to the Public Place) which focused on women's issues from the point of view of culture. According to Abaineh (1985 EC), the television program created awareness in the society regarding the harmful traditional practices inflicted on women in different parts of the country. It broadcasted programmes on genital mutilation, exclusion of women from the family during child birth and menstrual period, and body mutilation in the name of beautification that are practiced in different parts of Ethiopia.

Following the 1974 Ethiopian Revolution, the print media

started writing articles about the place of women in society and their struggle for emancipation. Opposing views on the struggle were entertained in all government and non-government media. A woman's column entitled Yetagaye Demetis (The Voice of a Woman Revolutionary) was launched with an officially declared purpose of creating consciousness in the society about the importance of women's equal participation in the affairs of the country. It is essential here to mention one gender sensitive private weekly newspaper *Magazine Gohe (*dawn), with a women's column entitled *Betelye Lesetoch* (Especially for Women) that used to feature women positively. In the paper, women's lives, their struggles for democracy, development and more importantly for their equality were focused. Very powerful poems that positively portrayed women and encouraged them to participate in public lives flourished. Few of the titles listed below show the powerfulness of the messages transmitted through the poems:

ድርብ ሰንሰለት በአመፅ ይበጠሳል (ከፍትጉ መስከረም 1969)

Dual chain will be broken through revolution (Fetegu, September 1969)

እስይ ጓዴ አምጨፂልኝ (ከእሳቱ ተሰማ ሐምሌ *1968*)

Wonderful my Comrade, let me see you revolt (Esatu Tesema, July 1968 EC)

እስይ ጓዴ ከሰማኸኝስ (በትበር ሰይፉ መስከረም *1969*)

Wonderful my comrade now that you are listening (Teberhe Seyifu, Sept. 1969)

ችቦ ለኩሺላቸው (የካቲት *1977*)

Inflame the torch (Feb., 1977 EC)

However, this very popular paper among the young, the educated and the revolutionaries created greater awareness within the society, especially in the urban areas, about the democratic struggle, the lives of the workers, the equality between men and women than any of the media, though it was short lived. Accusing the paper for disseminating "unit-revolutionary" information, the military government closed it and imprisoned the owner, of course without due process of the law.

In the first three years following the 1974 Revolution, there was very high involvement of the public in debating various issues including women's struggle, in radio and television as well as newspaper columns that entertained different views on various issues regarding the governance of the country, democracy and development etc. However, the military government barred the debates and discussions as it was worried by the revolutionary situation that the media intensified. Thereafter, all the radio and television as well as newspaper programmes were reverted back to their old characters; and, the ones on women were relegated to writing and broadcasting the activities of REWA.

In conclusion, the media by its very nature can visibly promote or distract the struggle that Ethiopian women are waging against the undemocratic culture that devalues them. Though men of democratic values can fight against the negative portrayal of women, the biggest responsibility should be taken by women and those who are working in the media as the act of devaluing women directly affects them. Women in today's new Ethiopia are seriously participating in many aspects of the country's development agenda both as agents of change and beneficiaries as well. Thus, those aspects of culture that oppress women and deny their equality have to be undermined and the ones that give dignity to women have to be strengthened.

CHAPTER VI
Women's Equality and the Derg

Women and the 1974 Revolution

During the 1974 February uprising of the Ethiopian people against the monarchy, working women, female teachers and students, Moslem women demonstrated together with men against the monarchy, for democracy, freedom, for the rights of women, religion and economic prosperity. For the first time in the history of the country a labour strike was called by the Confederation of Ethiopian Labour Unions which paralyzed the whole country. Here again women joined the strike. Women organized themselves and went to the streets demanding for "equal pay", for "paid maternity leaves", "the right to organization" etc. In the rural areas, peasant women joined hands with men demanding an end to feudalism. In both urban and rural areas thousands revolted, and women played parts in all cases. The February uprising was significant not only in challenging centuries-old rule of the monarchy, but also for dealing the first and most important blow to the idea that the 'women's place is only in the kitchen' (Combat 1977). Unfortunately, the February uprising, though it succeeded in removing the monarchy, did not usher in a democratic order for which the Ethiopian people struggled. Instead a military government took over power and proceeded to curtail all the rights that the Ethiopian people fought for; it banned the right to free speech, press, assembly and the right to organization.

In the early years of its exercise of power, the Military

Government tried to appear as one that addresses the demands of the people, as demonstrated by its declaration of Socialism as its ideology. Of particular significance regarding the Derg's approach to the socio-economic and gender issues is the 1975 Land Reform Proclamation. The Military Government's land reform of 4 March 1975 did not make women land owners. Rural land was nationalized and tenancy was abolished; however, the issue of land ownership by women was not addressed. Given the historical discriminatory practices where women were denied the right to own property, their equality in ownership of land should have been stated clearly and squarely in the document. Therefore, not to have done so was a setback for women who had struggled under the banner of 'land to the tiller' and the abolition of tenancy.

The Proclamation of 1975 calls on all farmers to register and be organized into Peasant Associations (PAs). The associations served as political and administrative bodies that had the power of determining the local development priorities, land distribution and dispute settlement, among others. But since women were not recognized as owners of land by the decree, only men were eligible for membership. However, those few women who were household heads were members of the PAs. Thus the majority of rural women had only indirect access to these important institutions that have a direct impact on their lives. The proclamation was amended in 1982 granting membership to all adult members of the family. However, the amendment too had little impact on membership of women in the associations. According to Allasebu (1988) women were not able to become members as their husbands were not willing to pay the monthly membership fee which was one of the requirements. Furthermore, husbands were not also willing to let their wives contribute their labour for fear that household chores, such as taking care of children and preparing food would be neglected if their wives spent time working for the associations. In fact many husbands not only refused to allow their wives to be members of the PAs but also threatened to divorce them in the event of their becoming members. Despite the immense contribution of women to subsistence agriculture most of them could not reap the benefit from agricultural extension programmes and access to credit, etc. as they were not members of the PAs. Only 12 per cent or 679,322 women were members of the Peasant Associations and about 7 per cent or 6,832 women were members of Producers' Cooperatives in 1985 according to Paluha (1988).

Women's exclusion or marginalization from PA activities had negative implications for their empowerment. Peasant Associations had political and administrative powers and a key role in the development agenda of their localities. Not participating in PAs meant not having a voice in important matters of development. One might argue that women's interests could be addressed by Women's Associations (WA) that existed at the time. But these women's associations functioned as supportive organs of the PAs, without the same power. As Paula (1987) has stated WAs could not have been an alternative to the membership of PAs.

Women were also marginalized by the Service and Producers' Cooperatives that were organized under the PA. Here, as in the case of the PAs, membership was reserved for the heads of households who were mostly men. The Service Cooperatives which were managed by the executive committees elected by its members decide on the types of products to be sold and had the right to borrow money for developmental activities of the locality. Only 7 per cent of women were members of Service Cooperatives in 1985. Hence, women's interests, desires and voices had no representation since the members of the executive committees in most localities were men.

Similarly, Producers' Cooperatives which had the important role of allotting point systems of labour remuneration were managed by elected committee members who were mostly men. In most instances, the work point system benefited men since high points were allotted for tasks that were traditionally performed by men. Women were assigned to horticulture, milk processing and store keeping all of which had low points.

After doing fieldwork in the rural areas, Desalgene (1993) states that collectivization has reinforced the traditional forms of sexual division of labour. He argues that so long as land, which is the critical element in collectivization, was registered in the name of the husband and other assets were controlled by the PAs, married women's security of property was impaired. Therefore, collectivization has not benefited women (p. 8).

Another attempt by the Derg to address the pressing demands of women was to organize them. Thus, in February 1975 a seminar on women's issues was organized. Some 55 women from various government and non government organizations participated. Various papers related to social, political and economic realities of Ethiopian women were presented. After deliberation on the various issues for seven days, it was concluded with the election of an eighteen-member committee known as the Ethiopian Women's Coordinating Committee (EWCC). The mandates of the committee were: (a) To raise political consciousness among women in the rural and urban areas; (b) to prepare leaflets and other publications and distribute them to the general public, (c) to disseminate research outcomes, information and the like pertaining to women through the mass media; (d) to organize seminars, conferences and discussion forums regarding gender issues (Tenesh 1977).

The setting up of the coordinating committee was a landmark in the history of the women's struggle. The programme of the EWCC stressed the necessity of creating political awareness about women's issues in society, to coordinate women's issues with the overall struggle of the Ethiopian people. More importantly the committee emphasized the urgency of setting up a Women's League; and as a preparation, it set up branches in factories and government offices. Furthermore, in April 1967 (E.C.) a second seminar in which 300 women representatives from factories, government and non government organizations, the informal sector including commercial sex workers, homemakers (housewives), domestic workers and individuals participated was organized in Addis Ababa. In this seminar that took about two weeks, many papers pertaining to the oppression of women, their lives, challenges and their needs were presented and thoroughly discussed. The members of the seminar resolved to work for the establishment of a women's organization. The members of the EWCC were expanded from 18 to 25.

The Ethiopian Women's Coordinating Committee, organized women to celebrate March 8, International Women's Day in 1968,

E.C. for the first time in the history of the country. The day was celebrated in Meskel Square*) for three days using different activities that demonstrate the miserable lives of women who have been oppressed both at home and in public. Poems were read, plays were enacted. I remember a very moving play by the women of Berhanena Selame Printing Press which showed how women workers were treated. This is the episode that a woman was pleading with her boss to let her take her son to hospital as he was seriously sick, and the answer she gets from the boss was "You women are like cats who produce babies", This reflects the view of many regarding women. On the day itseif, there was a big demonstration where students, proletariat women, women who work in offices, teachers etc. participated. The slogans carried by the demonstrators reflected the consciousness level of the women as they were demanding the recognition of democratic rights, the set-up of women's organizations, equal pay for equal work, for the release of labour and teachers' association leaders who were imprisoned at the time. A photo exhibition depicting the different activities of women was viewed by the public. On the eve of March 8, a film entitled "The Red Women's Detachment" was shown. This was the film that depicted how Chinese women who were given to landlords, as slaves, joined the Red Army and struggled heroically. Furthermore, pictures of how women in China have progressed because of socialism were shown in the exhibition. The speeches were delivered by the chair person Nigist Teffera and a representative as well as a member of the EWCC, Mrs. Aster Assefa (a proletarian woman). Both speakers emphasized the importance of having an independent women's organization as organized struggle was the only way that women can realize their true equality. Songs about the importance of organization were also sung to sensitize the participants and the general public who attended the programmes about the situation of women. I would like to quote two important lyrics here.

---

* The Meskel Square is the second largest public space in Addis Ababa, next to Jan Meda. All major public gatherings are held in the square. Recently, a monument and a museum have been built for the Red Terror victims at the square.

ይህች ጭቁን ሴት ምን ታየባት
ሴትነትዋ እንደ እቃ ያስቆጠራት
ይህች ደሀ ሴት ታለቅሳለች
ለእኩል ሥራ እኩል ክፍያ ተነፍጋለች
ተነሱ ሴቶች ተደራጁ እና ታገሉ
ጭቆናን አስወግዱ

What did you see in these oppressed woman?
Why do you consider her womanhood as a chattel?
This poor woman is crying
She has been denied equal pay for equal work
Rise up women!!! get organized and fight
To eliminate the oppression

There was also another long and very powerful poem entitled "I will revolt".

As if to give response to the song. Part of the lyric goes as follows:

አምፃለሁ ከእንግዲህ እነሳለሁ
በበዝባዦች በጨቋኞች በአድሀሪያን በኢምፔሪያሊስቶች
ላይም እዋጋለሁ ቆርጣለሁ ጠላቴንም እጥላለሁ
ከቶ አልሆንም ወላዋይ ከመረረኝ ከሰለቸኝ ድርብ ጭቆና ከሰበረኝ
ከእግዲህስ ከአሁን ወዲያ አምፃለሁ

I will revolt and stand up against oppression, reaction and imperialism,
I am determined to eliminate my enemies,
I will not waver for I had it
I am fed up of dual oppression
From now on I will revolt

The celebration of March 8, was really more than a festive moment, the occasion was used to sensitize the Addis Ababa dwellers about women's issues. It was actually the beginning of the spark of women's struggle for equality. The subsequent celebrations of March 8 during the Derg were neither as colourful nor reflective on the struggle of women. The day was rather used as an occasion to subject women to the Derg's propaganda in town hall meetings and use of their labours in cleaning cities. If at all the issues of women were raised in the meetings, it was in the form of how Clara Zetkien initiated the International Woman's Day. However, after the fall of the Derg, March 8 is celebrated in various ways and the day is used by women as a day where their challenges and achievements are discussed and new agendas for further improvement are charted by many government or non government women's organizations.

Some of the members of EWCC were also members of the EPRP with an ideology that the women's question being an integral part of the over struggle of the Ethiopian people, they supported the demands of the workers, teachers and students who were fighting for democracy and prosperity. It also called for the establishment of "People's Government" declaring that it was only through such an order that women's oppression would be abolished. On the other hand, there were also members of All Ethiopian Socialist Movement (MEISON) that has a policy of conditional support to the Derg. The two groups were constantly debating about organizational and ideological issues not only about the women's struggle but about the future of Ethiopia as a whole. Eventually the EPRP group gained support and control of the committee which made the Derg uncomfortable. Realizing that things were out of its control, the Military Government launched fierce repression against the EWCC leadership (some of them went underground, others imprisoned and few murdered) and eventually abolished it.

Though limited to women in the urban areas (mainly in the cities), this period galvanized many of them to rally for women's equality and articulate the issues from rights, equality and development rather than from a welfare point of view. It was also a time when men (in the urban areas) for the first time began seriously thinking about women's issues.

REWA, A Woman's Organization against Women

Unable to crush the people's struggle by force, the military government tried to woe women by creating an organization that seemingly would "address" their issues. Thus it set up an organization known as the Revolutionary Ethiopian Women's Association (REWA) under the auspices of the government, in 1980. The objectives of the Association were:

(a) To enhance women's political consciousness through socialist ideology,
(b) To make women take their rightful places in the production processes and make them politically and economically independent,
(c) To safeguard their rights as mothers and create conducive environment,
(d) To make them participate equally in the National Democratic Program to establish a Socialist Ethiopia,
(e) To defend the mother land from internal reactionary forces and external enemies to safeguard the fruits of the revolution,
(f) To create an opportunity where women have access to skill training.

To implement these lofty objectives requires a democratic environment where human and democratic rights are recognized and observed, where people freely participate in the organizations that they believe addresses their concerns and interests. For instance let us take objectives (a) and (b) : how can political consciousness be created in the situation where all democratic rights such as the right of expression, opposition, demonstration, organization have been curtailed by law. Or, how can they be politically and economically independent where social services like education and health are wanting and the economy is in shambles?

In fact, REWA's directives below show the dictatorial nature of the association.

(a) Every Ethiopian woman above the age of 18 has the obligation to be a member of the Association.
(b) The Association has the obligation not only to accept and implement the declarations, directives and regulations of the government but also to have them implemented.

(c) To safeguard the country from its enemies and anti-unity forces.

As membership and participation in the activities of the organization became mandatory, women throughout the country were forced to join the organization not to be leveled as anti-revolutionary which has strong ramifications, starting from losing their ration cards which is used to basic food items such as oil, sugar from the Kebele stores to being imprisoned or even killed. Every woman had to pay a monthly contribution in cash and also attend a study circle where Marxist ideology (something that they could not relate with their day to day lives) was discussed among them. In most cases the women did not have the right to elect their own leaders and there are cases where chairpersons are assigned. One freedom fighter told me a very interesting story that depicts how undemocratically and arbitrarily the organization was run. In small town called Mersa (north Ethiopia), in Kebele, a famous priest (a man) was the chair of the REWA branch of the Kebele. This priest naturally could not have been a member of the Association, (I don't think he would want to be a member of women's group either) and hence, the women did not elect him. According to my, informer the fighter, the authorities assigned the priest to the post as he was deemed to be the most trusted man of the community and the husbands would allow their wives to attend meetings that are called by him (Mesert, 2012). Well that is the Derg's way of making women politically and economically independent.

Participation in income generating activities of spinning, embroidering etc. to support REWA was also obligatory. Those who did not comply were fined. As the civil war in the country intensified and the government could not feed its army, REWA began to force all women in Ethiopia to prepare dry rations for the military and ensure that funds were raised for the war effort in the name of safeguarding the country from its enemies. Women did not have the right to reject but to comply with the rules and regulations in which they had no say.

The Derg tried to emulate the women's movements that are initiated by the states in socialist countries but it did not in fact could not genuinely address the issues. Experiences show that women in socialist countries have benefited from the system. For instance women in Cuba not only enjoy equal political, social and economic rights but husbands share domestic chores that are incorporated in the marriage law (Yeshi 1994). Many socialist revolutions also paved the way for women to join the professions as discussed earlier.

However, in the case of Ethiopia, women did not benefit from REWA. Equality between men and women became rhetoric through the constant talk about women's oppression by the government media, 'to the point of mockery' as Yeshi (1994) puts it. Far from emancipating women from oppression, REWA as an organization of undemocratic government, invoked the oppression of women and constantly talked about it; but it never fought against the patriarchal ideology in any form, not even by the mobilization of women against such issues as sexual division of labour, land rights, violence against women, early marriage and other traditional anti-women practices. REWA multiplied the burden of women by imposing additional labour and financial contributions. Moreover, having suffered under REWA, women vehemently rejected the idea of getting organized. For a long time after the fall of the Derg and the abolishment of REWA, many women invoked the negative experiences that they went through as a reason for not getting organized at all. It took so many persuasions and convincing for some to join organization. The only merit of REWA was its open acknowledgement of women's oppression and in an attempt to create awareness within the society.

Of course, in the absence of democratic rights to the people of Ethiopia, it would not have been possible for REWA to have women's equality achieved. An inherently undemocratic government cannot address and have the correct direction to solve issues of women (Roman, 2000). From the outset, it was clear that REWA was organized by the state to use women so that they could serve the purpose of the military government which wanted to give the impression that it was a democratic government that gave a voice to its citizens, including women.

Women's Underground Movements

Despite the Military Governments repressive measures, the

Ethiopian people, students, teachers, workers, the urban poor and the peasants challenged its rule by organizing themselves in different underground mass organizations or parties.

To consolidate its legitimacy and power the military regime formed a party called the Workers' Party of Ethiopia, (WPE) in September 1984. Subsequently a new Constitution was proclaimed on 1 February 1987 which defined Ethiopia as the People's Democratic Republic of Ethiopia (PDRE) (Claphm, 1988). With the exception of those created by the regime all mass organizations were banned. The formation of political or social organizations was prohibited as was any form of peaceful opposition. Even worse, in February 1997, a "Red Terror" against those who opposed the military dictatorship was publicly declared, with the intention of killing all the enemies of the regime (Keller, 1990). The military empowered its militias to summarily execute those suspected of opposing the government as a result of which the civilian population in Addis Ababa and other major towns was faced with massive killing, torture, and imprisonment.

Writing about the brutality and the atrocities carried out on the civilian population, Lefort remarks that the slaughtering of students and workers who demonstrated on 1 May (May Day) 1977 was the climax of the terror. He writes, "Officially there were 732 victims. In reality, a thousand, two thousand? No one can say. It was a delirious madness. The bodies of the victims were handed over only after payment for the bullets that had killed them. Addis Ababans dazed, wore mourning for as long as it was permitted to do so"(as quoted, by Balema, 2003). Subsequently, the military government became very repressive; many women, young and old were summarily executed. Those who were not killed were thrown into prisons where they were physically and mentally tortured by harsh interrogation techniques. Mothers were put in prison on the assumption that their sons and daughters were in the opposition. Some of them were also forced to witness their children being shot.

Since all democratic rights, including the right to form political organizations were curtailed, underground political parties of a national and multinational nature as well as mass organizations proliferated. In all of them, women became members and active participants. The predominant ideology of most of these organizations was left-oriented too. Thus the "women's question" was perceived as one of the questions of the whole society that will be resolved when Ethiopian society became free from class oppression. One of these underground parties that popularly attracted a broad spectrum of the masses, (that is, the military, city dwellers, students, trade unionists) was the Ethiopian People's Revolutionary Party (EPRP). The party challenged the military government in the struggle for democratic rights of the Ethiopian people, and the establishment of a "popular provisionary government" (Ghelawdewos and Kiros, p. 63). Still another leftist political organization was All Ethiopian Socialist Movement (AESM) or MEISON (its Ethiopian acronym) which advocated critical support for the military. Both organizations had unspecified numbers of women members. The EPRP, which had incorporated the equality of women in its party programme had organized a separate women's mass organization called **የኢትዮጵያ ሴቶች ትግል ድርጅት ኢሴትድ** (the Ethiopian Women's Organization for Struggle, EWOS). Both party and non party women became members and undertook underground activities to create consciousness about the oppression of women and mobilize them so that they would fight against undemocratic rule. Study circles were organized in the cities, towns and villages which discussed the cause of women's oppression and the nature of the struggle. EWOS distributed an underground paper entitled "**ድርብ ታጋይዋ**" (which translates as "one who fights against double oppression"). Though EWOS was a women's organization, like any socialist oriented mass organization, its primary concern was the class struggle.

Women and the Red Terror

The Military Government killed thousands of people regardless of gender, class, religion or nationality during the "Red Terror". Those killed belonged to all sectors of society; peasants, students, intellectuals and workers. They came from all ethnic and religious groups of Ethiopia in which women were included.

The 'Red Terror' lasted for two years, from September 1976 to May 1978; and, according to Bahru (2009), it is a period where people were massively and indiscriminately detained, and summarily executed. The period of *natsa ermejja,* an Amharic expression meaning an unrestricted license to kill, was sarcastically characterized by Bahru (2009) as terror that had become democratized! Kebele leaders, guards and the Revolutionary Defense Squads were given full authority to kill anyone who is suspected of so called 'antirevolutionary' activities.

The number of lives that were lost is very uncertain and the most conservative estimate states that "at the very least several thousand people were killed and thousands more imprisoned (Clapham, 1989). On The May Day rally of 1977, soldiers shot at students who were peacefully demonstrating and calling for the establishment of a "Provisional People's government" in Addis Ababa. The number of victims was estimated to be around some five hundred. Professor Kinfe Abraham who called The Red Terror "genocide" stated that "thousands" of educated Ethiopians perished during this period. Many writers and human rights advocates referred to The Red Terror as "State Terrorism". Thus, Tronvoll, Schaefer and Gimachew (2009) state that the Red Terror in Ethiopia was the most systematic and infamous campaign of human rights violation perpetrated by the Derg.

Every big villa in Addis Ababa and other cities and towns like Awassa, Gonder, Dire Dawa, Nazreth, etc., that were confiscated by the Derg were turned into places where thousands of political prisoners were detained. The peasants and others in the rural areas were not spared detention. Most peasant associations had their own prisons. Amnesty International reported that it was no exaggeration to say that Ethiopia had been "turned into one big jail" (quoted in Balsvik 2007).

Prisoners from all walks of lives and ethnic groups went through untold sufferings. The prison cells were tightly packed cells often including wounded prisoners. They were infested with cloth and hair lice, rats and pests. As the cells were so packed, prisoners often had to sleep in shifts. Detention by itself was tormenting, and to be confined in such appalling conditions was a constant torture by itself. Political prisoners were commonly tortured during interrogation with different forms of cruel and degrading treatment. Forcibly putting blood stained cloth in the mouth to stifle the prisoner and beating the soles of the feet was the most common form of torture. Others, such as submerging the head in dirty water, extraction of toe and finger nails, pouring boiling oil on the body, electrifying parts of the body, leaving the prisoner hanging by the shoulders was also used.

Execution of prisoners was also a common occurrence. Guards usually visited prisons around five in the evening to take prisoners out for execution*. Often executions took place just outside the prisons, so that prisoners could hear the shots. Relatives were not officially informed about the death of their kin. However, they would suspect the worst when the food that they brought in for the day was returned by the prison authorities. Often times, the bodies of those murdered were often displayed in public in the neighborhood of the deceased and in such cases relatives were forced to join the demonstrations supporting the elimination of "counter revolutionaries" (Balsvik, 2007). At other times bodies of the deceased were thrown into mass graves. The "lucky families" were allowed to take the bodies of their loved ones after paying for the bullets that killed them. Relatives were not allowed to mourn in the traditional manner. As mass killing became rampant, mothers came to regard detentions as a safe haven for their children and "A common exchange between mothers at the time ran like this: Is your child still in detention? "Yes, thank God", and then the mothers would embrace to express their satisfaction!" (Bahru, 2009). In the same line, my mother also told me that she rejected the idea of approaching the high officials through an acquaintance so that I get released from prison fearing that they would be reminded about my imprisonment and ultimately kill me.

In some cases, workers were picked from their work places and get killed right away. The brutal murder of Daro Negash is such an example. Daro was a labour union leader of *Berhanena Selam* Printing Press and a member of the Ethiopian women's Coordinating Committee.

---

* The pattern was such that inmates would guess the purpose of the visit of prison guards. If somebody was taken late in the afternoon and was instructed to bring his/her clothing along, then it was for execution. But if prisoners were taken in the morning then it would be for interrogation where torture was invariably used.

At the time of her murder, Daro was nine months into her pregnancy and her husband was also in prison at the time of the execution. However, the butchers could not spare her and they killed both Daro and her unborn child making her eight children motherless. Daro was murdered along with seven workers of the printing press and two of them, Workenesh Habtemariam and Zewdensh Wanna, were women.

Many committed suicide instead of falling into the hands of the Derg, Negist Teffera was one of them. Negist, affectionately called as Nigi among her friends, was born on 1940 (E.C.) in Addis Ababa and at the age of 13, her father the only breadwinner died after a prolonged illness which depleted the savings of the family. This was a turning point that thrust the family into a miserable financial condition and Nigi into being responsible for the family as she was the first born. At the time of the death of her father, Nigi, who was a primary school student in one of the mission schools named Nativity Girls' school, was faced with the reality of dropping out of school for lack of money to pay the tuition fee as there was no pension plan at the time for her father who was a government employee. Luckily, the administration of the school permitted her to continue her education while performing janitorial work in the school in the evening.

According to her younger brother Dr. Mekuria Teffera, from whom I had gathered information about the childhood character of Negist, she was a very responsible, duty minded girl who had the highest love and affection for her younger brothers and sisters. She was also a mentor to them who required of them to execute their responsibilities as well. Having a very high self-confidence, she vehemently hated dependency and instilled the same values in her siblings.

Nigi was a very hard working and intelligent student who unlike the other girls of the period loved to read books written by foreigners and Ethiopian writers like Addis Alemayehu, Kebede Micheal, Tolstoy, Dostoevsky etc. during her spare time. Her brother Dr. Mekuria remembers that the day she received her very first salary, she bought a book entitled *Gone with the Wind*, by Margaret Michelle, published in 1936.

Nigi was the top student while she was studying in Tereri

Meknonen School. Moreover, aware about the importance of women's education, she was one of the female students who challenged the school administration when they were denied the chance to take the Ethiopian School Leaving Examination to join higher education; on the pretext that the female students were being prepared to be secretaries as discussed earlier. After winning the cases, she was one of the four female students who joined Haile Sellassie University from Tefferi Mekonnen School for the first time.

Nigi who was exposed to so many life hardships at an early age, was quick to relate the problems that she and her family faced to the unjust system prevalent at the time. Thus, Nigi like many young women and men of her generation, became more involved in the student movement after joining the university. Unlike many senior female students in the university, Nigi and her mates joined hands with male students in a revolt against the fashion show that was discussed earler. In the event of the university administration closing the university because of the revolt and dispersing the students, she and other female students used to raise funds for the male students who had neither money nor family to feed them. Her involvement in politics was intensified after the murder of Tilahun Gizaw, the university student leader. According to her brother, Nigi tried to make her brothers to be aware of the socialist revolutions by narrating the books she read.

Negist was the chairperson of the EWCC, the inter-zone committee member of EPRP and was working in the Ethiopian Highway Authority after graduating from the Haile Sellassie University with a bachelor's degree in Business Administration. In September 1969 E.C. her name was put in the wanted list of the Derg. Once she miraculously escaped from being captured by the Derg security people who went to her office to arrest her. Having no picture of her on hand, one of the security men luckily asked her to show him Nigi's office, suspecting arrest; she showed him a wrong office and went out of the building. From that time on, she left her home, went underground, moving from one place to another within Addis Ababa while she was executing her responsibility as a political worker of EPRP. Nigest was a militant who never wanted to fall into the hands of the Derg, therefore, she always carried a cyanide pill so that it would come in handy whenever she wanted to commit suicide, instead of being detained. After two years of hiding she was apprehended along with others in a house where she was working as a maid while the Kebele Guards were doing their usual house to house search. Though the guards only knew that she was a maid when they took everybody to the Kebele prison, Nigest who has been hunted by the Derg did not want to give it the satisfaction of torturing and killing her, so she took the cyanide that was always with her and died a heroic death. Her family did not know her whereabouts for many years until they were told about her death by her friend.

Few women were untouched by the killings and imprisonment of the time. It was common to have lost either a family member or to know of a victimized family in the neighborhood. Very often mothers would spend their days carrying food and clothing for their relatives in prison. It was common also for more than one person to be imprisoned from a household in different places; it was, therefore, common for women to move from one prison to another delivering food.

Women in Prison

One of the manifestations of state terrorism during the military regime was silencing any form of opposition or expression of views. Kebeles (urban dwellers' associations) were empowered to imprison people and even carry out death sentences. Most nationalized villas and houses were turned into prisons of Kebeles. A number of prisons mushroomed as police stations, military camps, villas and other houses were turned into prisons. Even in the rural areas the peasant associations had their own prisons.

One of the methods of the government to hush the struggle for democracy was to arrest and put in prison anybody whom they thought was counter revolutionary. Since all sorts of democratic rights were curtailed by the decree (see the proclamation 2 Sept. 1967 declaration), peaceful demonstrations, gatherings or reading of non government papers, voicing one's grievances etc. were labeled as counter revolutionary acts; thus anybody who was suspected of being involved in such acts was labeled as counter revolutionary, which led to the arrest and imprisonment of many all over the country. In fact one does not have to be found doing any of the things defined as subversive activities to be either killed or be thrown into jail.

The following account is from my own encounter as a prisoner in five different prisons and also from interview of women prisoners. One of the worst prisons was called "The Military Police" where prisoners were interrogated and tortured; here is where you first encounter your interrogators and torturers.

Saba Kidane Mariam was a university student when she was detained in the military police. She was taken to the "Military Police" and kept in solitary confinement. She was put in a small room with no natural light and was kept alone after being tortured during interrogations. She said that she used to sing to herself and continuously walk within the small room going from one corner to another after giving each of the corners well known area names of Addis Ababa such as "Sidst Killo", "Kasanshes" etc. She did this to keep her sanity and also pass time. She said that the continuous singing and walking kept her sane as she was confined within a small room (2m × 2m) alone. She banged the walls so that other inmates in the next room would bang back, which gave her a sense of communication with people. The only time that she could recognize whether it was day or night was when the prison guards opened the door for her to go to the washroom. As she was a woman prisoner some guards took pity on her and let her go to the washroom whenever she wished; otherwise the general rule was to let prisoners visit the washroom only twice a day (early morning and in the evening).

At the beginning of her detention, Saba could not move and walk because of the torture; therefore, women who were in the bigger prison cell used to beg the guards to let them clean her, assist her to go to the washroom, and feed her. Those women prisoners in the bigger cell were students and mothers, some with children. As they were not in solitary confinement, they were allowed to stay outside their rooms for one hour. And during this hour, they would help Saba, provided that there was a sympathetic guard who let them go into her cell. However, Saba never told them or showed them any sign of her sufferings so as not to disturb them.

After suffering a lot in solitary confinement, Saba was allowed to join the rest of the prisoners, which according to her was a relief and as good as being freed. Saba started appreciating the importance of being with others in prison. "You could share your sorrows, plights, even the possibility of being talked back," she says.

The military police prison was one of those prisons where political prisoners and prisoners of conscience were confined. Apart from cells of solitary confinement, it had cells for men and cells for women too. Doors of the cells were always closed, being opened only in a situation where someone was sick. However, women's cell doors were kept open for one hour since the administration realized the need for washing. In many prisons the norm was that prison cells were to be kept closed, but in some areas where the prison administration was sympathetic, they allowed prisoners to stay outside and/or walk within the compound for a few minutes.

As food was not provided by most prison administrations except in the central prison called *Kerchele*, families of the prisoners used to bring food. But the food was shared among all prisoners. This was done voluntarily since poor families could not afford to bring food. There were many agonies that mothers, sisters and wives went through to feed their loved ones. Every morning you saw lines and lines of women in every prison in Addis Ababa and throughout the country offering whatever they could bring to the prisoners.

The plight of these women didn't stop at bringing food to prisons. Many of them were told to take back the food as the inmates whom they were visiting were not in the prison any more, signaling that he/she was killed the previous night. Saba remembers that all 37 cellmates, who were imprisoned adjacent to the women's cell, were taken out of the cell one evening and never came back, all had been killed. The prisoners allegedly were planning to join the E.P.R.P. army; thus, they were rounded up, locked up and finally killed without due process of the law. There was neither pattern nor known reason as to why a prisoner was killed or released. Some were killed a few days after they were detained. For instance, I remember Greeky Chala who was a very bright young woman of about 20 years who joined Ethiopian Airlines Technician Training after withdrawing from the university. She was taken out of prison about fifteen days after her detention never to return to the cell. Others were killed many months after detention, usually after their wounds of torture had healed. Such prisoners hoped against hope to live. Saba remembers one inmate by the name of Abebech Haile who was killed after a year of imprisonment. Abebech was working at the "Alert Hospital" and was suspected of being a member of the EPRP and she was tortured terribly during interrogation. Saba also remembers Abebech's mother, who she says always had a sad face and did not stop coming to prison in the hope of finding her only daughter.

People used to be picked up from the streets if they looked "suspicious" which often meant that they were young wearing an "Afro" hair style, or wore jeans, jackets and pants, etc. There was a prisoner in our prison who was detained because she reacted spontaneously to an execution; her name was Abozenech. She was working as a domestic worker for a family. Her crime was that she cried "stop" when she saw a young boy of her neighborhood being shot by a policeman. She was imprisoned for one year just for showing sympathy for a boy whom she knew. Abozenech at the time of the incident was going to a store to buy coffee beans. I also remember Menber Kifle a very young girl, in her teens who was killed after six or seven months of detention. I remember her very clearly because she was very cheerful and at times cried a lot because she said she missed her mother. Having had limited movements in prison, she was one of the prisoners who had serious intestinal problems. Her crime was to be a member of the Youth League of EPRP.

Saba also told me about her inmate Mheberat, who went insane after being imprisoned because a pamphlet, which was widely distributed in Rome about Eritrea, was found in her possession when she was searched at the airport. Mheberat had gone to Rome to work as a maid and was coming back to Ethiopia to visit her family when she was detained at the airport. When they apprehended her and tortured her about the pamphlet, she repeatedly told them that it was a free paper distributed in Italy and that she brought it to give it to her brothers. Mheberat was apolitical and did not understand why the military government was worried about her having those papers. The agents who were not impressed by all her responses and acts assumed instead that she was a big political activist and put her in chains. Then Mheberat stopped eating, started loudly murmuring something in Italian and finally went crazy. According to Saba, Mheberat was a poor woman who had a dream of building a house for her mother but instead ended up insane. As with Saba, the military government indiscriminately put the innocent, the sick and even children in prison. Saba also remembers a prison mate who was a breast cancer patient, suffering so much from lack of treatment. This cancer patient, instead of being hospitalized, was separated from the rest of the inmates and put into a small room which became very cold during the rain and very hot during sunny days; her inmates could not provide her help of any kind because it was not allowed. After a few days, she was taken out by the guards and nobody knows what happened to her.

Saba is at present heading an International NGO, IPAS that works on women's health. After she was released from prison, she graduated with a BA in Economics and MA in Organizational Leadership. As discussed above, there are many untold stories of how women suffered in prisons. Some were imprisoned while pregnant and others just after delivery, leaving their babies at home. RG was detained barely eight weeks after she gave birth. Apart from being separated from her baby boy, she was barbarously tortured.

Gifti Abasiya was another prisoner who was four months pregnant when she was detained. Gifti, who was a high school student, fled her home town of Jimma after the administration decided to kill her and her friends who were active participants in their school's student movement. She had to go to Addis Ababa, hoping to escape persecution. From Addis Ababa she went to another place called Bati in order to join the armed struggle in Assemba (the army base of EPRP) in the north. However, while waiting in Bati, she was told to go back to Addis Ababa since it was impossible to continue her journey to the army base.

In Addis Ababa, Gifti continued with clandestine work of agitating, distributing pamphlets etc. But a few months later she was identified by one of her old friends who were working as an informer for the Government. The informer, who considered Gifti was a big trophy, took her straight to what was called The "Derg" Office. This was the office of Mengistu Hailemariam, the president of the country; it was also a notorious place where people were interrogated and tortured under very harsh conditions.

Gifti was not spared all sorts of torture though she was pregnant. Reflecting on her experience in the notorious "Derg" office where she was tortured, Gifti said that everybody in the compound starting from the simple guards at the gate, to interrogators, office boys, etc. all showed readiness and happiness in kicking, slapping and humiliating prisoners. After going through grueling interrogation, Gifti was sent to one of the prisons (the 6th Police Station) and shortly after that to the central prison or *Kerchelle.* Since her family lived outside Addis Ababa, Gifti had to depend on a few friends and prison food, which was mainly a very dry loaf of bread and over-cooked cup of tea. She says that on Sundays some meat was put into the stew, meat which could not be easily chewed. Gifti and the other pregnant prisoners (there were some) obtained some help from their fellow inmates.

In the Central prison, there were women of all ages, professions and walks of life. There were members of the Royal family, wives of the officials of the Haile Sellasie Government (some of whom were summarily executed), students, journalists, nurses, airline hostess, etc. Some of the prisoners had left little children at homes; some have been imprisoned with them while others gave birth in prisons. There were also elderly women.

Gifti vividly remembers how the women guards treated her when she was in labour. Her inmates were knocking at the closed door appealing and pleading to take Gifti to the hospital. The guards did not care even to open the door and find out why all the inmates were pleading. With luck, Gifti gave birth in the hands of a trained nurse by the name of sister Hawelt and an air hostess called Yayeneshet (who were women prisoners themselves) under unhygienic and congested prison conditions. In the morning the prisoners had to appeal again to the guards so that the new born and the mother were taken to the hospital because Gifti needed stitches. But then again the guard turned a deaf ear to these pleadings. It was a weekend and Gifti had to wait until Monday to appeal to the higher authorities to be permitted to go to hospital. Finally, after three days of suffering, she was admitted to a hospital and had to stay for twenty days until she was diagnosed as fit to go back to prison. Of course she was guarded by a policeman 24 hours throughout her stay in hospital. Gifti said that she was indebted to all the inmates particularly to Sister Hawelte and Yaneshet as well as to two elderly ladies, Mrs. Tsion and Mrs. Yeshemebet Guma.

There were several others who gave birth in prison. I particularly would like to say few words about Tadellech Hailemikial who was detained for 13 years. Tadellech was pregnant when she was caught in Wello area while guiding her comrades to the base of the armed struggle that was led by her husband, Berhane Meskelle Reda, who was one of the student movement leaders and founder of EPRP too. Though suffered in the hands of the torturers, Tadellech gave birth to HB, a healthy and beautiful baby girl. The HB was seven years old when she left prison to attend school, living with her grandmother who was already taking care of Tadellech's older daughters.

I had the opportunity to ask Tadellech, one of the longest imprisoned woman, how she endured prison for such a long time not only as a nursing mother but also as one who had left two small daughters behind and as a widow? These are her words:

> "The fact that I was pregnant was in a way a good omen. As I came to know after my release I was given a death sentence (without due process of the law) which was suspended because of my pregnancy as the Derg had decided not to kill pregnant women until they give birth after Daro's incidence that shocked the Ethiopian society. After I gave birth, I was ordered to give my child away to which I appealed that I had no one to take care of her. Finally the death sentence was revised since they found me no threat to the government. I heard about the death of Berhane and the other comrades caught with us after I gave birth to my daughter. Though I knew deep at heart that he would not be spared, I was bull versed the day I know about his execution. I used to miss my two

> daughters, who were growing without their parents, dearly, however; raising a child in prison gave me a purpose to live. Taking care of my child, attending to her every day needs, like preparing food, helped me even to forget the prison condition focusing my attention around her life and wellbeing. She was both the source of my strength and motivation. I was determined to survive for her and her sisters". (August 2013)

True to her words, Tadellech was determined not to be crushed by the Derg and came out of prison strong and serene. After the fall of the Derg, she pursued her political mission to serve as the first Minister of Women's Affairs to promote for women's empowerment.

Growing up in prison had a negative impact on the socialization of the children. According to Gifti, most children born and brought up in prison were scared of men as they rarely saw them growing up in the women's prison. The children used to cry petrified by either an appearance or voice of a man. Gifti who was released when Aman, her son was two and half years old, had a hard time to make him socialize with the outside world. This was also true of other children born in prison.

The inmates also developed psychological and physical problems. Many complained of respiratory and urinary tract infections which are commonly associated with prison conditions. According to Gifti and many others, they had difficulty adjusting to the outside world, developed claustrophobia, got panic attacks when doors were shut at night or somebody knocked at the door. I knew one inmate in the criminal investigation prison who used to throw up every time after she ate or drank. She stayed in prison a little over a year. By the time she was released, she had lost so much weight that it was difficult to recognize her. But a few days after she was released, she stopped throwing up.

Sunday was the most memorable day in the Central prison where families would be allowed to talk to prisoners. It was also the day when food and fruits especially oranges and bananas were in abundance. In fact, prisoners learnt how to dry bananas and use them later.

Inmates supported each other and shared food in groups. According to Gifti, it was because of the support she got from the inmates in terms of clothes, food and milk that she could raise her son with little difficulty. She appreciates what the inmates did for her. She fondly remembers Mrs. Tsion Andom who made her a baby cot out of cardboard. Mrs. Tsion who was detained at the age of 53 and released at the age of 60, for being a sister of Aman Andom one of Haile Selassie's Generals who was head of the Derg but was later summarily executed by it. Mrs. Tsion, who was referred to as Emma (mother) Tsion, was one of the much appreciated prisoners since she rendered a helping hand to inmates. An enterprising lady on her own right, Mrs. Tsion modernized the *abesh kemisse* (Ethiopian national dress) so that it could be used for different occasions.

Prisoners not only support each other materially but also encourage and comfort each other so that the detention is bearable as much as a prison can be. They sang, played and joked about each other, consoled each other etc. I remember a unique prisoner, Azeb Girma, who was a very courageous and militant woman, who always comforted and encouraged prisoners whose morals were down. I met Azeb in Number One Police Station Prison when I was taken there after being detained in the famous Derg Investigation Office and she was detained about two weeks before me. As there was no women's ward in the police station, about 60 of us were put in a small tin roofed and walled security guard room. Since there was not enough space to make all the inmates sleep or sit, they had to do it in rotation, that is some sat/slept and others stood and *vice versa*. However, tortured prisoners who could neither stand nor sit were given enough space to lie down. Azeb was barbarously tortured, therefore, she had the 'privilege' to lie down. As a tortured prisoner, I was also given space next to her which was the beginning of our bonding.

Azeb was a university student at the time of her detention. She was initiated to the Ethiopian Student movement while she was a first year student at the University. Azeb joined a study circle where like minded students discuss politics, social and economic issues such as, land to the tiller, the famine in the country, education, the Eritrean question etc. Her involvement was not limited in discussing issues but also participating in demonstrations, class boycotts and the like. As a second year student, Azeb was suspended from her university education for her involvement in the student movement. Suspending students for a number of years was the punishment given to students when they got highly involved in the student movement. From student movement participant she became a party member of EPRP and was assigned to the Youth League (This is the youth branch of the party) until she was captured by the Derg security while attending a political meeting. According to her friends, Azeb was a very serious participant of the movement who devoted every aspect of her life to the struggle selflessly.

Azeb was not only very clever and wise but also mature and compassionate who understood people's problems. Though younger than me, Azeb was my source of inspiration and encouragement whenever I felt low. Once in prison, I was so disturbed and felt guilty for missing my children instead of forgetting them. Then I confided my feeling to Azeb who told me that it was human to miss one's children but the most important thing was not to do something that harmed the struggle, such as being an informant, or giving organizational secrets away to the Derg in order to be released.

As I admired Azeb and wanted to understand about her upbringing and childhood, I contacted her sister Nahu Senay Girma and her brother Antneh Girma in order to know more about Azeb. Naho said that Azeb was a very kind hearted child who shared her belongings including her school uniforms with the needy students so that they were not expelled from school for not having uniforms. Furthermore, according to her sister, Azeb was a very focused and serious child who never wavers when it comes to putting her principles in practice. Naho informed me that she was sure that Azeb would be killed by the Derg (and also told her mother) when she was informed about her sister's detention. I asked why? The answer was very simple for Naho who said, "I knew Azeb will not give away anything to the Derg that implicates her movement and her friends as she would rather die."

I asked her brother Antenhe Girma how he remembers his sister as a child, especially about her values, principles and the like. The following is what he wrote. As it succinctly describes the Azeb I knew as a prisoner and a friend, I thought that I should reproduce it here so that the readers understand the kind of young men and women that the country lost during the Red Terror.

> "That she was the brave foot soldier of the poor, the feisty and unbreakable vanguard of the downtrodden and the destitute, my gallant sister AZEB and try to seek out if there were traces of the unwavering dedication and the unbreakable will to stand up for what is fair and just that had become her trademark in her short life was present even then.
>
> "I knew from when I was very young that my sister was very special. She was brilliant, her mind was broad she loved to read and she encouraged me to read and I became an avid reader. She was also very kind. I remember once when I was about thirteen or fourteen I came home from playing outside and found her crying and found out she was crying because she was listening to a drama transmitted on the radio about this "GAREE NEDIGE" who had fathered about 8 children and who was not able to make enough money to take care of his family and decided to take his own life. She always commanded respect from others, even people who were older than her. Most of us were careful not to say the wrong thing in her presence. It felt like you were in front of a judge where you must tell the truth and that you will have to be at your best behavior. She commanded that kind of respect. It was no surprise to see Azeb's involvement in the student movement. The student movement has only given her a platform to fight for justice which she had believed in long before that. We all followed in her footstep because we all knew Azeb to be true and just".

True Azeb was a very committed fighter who never gave an iota of organizational or personal information to the security even when she was tortured in such a manner that one of her arms was broken as well as both her legs and feet were terribly wounded to the extent that inmates had to carry her to and from the toilet for a long time.

Azeb was courageous enough to send and receive information through her mother under the nose of the prison guards. Azeb was brought up by her mother alone as her father died when she was only five years old. Her mother Emama Belayenesh was as courageous as Azeb herself who brought up four children after the death of her husband when she was only 24 years old. Emma Belayenesh was very popular among the prisoners as she was our contact person with the outside world. Because of her love for her daughter, Emma Belainesh was always the first one to arrive at the gate of the prison to deliver lunch box to Azeb every single day. She was a very devoted mother who brought organizational and other information written on a piece of paper to her daughter hidden in lunch boxes, thermos flasks, seams of dresses etc. Emama Belayenesh was not an ordinary mother but a revolutionary in her own right.

Azeb was killed after seven months of detention in both First Police Station and The Third Criminal Investigation prisons. I clearly remember her face which did not show any emotion though she must have suspected that she was being taken to be killed as the time was about 5 o'clock in the afternoon and she was told to bring her 'gabi', which was the signal for a death sentence without due process of the law. She lived and died courageously.

Elderly ladies who had no political inclinations were also detained for being relatives, mothers and/or sisters of political suspects. I remember Mrs. Teseme who did not have any clue as to why she was imprisoned. Having a traditional notion of a character of politicians, she used to be very furious when the inmates said to her that she was a political prisoner. According to her understanding, a politician is a liar and talkative who is good for nothing; therefore: she said that she had nothing to do with them. Emma Kejenesh was also an older lady who was imprisoned after her son was killed and his body exhibited in the neighborhood as a deterrent for others.

Coping with Life in Prison

This is an account of how the inmates attempted to make prison life bearable which otherwise would have been very difficult on account of my experience in three different prisons. Though I had stayed in *Kerchele* (the main prison), for about eight months, it is not included here since those who wrote their prison experiences before me have extensively and beautifully described them. Thus the following accounts are about prison lives in First, Third and Six Police Stations. As there are three prisons known by Third Police Station, what is referred to here is Wongel Meremer but not Maekelawe (the most notorious prison where many are detained). All the three police stations were originally used to detain criminal offenders until they appear to court. However they were turned into full-fledged prisons by the Derg like some of the confiscated villas in the cities.

Most of the women prisons in The First Police Station were brought to The Station by the Derg Investigation Bureau after they were interrogated and most of them tortured. Different methods of torchers such as application of electric shocks, pulling of nails, biting of the soul of the feet while gagging the prisoner with blood and saliva soaked cloth ball in the mouth, etc., were used during interrogation in order to make prisoners give out information about their roles as "counter revolutionaries", secret documents, hide outs of other "counter-revolutionaries. As the police station did not have the experience of dealing with large number of political prisoners, there were problems of space and how to handle them. Women prisoners were put in a small tin roofed and walled guard room.

The door was always locked from outside and the guards often ignore our plea for having the door opened for air or to go to the toilet before the specified time. Prisoners were allowed to visit the toilet only twice; early in the morning and at 6 o'clock in the evening. The door is also slightly opened at mid-day to receive the food brought to us by our families. As we eat, sleep and sit in the small room, without fresh air hair, cloth and dedbugs were all over our bodies and clothes and big rats, attracted by the leftover food were our constant companions. Because of lack of fresh air, suffocation as well as infrequent use of the toilet, some inmates developed respiratory and urinary tract problems.

Our plight in the First Police Station ended, thanks to visit of Colonel Atnafu Abate, the then Deputy Chairman of the Derg, who saw how suffocated and jammed we were in the small cell. Colonel Atnafu, could not enter into the cell but peep through the jarred door since he could not stand the foul smell of the cell. Later on we were told that he had given instruction that we get shifted to the Third Police Station which had a bigger prison cell for women. Sadly we heard over the radio a few weeks after our transfer that "*Abeytawe Remeja*," was inflicted on him, meaning that he was executed. One of his "crimes" was that he had a soft heart for "counter revolutionary" prisoners as he wanted us to be treated humanely.

Once we moved to The Third Police Station, we felt that we were "freed" as the room was so large we each could have wide space to sit, sleep, even do a little exercise; we were allowed to shower in big shower rooms; allowed to sit in the open air for about half-an- hour each morning and afternoon. Well, comparing with our previous prison conditions, we felt as if we were finally released.

One good thing about this prison was that the clinic that is used by the staff and non-political prisoners was near our cell, therefore, tortured prisoners had the advantage of their wounds being treated. In fact for the first few weeks of our arrival, the seriously wounded and injured were referred to hospital for treatment. However, when the Derg authorities knew about it, this was stopped

It is here that we organized ourselves in different committees such as food, hygiene, entertainment etc. to make our lives as comfortable as possible. Most of us in this cell being members of EPRP, we shared the same view point though the level of our consciousness varied, we treated each other equally, shared our belongings and discussed problems pertaining to our lives in the prison. Thus, no one claims on the food (unless it is specially prescribed food for the sick) cigarettes, money, toilet paper etc. we share everything according to our needs.

Once the door is closed at 6 o'clock, we start singing (in inaudible voices), dance of course, no clapping, as we are not allowed to make loud noises. We tell jokes as well as we make fun of each other. If any of the prisoner does not join in the fun we sing a special song pointing at her. Short theaters were shown, poems depicting our lives and deeds were read organized by the entertainment committee.

እኛ ምንቸገረን መደሰት ብቻ ነው
የከፋው ሲመጣ በሩን ማሳየት ነው

We do not care about anything but to be happy
When we see someone who is sad, we show her the door.

Since we believed that we were in prison for a cause and fighting against the Derg, and also realizing that our fates were not in our own hand we chose to sing, dance and make fun of each other than sit broodingly. This act is specially intensified when one of our inmates is taken to be killed, as if to say to the Derg that our morale was not crushed by its brutality. Elfenshe, who was referred to as *Tenkole* for her sense of humor and Teberhe for Eritrea and *Shewaye* from *wollo* were real entertainers.

Sometimes, serious discussion and evaluation is made regarding our behaviours. I remember a discussion and debate about stopping cigarette smoking. Unlike other debate, it took many evenings to reach a consensus to stop smoking cigarettes as the smokers defended their positions against many plausible financial and health problems associated with cigarette smoking. Criticism and self-criticism is also held when an inmate's behaviour disturbs our peaceful coexistence, shows undemocratic behaviour against anyone, becomes selfish or does not respect the rule that was agreed upon. Through the process of the discussion most of us learnt fundamental values of shared living and tolerance. We also tried to learn different Ethiopian languages such as *Oromifa* and *Tigrigna,* however, we did not succeed much in our endeavors.

Books were not officially allowed, however, some of our friends; families sneaked them in specially during the shift of guards who were very sympathetic with prisoners, so we read the books at night and shared the stories with those who did not read them. Sometimes, authorities conduct a sudden search for forbidden elements such as radio, books or the letters and the like. In most cases they don't find what they want as we were always alert about such searches. During the day, we do knitting and needle work and read books that were openly allowed. Some of us who have children made knitted clothes for; later on we started to sell the knitted sweaters and clothes to raise money for the upkeep of our children. I remember Adanch who had to send her one year baby to the rural areas to her mother since she had no relative in Addis to look after her child. So most of the prisoners made knitted sweaters, pants etc. for Adanach's baby. Adanach along with her friend used to tell us the plight of prostitutes as they were working in a bar when they were detained.

We secretly communicate with outside world through written notes that were brought in and taken out inside the hems of dresses, trousers and bottoms of thermos flask as discussed earlier. As anything that is brought into the prisons and takes out is thoroughly searched for poison, written messages, forbidden items like the radio, newspapers and certain books, we were very careful about it and we often do it during the shift of sympathetic guards.

As our stay in the prison was elongated, food became very scares, I remember few occasions when we had to buy Kollo-dried barley and chickpeas to share among us; and we had only a handful each as our dinners. In order to solve our problem, we petitioned to the prison administration to be transferred to Kerchele where we heard food ration was available for prisoners.

Well the administration had a better idea; they took back half of the prisoners to First Police Station and the others half to the Sixth Police Station where there was no food ration.

Despite lack of food ration for prisoners, the handling of prisoner in Sixth Police Station was similar to the previous prison so those of us who were transferred there did not face much problem in terms of space, air etc., in fact it had an added advantage of having toilet which we can visit as frequently as the need arises. As the Station was housed in an old Italian built ground plus one villa with number of rooms, and as they don't have a place for women prisoners, we were put in the lower floor of the villa with, few inmates in each room.

As prisoners were allowed to come out of our rooms when food was brought to us, we could see our relatives and friends from a distance, and sometimes the guards give us permission to bring our own food which give us a chance to talk to them. On weekends where the prison authorities do not come to office, some sympathetic guards allow small children to visit their imprisoned families, that is when some of us saw our children who grew up without us for the first time. I remember that in one occasion my youngest daughter who was only a year and five months when I was detained gave me a perplexed face and asked me if I knew him, when I asked her if she has visited Taddy, (then my husband who was also imprisoned *in Kerchele*). It took a long time for my younger daughter to accept that I was her mother, and used to repeatedly ask me if I were her real mother until she was in her teens. At another occasion, my eldest daughter brought me Ethiopian 10 cents and when I asked her why. She said: "I know you are always hungry so please buy bread with it." Though I was somehow aware how our families suffer emotionally and the likes, but I did not realize its magnitude until my children started to visit me.

Mothers' Involvement in the Struggle

Many mothers joined their children in the struggle since the Ethiopian people's fight against the military Junta was intensified. This was the time when the Government was trying to quash the struggle of students and the peasants, declaring what it called Netsa Ermega where revolutionary guards were given a free hand to shoot and kill as well as detain whomsoever they suspected to be counter-revolutionary.

In order to intimidate the people, the Derg conducted psychological warfare. For example, they would kill children in front of their mothers, brothers, sisters and other relatives. They would also make school children stand around a dead body of "anti-revolutionary" and sing.

Most of the time the revolutionary guards went around houses searching for so called "Counter revolutionaries" and detained any young student found in the house. During such times mothers in many neighborhoods of Addis Ababa were advised by the EPRP to make outcries (in Amharic UUTA). Women made the outcries in unison both to warn people that the revolutionary guards were in the area and to make the attrocities of the Derg known to the public. Furthermore, mothers in several neighborhoods were organized to provide information to EPRP members and support them in their movements.

Many mothers have been imprisoned and tortured for such acts. For example Abekelesh who lived near *Tekehaimanot* was detained in The Third Criminal Investigation. She gave her account of how mothers participated in a revolution supporting their children. The accounts of her exploits and those of her kind are reminiscent of similar developments during the Bolshevik revolution in Russia.

There were also women who did intelligence work among the peasants and urban dwellers during the armed struggle. Some women prepared dry rations for the fighters, while others let their houses be used as meeting and hiding places for the fighters. Furthermore, many mothers encouraged their children to join the armed struggle very well aware that their children might get killed, wounded or crippled in the war. When asked why they did this, most said that there would be no peace and, therefore, no education as long as the military government ruled, so resistance was the only way out (an interview with Netsanet Aberra, 2010).

Such was the general view of most of the mothers. One can imagine how unbearable the atrocities and injustices inflicted on the population must have been for mothers to push their children to join the armed struggle with clear understanding that they might be killed. For example in Gonder, the then administrator and member of the Derg called Melaku Teffera has done many inhuman deeds on the youth. Mothers in Gonder suffered so much that they considered having children as a curse rather than a blessing. This view is expressed in the following poem.

መላኩ ተፈራ የእግዜር ታናሽ ወንድም

ዘንድሮን ማርልን ወደፊት አንወልድም

Melaku Teffera, God's younger brother,
Please have mercy on us for now
We shall not have any more children

Well, because of their struggle, now the mothers of Ethiopia including those of Gonder have achieved respite from atrocities and suffering. Melaku Teffera has been brought to justice.

Among those mothers who were supporting the resistance

movement was Mrs Berhan Abera. She was a dweller of Sekota, a small town in the north where the EPDM launched the armed struggle. I had a conversation with Mrs. Berhane in August 2010 and here is her story. Berhane is known as "Mother" among the fighters. "Mother" was a housewife who had seven children. She joined the struggle as an underground worker in whose house the fighters conducted meetings, lived and used it as a meeting place for the members of the resistance. She used to be a messenger, passing information from one area to another; and, served as a transit point for those who were going to join the armed struggle. As she was working as an undercover member of EPDM, the administration in *Sekota* detained and released her with strong recrimination and a warning.

However, "Mother", had eventually to close her doors, leave her husband behind and join the struggle with all her children, the youngest was just a five year old boy. Before she joined the war front herself, "Mother" had recruited and mobilized all her older children and sisters, nephews etc. even her domestic help to join the struggle. Like all mothers of the time, she had one thing in mind and that was to be liberated from the yoke of subjugation. For her, marriage and family came after the liberation.

Mother proudly remembers her bookkeeping work as a casher in the struggle where she carefully kept and guarded the money of the organization. She also remembers the hardships such as hunger, doing away with water for days and days, the long walks, the anxiety of the loss of her fellow fighters in the war.

"Mother's" daughter, Tarik Fente who joined the resistance movement at a very early age was assigned to train new entrants into the army. However, believing that to be involved in the actual fighting was more important than training fighters, she insisted on being part of the army as many women did (Many fighters preferred to participate in the war than do something else). They believed martyrdom for the cause was honourable so Tarik insisted that she be assigned to the war front where she was killed in an air bombardment by the military Government. I asked "Motner" about her feeling when she learnt about the death of her daughter for which she answered. "As a mother, I felt very sad and had to go to a very remote place away from everybody and cried my heart out; I feel sad whenever I remember her, but I am very proud of her and other martyrs. It is because of the sacrifice of their lives that we are living in peace. I have neither remorse nor guilt".

Mother is also proud that women's legal equality is acknowledged. She remembers the time where she has been miserably treated by the officials of the Police Station in Sekote where she went to appeal for justice since her husband had brutally hit and cracked her forehead with iron paddle. The "justice" she was served was insult, dehumanization and reprimand for taking her husband to justice.

I asked mother how she felt when saw women doing everything that men did, fighting in the actual battle, in administrating and even leading political discussions. She said that she was amazed when she saw highly committed peasant women with arms fighting along with the men, and, felt proud when women make political analysis in meetings. Though Mother has come across many courageous women fighters, she singled out Serkalem as the most committed and gallant one.

At the end, mother told me that she was very happy that her country was progressing and women were part of the progress. Women's equality was unheard of when she joined the struggle at the age of 43; she used to feel irritated about how women were treated. She is happy, that women's equality is being realized during her life time. She believes that what she had gone through in the struggle was worth it.

Women faced the worst sufferings under the Derg government that preached women's "equality". They were put into prison for demanding freedom of expression and organization; for equality of nations and nationalities, women and religious groups. Women were imprisoned, faced sexual violence, tortured, executed without due process of the law and were even used as labourers who prepared food ration to the army that killed their children, husbands, brothers and loved ones. However, the women did not relent in the face of all these atrocities rather, they withstood and courageously opposed the Mengistu Government as their grandmothers and mothers did during the Italian aggression.

CHAPTER VII
Resistance with Arms

As the repression by the military regime became unbearable and peaceful opposition impossible, many national liberation movements took up arms to fight for their human and democratic rights. Towards the end of the military regime, there were about 17 organizations of nations and nationalities waging armed struggles in different parts of the country. National Fronts, such as the Oromo Liberation Front, the Tigray People's Liberation Front, the Afar Liberation Front and the Ethiopian People's Democratic Movement, which was a multinational organization, were a few of the fronts that were fighting against the military regime. The other major forces that fought both the monarchy and the military regimes were the Eritrean Liberation Front (ELF) and the Eritrean People's Liberation Front (EPLF)

The Amhara Nation Democratic Movement (ANDM), was a movement that was organized by a group of young men and women who split from the EPRP. The latter, as I have pointed out earlier was an organization that had mobilized many students and urban dwellers under the banner of "Provisional People's Government". However, EPRP disintegrated because of the erroneous strategy it adopted in regard to the urban armed struggle and the undemocratic practices within the party. As discussed in the preceding chapter, many young men and women were subjected to the merciless killings of the Derg partly because of the wrong direction followed by the EPRP. The leadership of the organization blindly continued the urban warfare even when thousands of courageous young men and women perished without any protection. Though some members of the party disagreed with the urban guerrilla welfare and called for discussion, they were denied by the leadership of the party since there was no internal democracy within the organization.

Those members of EPRP who survived and joined the armed struggle abandoned the struggle and went to the Sudan, others surrendered to the Derg, and a few continued the struggle reorganizing themselves under Ethiopian People's Democratic Movement (EPDM) which later changed into ANDM.

Due to lack of information about women's involvement in other organizations, only the women's role in TPLF and EPDM is discussed here.

TPLF and EPDM started their resistance movements in different localities until they joined as a united front in 1990. The armed struggle lasted for about seventeen years and women joined the movements from the very beginning. In fact, out of the 37 founding members of ANDM, two, Gennet Taddesse and Assefash Tasew were women. I had the opportunity to interview both Gennet and Assefash about their motivations to join the armed struggle and their roles in it. Gennet has always been in the army in fact she was commander of *Haile, which was the highest army division at the time; while A*sfash was a cadre working in mobilizing the community. Assefash who had participated in EPRP longer than Gennet when the idea of continuing the armed struggled was entertained. As discussed earlier 37 ex-members of EPRP reorganized themselves in a new organization, EPDM, and Gennet and Assefach were the only women founding members.

As I was curious to know their reasons for opting to continue the armed struggle despite the fact that EPRP had disintegrated, many of their comrades had either fled to Sudan or surrendered to Derg, both said that though they were aware about the difficult circumstances they felt that fleeing or surrendering should be the last option to take when and only when it was absolutely impossible and all avenues are closed to fight for the cause for which they joined EPRP.

"Yes, EPRP has disintegrated, but the questions for which its members struggled are not resolved yet, moreover, abandoning the struggle means failing those parents whose children have been killed, imprisoned and or disappeared; failing those farmers whose farm has been burnt, houses destroyed. We also owe it to our comrades who perished fighting until democratic and human rights, the equality of nations and nationalities as well as women are achieved. Furthermore, it would have been very painful to go back and face the people as failures. No discussion, no promise of comfortable life would have persuaded us to abandon the struggle". (interview with Gennet Taddesse and Assfeash, 2012).

Though Gennet and Assefash never met during their work in EPRP and did not know each other to consult on the matter, both decided to face the hardship carrying the banners of the failed organization under renewed commitment of EPDM. However, their decisions to join the new organization was not readily accepted as some members were of the opinion that accepting women in the armed struggle would distract men from focusing on their fights.

Characterizing women as destructors of the struggle was a view within the organization despite the fact they were active participants. I remember, B.A., a member of EPRP, who told me once that he was shocked to know that Berhane Meskel Redda, one of the leaders of the EPRP, was married.

Surprised by his statement, I asked "Why"?

In an angry tone, "Because women a the struggle" B.A answered.

This time shocked, "Do I and other women members distract the Party work, the struggle"? I asked him

"You are different" was his answer which is the usual response given when people are confronted with their chauvinistic views.

Well, it was the EPDM's decision that women join the armed struggle sooner than latter. Saddly, there numbers were only two. Gennet and Assefach hoped that other women would join them which they did. Being the only women and living as a fighter in the bushes was very difficult, however; both are grateful for TPLF fighters who attended to their needs and provided them sanitary materials and also gave them moral support. Among all the hardship, both still remember how they treat their cracked feet and heals. Often they soften the cracked heels by putting a very hot lard (animal fat) on them and stitch them with ordinary (not medical) needle and thread. Having no luxury of taking care of the feet, they had to walk while bleeding. A farmer who had observed the suffering of the women in the struggle once approached Gennet and said: " I know, *mewagate lewendoch yabate new,* (*it is traditionally expected for men to participate in wars*) *why you.* Let me find you a good husband, I make sure that you have everything you need; so instead of suffering please stay behind get married and have children as a woman should".

Whenever, Gennet complains about anything, even after the struggle was over, her comrades tease her that she should have acted on the advice of the farmer and pursue a "comfortable" life as a wife.

Within eight months of its formation a woman by the name of Kahassi, had joined the TPLF. She was followed by other women from AAU like Mulu Haggose and Mebrate Beyen. Mebrate is The Charge D'Affair of the Ethiopian Embassy in Stockholm now. University graduates like Aregash Adane, who became the first Central Committee member of TPLF, and many girls from high school also joined the struggle as "The Red Terror" was intensified in cities and towns. During the course of the struggle many young women joined both organizations. It is estimated that by the time the Military Government was defeated, one-third of the members of the fighters were women (Netsanet 2007).

As it was the case with EPDM, the issue of accepting women in the army at the early stage of the organization was debated, in TPLF too, the bone of contention was the biological nature of women as quoted by Hammond (1989).

> "We are poor. We often have to do without food. We have to travel fast. How can we provide such things as panties or pads for menstruation? Even if pads cannot be provided, there have to be clean clothes and this is not possible. If People are starving, how can an organization provide pads, when we have not even enough clothes to cover ourselves from the rain?" (p. 46)

In order to dispel the attitude of some men fighters and prove that they were equally capable of participating in the war situation, the women fighters tried to proof their endurance by participating in all physical activities. In this regard Regebe Tsegaye* with whom I had a discussion, said that, the women worked harder and demonstrated their equality overzealously carrying heavy guns, ammunitions, rations etc. as if gender quality means physical equality. Furthermore, Regebe says:

> "We often consulted, encouraged and supported each other and our mantra was "Never show that you're tired. Don't carry less than what the men carry". There was no way we'd stay behind in any of our assignment, always tried to be ahead of the men. Whenever, we find one of our women comrades a bit tired, we help her out so that she does not lag behind by carrying her guns in addition to ours guns. A woman who is menstruating is not supposed to participate at the battle; however, most of us do not take this advantage. In the same manner, a pregnant woman is not allowed to participate in a battle, here again the women don't reveal their pregnancies. I remember a women fighter by the name of Senait who was in the same regiment as I. One day while we were under training in *Talem* 02 (an army training centre), she became very sick and when taken to the clinic it was discovered that she was in labour. No one, even those of us women fighters knew about her pregnancy. Such was our courage and over zealousness to prove our equality. Such was our commitment to the struggle (2010).

Though women's issues were raised during the student movements, it is during these armed resistances that it was addressed practically. The organizations viewed women's issues as societal problems that need to be tackled through the joint efforts of both women and men. Efforts were made to change the

---

* Regebe Tsegaye was a fighter who joined TPLF in her teen and is now serving as a Diplomate in The Ethiopian Embassy in New Delhi.

attitudes, practices and values that limit the empowerment of women. During land distribution in the areas that were under the control of the resistance movements, it was made imperative that women have equal access to and control over property (land) as men regardless of their marital status. Furthermore, the laws and proclamations that were legislated to administer the liberated areas acknowledged that women:

- were equal to men in every respect,
- were entitled to own and control property, including land,
- could have equal right to vote and be elected to any office,
- had the right to organize themselves,
- shall have the right to education,
- were entitled to marriage based on the consent of both partners,
- have the right to fight for the elimination of harmful practices,
- could seek divorce since it was the right of both men and women equally.

As noted earlier, land within the context of Ethiopia's agricultural economy is a very crucial element, and many have paid with their lives for land distribution to the poor. Entitlement to land fundamentally changed the lives of women in those areas under the administration of the resistance movements. Commercial sex work, which was the main occupation of the landless single women decreased according to a study, entitled *The Women Question* in Zana (Netsanet). In a small town of Derba Kerbe where there were 317 prostitutes, their number decreased to only 17 three years after land was allotted to women (Netsanet A. 2007). Marriage that used to be easily dissolved through divorce, whenever the husband wished to do so, also decreased since men started to respect women and safeguard their marriage lest they lose half of their land if they were to divorce. The incidence of early marriage, which was widespread also decreased as men wanted to marry girls who already had land and it was distributed only to those who were older than 17 years (Netsanet A. 2007). The law also protected the rights of children by illegalizing early marriage and eliminating the concept of illegitimate children. In most Ethiopian cultures, especially in the north where the armed struggle was waged, those children who were born out of wedlock were regarded as 'illegitimate'; some were not recognized by their fathers. However, the law stipulated that in those cases where the father denied paternity, fatherhood would be established through the word of the mother. This was done, of course, after many verification processes were undertaken in the community. In Tigray, unlike other parts of Ethiopia, the family of a bride had to give dowry to the bridegroom in order to marry into a wealthy family who had land. But this practice also decreased as women got land in their own right. Thus, the provision of land for women who are more than 17 years old resolved the problems of early marriage, divorce and the question of paternity.

Women were also elected to political posts such as administrators, judges with responsibilities in Kebels and Woredas. Moreover, they were military leaders and most importantly served as members or chairs of law and justice committees. All these positive changes in the lives of women did not come easily. There were many hurdles and challenges faced by the women starting from the chauvinistic attitudes of the male members of the liberation movements to physical hardships such as walking for long hours through the mountainous terrains of northern Ethiopia carrying rifles and ammunition as well as braving hours of hunger and thirst. In order to create awareness about the issues of women within TPLF and the society at large, there were women's organizations within the armed struggle in which both women in the army and civilians in the liberated areas were members. The organizations served as forums where awareness about gender issues was created; and experiences pertaining to their struggle shared among them. The women's organizations played a pivotal role in making the laws that govern the resistance movement become gender-friendly. Netsanet (2007) affirms that gender sensitive laws were promulgated because of women's organized struggle, correct political program, as well as commitment of both men and women in the resistance movement.

The first woman fighter to join the TPLF as pointed out above was Kahassi known as Kasu in short. Kasu joined the struggle eight months after the armed struggle was launched. Kasu was a peasant woman who went to Eritrea looking for a job. There, she met women fighters who were member of the Eritrean People's Liberation Movement (EPLF) that was fighting for the independence of Eritrea from Ethiopia who motivated her to join the TPLF. Kasu was renamed Marta in memory of Marta Mebrahtu who was one of the women political activists in the Ethiopian Student Movement (ESM). Kasu hereafter will be referred to as Marta. Marta was an illiterate when she joined the struggle but she was bright enough to be able to read and write in one month. Unfortunately, Marta was martyred in battle in 1980 shortly after she joined the armed struggle (Hammond, 1989). Many women joined the army a little while later, and unlike Marta, most of them were from better-off families and better educated in the towns of Tigray. Many were influenced by the Ethiopian Student Movements in the university and high schools (Hammond, 1989).

TPLF had programmes such as education, family planning, skill training to empower both the fighter and civilian women that run in parallel with the armed struggle.

I learnt about these activities from Roman* with whom I had many conversations about the women in the army.

As the number of peasant women joined the struggle, it become necessary to educate them so that they would be better fighters. Thus two schools were opened, one for the fighter women and another for the village women. One of the schools was called March 8 and the other one was Martha. March 8 gives political training for the fighters with an aim of training women to be better fighters for both the society and women's equality. Hence political education including gender issues was taught. As the male members of the movement were also socialized in the patriarchal values and attitudes about women, the chauvinistic views and actions in the resistance movement was not easy. It was necessary

* Roman is one of the women fighters who joined the armed struggle from its early years. She has assumed many responsibilities in the struggle including being the chairperson of the Tigray Women's Association. She is now a member of the House of the Representatives and The Whip of TPLF with a title of State Minister.

that the women had to combat male chauvinism in the movement and in the larger society too. The Martha School offers health, agriculture, home economics and language related programs other than political education. The motto of the educating women in the struggle was based on the conviction that "teach the women and they can do what men can do" (Jenny Hammand, 1989).

Hence, women were taught about personal hygiene and sanitation, reproductive health including menstrual cycle and family planning. In order to improve the life styles and the health of the families, subjects like the use of bed nets in malaria infested areas as well as hygiene were stressed. Included in the curriculum were economics, nutrition, gardening, growing vegetables, as well as soil and water management. Basic skills trainings in producing household utilities such as pottery, basket making and spinning and weaving were also offered in the schools.

The women who joined the armed struggle have advanced to the ranks of commanders and commissioners at the war front. Moreover, they also:

(a) Mobilized the peasant and town dwellers to resist the military Government's rule.
(b) Engaged in giving political and military training to new recruits or entrants to the organization.
(c) Provided health care services to the wounded and the sick, etc.

Most women fighters withstood the problems they encountered because of their womanhood. For instance, since pregnant women were not allowed to be in the front line of the war, some never revealed that they were pregnant when they join the struggle to go to the war front. One can imagine how difficult and painful it could be for a pregnant woman to travel long distances through difficult terrain carrying arms and ammunition. This was the highest demonstration of both physical and moral strength of these women. Such strength was exemplified by one of the women fighters called Serkalam a member of EDPM, whose story is briefly presented below.

Serkalam was between 16 to 20 weeks pregnant when she

was captured by the Government in a battle. Her capturers were very delighted to capture a woman whom they thought would easily reveal and give them all the secrets of EPDM. On the contrary, she is said to have taught them a lesson about the resoluteness of women. Under repeated torture she kept saying "I am a daughter of EPDM, a democratic organization; I have nothing to tell you, you fascists, as your job is to kill people, kill me" (interview with Netsanet Aberra* 2010). True enough, they killed her. Serkalam was an example of many brave women who fought under unimaginable sufferings and sacrificed their lives for democracy, for women's equality and the prosperity of Ethiopia.

Bearing the consequences of marriage as well as having sex in the movement, was not allowed. Giving propriety for the cause of the struggle, young men and women withstood the temptations of having sex as it was illegal; and those who were caught were severely punished. However, towards the end of the war, as the movement became successful in liberating and controlling more areas, marriage was allowed and women fighters started having babies. Wondering how these women managed having and raising a child while fighting in a situation where there were not many facilities, I asked Mrs. Elsa Asfeha, a veteran, who had the first child in the struggle about her feelings and troubles. She told me that though there was pleasure in being a mother, it was not very easy to raise one too. Most mothers worry about the future of their children in case the struggle is protracted, they worry about their health, the danger they might face in case of air attack, etc. As the mothers have to execute their assignments they did not have much time for all the motherly functions and affection that the babies needed. Elsa painfully remembers an event where she had to leave her sickly, thin baby girl behind to attend a meeting for about three days while the baby was suffering with cerebral malaria. But the saving grace of the situation was that babies were

---

* Netsanet Abbera is one of the female fighters who joined EPDM and the armed struggle while she was a high school student, and today after completing her college education is working as a Director in The Ethiopian Revenue Authority.

considered as the children of all; therefore, they were taken care of by the fighters, peasants and the community in general.

Reactions of the Community to the Women Fighters

The participation of women in the actual war was against the popular view because at the time women were considered to be supporting man but not participating in the actual fight. In fact, there is a saying in Amharic depicting such a view, "Unruly woman uses sword as a belt".

When armed women fighters went to the villages to mobilize other women, the villagers were scared of them as they had bad experiences with people with arms. It took much convincing for the women fighters to be accepted by the villagers since the villagers thought that the fighters were either bandits or members of the military government. Furthermore, it was also strange for them to see armed women wearing pants, without ornaments but with short hair.

Questions such as: "How can a woman go fighting?" "How can a woman hold a gun?" "Are you really women?" were questions frequently asked by the villagers. They also had to show them their wounds to make them believe that they really participate in the war since the villagers' comment was that "May be when your comrades go to the front line, they leave you at home," (Hammond, 1989). As the mistrust gave way, a life-long bonding between the fighters and the village women was established. However, as the women were convinced that they could take up arms, their husbands were not comfortable that their wives were exposed to such political education. They thought that if the women were politically conscious there would be disagreements in the family. It took a lot of persuasion and education to convince the men about the importance of women's participation in the struggle (Hammond, 1989).

The armed struggle where women fought gallantly and sacrificed their lives, their youth and property not only liberated the Ethiopian society from the shackles of dictatorship, national oppression and famine but also shattered the patriarchal attitude that women were inferior to men. Women started to develop self-esteem and confidence in the process of the struggle. The core of patriarchal thinking that sanctioned the oppression of Ethiopian women in every sphere of their lives had been challenged. This was because the women in the struggle demonstrated not only unprecedented gallantry in the military assignments that they undertook but also competence in political leadership and good administrative skills in the work that they were assigned. The anti-chauvinist struggle waged within the organization has surely created gender sensitivity among the male members as well. In general, the armed struggle has paved the way to a women's empowerment within the Ethiopian society.

In January 1989, the two organizations that waged armed struggle (TPLF and EPDM) formed a united front after eight years of collaborative efforts. Later, in 1991, the Oromo People's Democratic Organization (OPDO) and the Ethiopian Democratic Officers Revolutionary Movement (EDORM), (these were military officers who defected from the government's army) joined the front (Balema 2003). Thus the front known as Ethiopian Peoples Revolutionary Democratic Front (EPRDF) intensified the armed struggle and finally defeated the Military Government in May 1991.

As the case of women in some liberation struggles, the women did not revert back to their household once war was won, with the exception of some, they rather continued to work in the economic and social developments of the country. This was possible because, right after the end of the struggle, the leadership had planned how to integrate them into civil lives that required different skills, trainings and experiences. As most of the fighters were either peasants or were not advanced in their schooling, it was necessary that they get education. Thus special schools for fighters that enable them to complete primary and secondary education within a period of six years, instead of twelve were established in various areas of the country with a curriculum suitable for adults. Many women fighters took advantage of the opportunity and furthered their education to a graduate and post graduate levels which helped them to work in various government and non government places. Those who are retained in the national army have reached the ranks of colonel and recently Mrs. Askale Brhane (a fighter) has been promoted to the rank of General.

To conclude, there are many exemplary deeds of women in the armed struggle which need to be written and researched extensively. It was possible for women to excel in the war efforts because of the democracy that was prevalent in the struggle, the commitment of the fighters for the cause and respect and egalitarian relationship within the army. The armed struggle was led with internal democracy where every fighter has the right to dissent, express his/her views, disagreements and likes. This was also the army where a domestic help, a peasant or any person with humble background can reach the highest position in the army provided that he/she has the abilities (Roman, 2011). The victory of EPRDF ushered in a new democratic era in the Ethiopian political and economic landscape.

Source: Ethiopian Press

Photo 1: Students exposing the hidden Hunger of 1974

Source: Ethiopian Press

Photo 2: Secondary School Student's demonstration against Derg

Source: Ethiopian Press

Photo 3: Students demonstrating against DERG

Source: Ethiopian Press

Photo 4: Women demonstrating for Women's equality

Photo 5: The Cover of the first Female Students Magazine in 1964 EC

Source: Ethiopian Press

Photo 6: Demonstration

Source: Ethiopian Press

Photo 7: Women Celebration on March 8, 1975

Source: Ethiopian Press

Photo 8: March 8th Celebration

Source: Ethiopian Press

Photo 9: March 8, 1975 –Nigist (the Chairperson addressing the gathering)

Source: Ethiopian Press

Photo 14: Prisoners during the Red terror

Source: Ethiopian Press

Photo 15: Mothers mourning their children after the fall of Derg

Part Three

The chapters in this part discuss the concept of women's empowerment, the benefit that Ethiopian women have gained as a result of a struggle in terms of legal entitlements as expressed by the Constitution of 1995, the revision of the Civil and Penal Codes, the institutional set-up for their empowerment.

CHAPTER VIII
Empowerment for Equality

Introduction

The Ethiopian people in general, and Ethiopian women in particular, have for long been struggling for empowerment. To be empowered means a lot more than just making one's voice heard or increasing one's role in economic, political and social activities. Among other things, it encompasses changes in the legal arena, in the area of policy formulation and implementation, as well as in the area of decision making. This is not always appreciated however. It is, therefore, necessary, before we discuss the issue of empowerment of Ethiopian women, to look into the concept of empowerment itself.

The Concept

The concept of women's empowerment emerged out of the feminist debate on the question of power. According to Btliwala (2007), this concept evolved from the critique of the women's movement in the Third World where there was growing discontent with the largely apolitical and economist models of the development agenda. As women's movements in the global south (particularly in South Asia and Latin America) created their own distinct approach and added their own voices, women's empowerment as a transformative idea of struggle against patriarchy, class, race and ethnicity was developed. Thus empowerment was about shifts in political, social and economic power between and across both individuals and social groups (Btliwala, 2007).

Women's empowerment has been internationally acknowledged as an important means of bringing about social, political and economic development. Though there is wide acceptance of the importance of the empowerment of women for development, ways of measuring and monitoring changes in the levels of empowerment are not well established.

As with race and ethnicity, gender is a social construct that defines roles, rights, responsibilities and obligations of women and men (Grown, Gupta and Khan, 2003). Society interpreted the biological differences between the sexes that led to the creation of a set of behaviors deemed appropriate for men and women. These socially constructed behaviors determine the differential access to rights, resources and power of the sexes.

Every democratic society that aspires to social justice and human rights regards equality as its cornerstone (UN 2002). Hence, gender equality which is defined in many ways has been the subject of considerable importance in any development agenda. The United Nations Human Development Report (1995) defines gender equality in terms of capabilities (education, health and nutrition) and opportunities (economic and decision making). Likewise the World Bank (2002) defines gender equality in terms of equality under the law, equality of opportunity and equality of voice, the ability to influence and contribute to the development process. Therefore, the definition given by both the UN and the World Bank identifies three major components of equality between women and men. These are capability, access to resources and opportunities and the ability to influence outcomes. While the first component refers to education, health, and nutrition which are the most fundamental to achieving equality, the second refers to economic assets such as land, property, income and employment. The last component is the defining element of the concept of empowerment which refers to the ability to make choices and decisions that can alter outcomes (Grown, Gupta and Khan, 2003).

The concept of women's empowerment has two defining features. The first is process and the second is agency (Kabeer

2001, Oxaal and Baden 1997). Women's empowerment is thus defined as a process by which they play an active role to take ownership of their own destiny through expansion of their choices. Therefore, empowerment cannot be given to someone or a group. It has to be driven by the actor or actors themselves. In essence, women as individuals or as a group have to have an active role in the process of empowering themselves. Thus, whatever measure or action is taken to empower women would not be effective unless the women themselves take effective roles in the action itself. There are ample examples in Ethiopia to illustrate the fact. For instance, some authorities and NGOs tried to provide social services such as health, potable water, credit scheme etc. that failed to achieve the intended purposes because the women for whom these services were provided did not participate in the process of planning, implementation, evaluation of the projects etc. Hypothetically, there could be improvements towards gender equality through various measures undertaken by others. However, unless the intervening processes involved women as agents of change rather than as mere beneficiaries, the desired outcome cannot be achieved.

A good deal of literature also emphasizes the importance of resources. Here resources are not seen as a feature of empowerment but as an enabling factor or tool for empowerment, though access to resources alone does not empower women right away. Women must be able to use the resources for the purposes of their own choice. Women must be able to take the drivers' seats in the process of decision making and negotiation required to effectively use resources. The clarification of resources as an enabling element is useful in the context of policy and evaluation. In particular, many of the variables that have traditionally been used as indicators for empowerment such as education and employment might be better described as enabling factors (Kishor 2000).

An individual's ability to control economic resources such as land or property, credit etc., will determine his/her power. For instance, wives who are involved in income generating activities outside the home are relatively more empowered than those who are engaged in unpaid housework. For example, in the discussion I had with Women's Association members in *Ambassele,* one of the districts of South Wollo in Ethiopia in 2012, I learned that those women who are involved in such income generating activities of spinning, basketry and coffee production have started making joint decisions with their husbands in matters of acquiring or disposing of their properties, children's education etc. which is an emerging feature in the society.

As control of resources is power-bearing, earning income through paid employment is likely to be empowering too. However, factors such as tradition, employers' practices, government policies and the like can negatively affect the impact of earning income and controlling its use. A study done in a Malaysian rubber plantation where the wages of married women were given to their husbands proved that wage employment did not empower the women since they did not control the use of their wages (Jain 1970).

There are variable relationships between women's paid employment and various aspects of their empowerment. A study undertaken by Mason (2005) in five countries revealed that though paid work was positively associated with having greater say in the household's economic decisions in all the countries studied, the strength of this relationship was weak in some and strong in others. In three of the five countries, women's paid job was unrelated to having a say in certain decisions like family size, freedom of movement and disagreement with the husband on issues. Therefore the study concludes that though engaging in paid work is not a guarantee to have a say in important household decisions, it influences women's empowerment. Access to education, health, or paid employment may contribute to women's empowerment; but they don't necessarily determine it since their impacts are affected by the social norms and ideologies that define the rights of women and men (Kabeer 1998).

The Role of Government in Women's Empowerment

Introduction

Though women should be major players in the process of changing their fates, it does not necessarily mean that they alone have to do everything on their own to improve their lives. Actors such as the government have to create an enabling environment to empower women. In fact it is the responsibility of governments to promote policies that strengthen gender equality through various means including legal and political reforms. Women as citizens should also have the right to demand access to resources. However, the question of citizenship which is an important element in the empowerment equation is still an unresolved agenda in some countries.

A dilemma in the idea and practice of citizenship is the way in which citizenship as a relationship between the state and the individual is influenced. In reality a relationship between the state and the individual as well as between the state and groups representing particular identities are constructed sometimes based on religion (as some in South Asia and in the Middle East and in the North Africa region) and/or on kinship groups, tribes, ethnicity and other formations.

Citizenship involves the mode of incorporation of individuals within the framework of a social and political community. In some societies, the incorporation process is done *via* their belongingness as individuals to kin-based formations. Thus, far from being a vestige of the past, lineages continue to occupy a central place in social relationships. And as the link between politics and gender relations, they shape the position of men and women in the family and the larger society. Therefore, women become subjects not only to the power of their husbands, but also to the power of their kin. Since the state is one of the key social actors involved in the construction of citizenship, its power to affect changes in gender relations and to promote formal and substantive equality is dependent on the extent to which the state in question is autonomous of kin-based structures in society or its secularity.

Women and Full Citizenship

Because of the rise of international rights movements in the wake of the 'good governance', agenda in development studies have started focusing on the concept of citizenship. Another factor that stimulated interest in the concept of citizenship was the understanding that programmes of poverty alleviation would not succeed unless marginalized groups like women had a say in decisions affecting their lives (Mukhopadhyay and Meer 2004). Thus, citizenship in development moved away from a solely legal conception of rights and formal status to conceptualization as a form of personhood that links rights to ability to make one's own decisions through participation.

However, the recognition of the right to participation did not automatically look into gender relations for social inclusion. Some views on citizenship do not accommodate differences resulting in exclusions and the denial of rights to certain categories of people such as women, who as a group were denied access to equal rights. The liberal conception of universal rights puts forward the idea that a person is entitled to the same rights and treatment irrespective of his or her race, class, caste and gender.

Such universal rights have been challenged by women's groups, race and disability activists. They have debated that rights standards while seemingly neutral from class, caste, ethnicity or race are, in reality, standards built with elite males in a given society as the norm. Thus, entitling all citizens to the same rights does not necessarily promote equitable outcomes, and formal rights do not ensure substantive equality.

Being a citizen means not having to make claims based on norms, charity, benevolence or patronage (Mukhopadhyay 1998, Kabeer 2002). For women, this should mean that their identities are as persons in their own right and not in relation to a man as a mother, sister, daughter, wife or member of ethnic, religious or other particular groupings.

Literature has also highlighted instances of explicit outright denial of full-citizen status to women. For instance, such practices are manifested by citizenship laws that allow men to pass on citizenship to their foreign wives and children while denying the same right to women married to foreigners. In many sub-Saharan African countries such laws continue to exist (Ncube 1998 on Zimbabwe; Pereira 2002 on Nigeria). These restrictions are present even in some recently revised constitutions. For instance, Section 26 (2a) of Nigeria's 1999 constitution, grants Nigerian men the right to confer citizenship by registration to their foreign wives, but no such right is granted for Nigerian women married to foreigners (Pereira 2002; Okoye 2002). Recent reforms, such as Uganda's 1995 Constitution, South Africa's 1995 citizenship law, and Botswana's amended citizenship laws do away with these restrictions. Until ratified by the present Constitution (1995), children born of an Ethiopian mother and a foreign father were not entitled to Ethiopian citizenship unlike the case of the child of an Ethiopian father and a foreign mother.

Inaccessibility of institutions of justice also restricts women's citizenship rights. In many sub-Saharan African countries, access to justice institutions are restricted because of factors such as geographical location, affordability, language and absence or inadequacy of legal assistance services as well as lack of legal awareness on the part of women (Kuenyehia 1990; Butegwa 1990).

Disparity in access to and control of resources is seen as one of the most important indicators of gender injustice. In regard to property relations, gender-based inequality in access to and control of land characterizes the realities of many African countries where land is the most important resource. In an agricultural society like Africa, land is also central in defining social status (Mbaya 2001).

Few state programmes address landlessness in general and landlessness of female-headed households in particular. The few incidents of state-led land reform have either lacked a gender component altogether or were inadequate. For instance, reforms might simply provide poor women with land without the necessary inputs to make the land productive and valuable (Meer 1997; Gaidzanwa 1995; Ishengoma 2002).

Under-representation or complete absence of women in key decision-making institutions on land and other key resources had not been addressed at all by some countries while others have made recent changes stipulating minimum representation for women (for instance, Uganda and Tanzania's 1998/9 reforms in land laws).

Despite constitutional promises of equality before the law regarding the right to property and entitlements in the family, women in many parts of the world are still subordinate to men in domestic affairs such as marriage and divorce. Customary and religious laws are often invoked to maintain this inequality. Sometimes the cultural specificity of a group is also cited as justification (Nyamu-Musembi 2002).

In summing up, in any development agenda, the equal participation of women has been the subject of considerable importance. As women have been marginalized in the past redressing the old discriminatory laws and structures are required to pave the way for their equal participation. Furthermore, provision of social policies that capacities women, economic resources as well as opportunities and voices to make their own decision are required if women have to participate in any development in earnest.

The preceding chapters have shown how Ethiopian women resisted and struggled against both dictatorship and patriarchy in order to empower themselves and play an active role in the development and progress of their country. Thus, in the chapters that follow, how far women have fared in their aspiration to achieve their empowerment within the Democratic Development state of Ethiopia will be discussed. As Ethiopia has legislated a new Constitution in 1995; it will be discussed in relation to its acknowledgement and protection of women's rights. The provision of social services such as health, education, water will be evaluated in the light of their contributions to women's empowerment. Access to economic resources such as land, property as well as women's opportunities in decision making will also be looked into to see how far women are empowered.

CHAPTER IX
Constitutional Entitlements

Introduction

As we have seen earlier, Ethiopia is a country with many ethnic groups each having its own culture, religion, language and traditions. However, the unitary form of government of the country not only failed to recognize diversity but also oppressed and exploited them. Though the country is a multicultural one, the organization and practice of the government was exclusive rather than inclusive denying the basic human and democratic rights of the people. Most felt that they were subjected to second class citizenship in their own country.

Those who did not belong to the nationality and religious affiliation of the ruling elite were marginalized. For instance, only one Ethiopian language (Amharic) was recognized as a 'national' language and used in government administration, courts and schools despite the existence of more than 80 different languages and dialects. Similarly, there was also religious discrimination as the state far from being separate from the church, was in fact partial towards the Orthodox Church.

As a result of such exclusion and discrimination, many of the different ethnic groups organized themselves under various national and multi-national movements and took up arms to assert their rights. The country was on the verge of disintegration when a coalition of national liberation movements defeated the Derg and took over power. In 1995, a new Constitution was ratified. The distinctive characteristic of the new Constitution is that it began by recognizing the ethnic, language and religious diversities of the people.

The country had successive constitutions since 1928 (E.C.); however, none of them recognized the multiculturalism of the country and the sovereignty of its people. The first and second Constitutions of 1923 and 1948 (E.C.) bestowed the supreme power on the king or the royal family and treated the citizens as their subjects. In fact, the Constitutions were considered as goodwill gestures of the king for the wellbeing of the people. Pursuing the 'Socialist' ideology, the Derg ratified the 1980 Constitution that bestowed supreme power on the "working class" despite the fact that their numbers were negligible.

In the first parliamentary election, those who were elected to parliament were property owners, and the people were not allowed to participate even as voters on the pretext that they were not ready for such practices; they had to wait until 1948 to elect their representatives from among the property owners. As a one party system was practiced during the Derg rule, only members of the EWP (Ethiopian Workers Party) were allowed to run for election.

Shortly after the defeat of the Derg and the establishment of the Transitional Government, a Constitution Draft Commission was set up. The Commission recognized that it was important that, because the Constitution was such a vital document that was to shape the future of the country, it should be prepared through a participatory process. Therefore, a Constitutional Assembly was formed through direct election where every 100,000 people had one representative. The important tenants of the draft Constitution such as land rights, the rights of nations, nationalities, women, democratic and human rights were debated in Kebele meetings where the dwellers, including women, in which the meetings took place, participated in expressing their views and concerns. Furthermore, issues raised and views expressed in those meetings were used as a inputs by the Constitutional Assembly. The Debates at the Kebeles as well as in the Assemblies were aired and televised which was a political sensitization exercised by them.

It is important to note that women played a pivotal role in the ratification of the Constitution. In the Constitutional Assembly that was elected to ratify the Constitution, the number of elected women were few (only 24 out the 544 elected members were women). However, women members of EPRDF, and non-members from Addis Ababa and Regional States played a key role in making the Constitution gender sensitive by challenging the first draft which had only one article stating that "women, children and physically challenged people will have special provisions". The women organized discussion forums in Addis Ababa and made sure that their voices were heard in the various grass root meetings held to discuss the draft Constitution so that it explicitly and exhaustively put the rights of women from many angles. Thanks to the experiences that they had in the armed struggle, women members of the EPRDF put the Constitution Drafting Commission on notice to the effect that they would not accept any less right than they had fought for in the armed struggles.

The efforts made by women in the process of ratifying the 1995 Constitution of Ethiopia by tabling their concerns to make sure that the democratic, economic and political rights of Ethiopian women are acknowledged; and the discriminatory values, practices and attitudes that governed the society redressed was exemplary. The fact that the Ethiopian Constitution is one of the most gender-sensitive constitutions in Africa is due mainly to the participation of women in the making of the Constitution.

The New Constitution of 1995

The Constitution of 1995 is completely different from the previous ones in its content, values and intents.

The Constitution acknowledges the rule of law rather than the rule of the rulers. This important pillar of the Constitution has many ramifications for the democratization of the process. As the sovereignty of the people is recognized; only those who have their votes can take power from the ballot box rather than by other means as was the case in the history of the country. The separation of power between the legislative, the executive and the judiciary, (as well as the independence of the judiciary) and the setting up of institutions such as Ombudsman and the Human Rights Commission safeguard the people's rights that are enshrined in the Constitution. During the monarchy, it was inconceivable to question the king's authority and his officials. Not even a policeman's authority was questioned. As depicted by the following poem:

> **ፖሊስ አይከሰስ እሱ ራሱ ዳኛ**
> **ይምታሽ ይደብድብሽ ምን እናርግሽ እኛ**

> A policeman cannot be accused as he is a judge himself,
> let him bit you till you die since we cannot interfere

Aware of the shortcomings in the liberal conception of entitlement, the Ethiopian women's organizations as well as ethnic based political organizations had to fight for the inclusion of group rights in the Ethiopian Constitution of 1995. Thus, Ethiopia being a multi-ethnic, multi-cultural, and multi-religious society, its constitution recognizes and gives equal acceptance to both group and individual rights where the rights of women both as individuals and as a group are enshrined.

The federal structure of government that is propagated by the Constitution empowers the people of Ethiopia through self-administration and participation in their own affairs. Based on such principles a number of structural changes are undertaken. The administration is decentralized to the lowest level (district) so that people at the grass roots level exercise self-administration, elect their own leaders, and recall them when not satisfied with their performance.

The Constitution separates State and Religion and by so doing it proclaims Ethiopia to be a secular state. Such separation addressed the historical discrimination in favour of one religion over the other. Moreover, as some of the discriminations and oppressions of women by the governments were based on religious practices, the separation of State and Religion has far reaching implications for women's empowerment.

The Constitution also laid down rules that would govern the economic, social and political principles to be followed by the government. A brief attempt is made here to show how women are constitutionally and legally empowered.

Through a new Constitution, the history of the country entered a new chapter in terms of setting a plural and multicultural democracy through its recognition of the diversity of the people.

Thus, the Constitution recognized the political, economic, social and cultural rights and entitlements of the Ethiopian people. A brief review of some of the articles of the Constitution speaks for itself.

Article (6, l): It stipulates that any person of either sex shall be an Ethiopian National, where both or either parents are Ethiopian. Unlike in the previous ones which did not recognize the offspring of an Ethiopian woman by a foreign husband, this article recognized the offspring of an Ethiopian woman regardless of the nationality of the father.

Article (8): The Constitution enshrined both human and democratic rights of the Ethiopian nations, nationalities and people for the first time in the history of Ethiopia closing the chapter of ethnic discrimination and inequality. It also recognizes that sovereign power resides in the nations, nationalities and people of Ethiopia. (1) Whereby their sovereignty is expressed through their representatives elected in accordance with the Constitution and through their direct democratic participation.

Thus direct democratic participation of citizens has become an integral part of the Constitution to ensure their involvement toward safeguarding their economic, political and social interests. The Ethiopian people would no more be passive receptors of oppression and exploitation as they were in the past. That they are the real sources of political power at every level of government has been recognized by the Constitution.

Equality of all the Ethiopian languages, beliefs, traditions, cultures etc. is constitutionally ensured without any discrimination. Accordingly, no language, religion, belief, tradition, culture etc. can be legally discriminated against. This is quite a new political chapter in the history of the country.

Article 10 (l, 2): It equally recognizes the rights of individuals and groups. In many constitutions one cannot find both individual and group rights enshrined together. While some recognize the rights of individuals alone, others recognize only group rights. But, in the case of the Ethiopian Constitution we find both individual and group rights recognized. This is because it is believed that in a country where there are many ethnic groups, recognizing the right of the individual alone will not enable them to promote the interests of the ethnic groups as a whole. Recognizing individual rights as if it is neutral and context blind does not address the issue of ethnic, linguistic, religious marginalization. Treating everyone the same without distinction of social, political, economic context does not guaranty equality. For instance without addressing the cultural marginalization of women in Ethiopia, granting them equality to education will not enable them to take full advantage of the right. Thus, in order to make the different groups including women have the right to fully participate and also effectively benefit from the political and economic life of the country, group rights had to be equally acknowledge as individual rights.

Furthermore, the Constitution did not only put down general principles about democratic and human rights, it has also adapted The Universal Declaration of Human Rights, International Covenants on Human Rights and international instruments.

One of the inequalities that were suffered by the people of Ethiopia prior to the establishment of the Federal Democratic Government and the 1995 Constitution was religious inequality. In fact during the monarchy, religion and state were not separated and the Orthodox Christian Church was the official church of the state according to Article 126 of the 1955 Constitution, but this situation has been changed now. Therefore, regarding religion, the Constitution enshrines that:

Article 11, Separation of State and Religion, (a) State and religion are separate, (b) there shall be no state religion and the state shall not interfere in religious matters and religion shall not interfere in state affairs.

Article 27, Freedom of Religion, Belief and Opinion, (1) everyone has the right to freedom of thought, conscience and religion. This right shall include the freedom to hold or to adopt a religion or belief of his choice and the freedom, either individually or in community with others and in public or private, to manifest his religion or belief in worship, observance, practice and teaching.

Regarding the democratic rights of individuals, Article 29 stipulates the Right of Thought, Opinion and Expression. Moreover, the same Article (3) states that freedom of the press and other mass media and freedom of artistic creativity is guaranteed. Freedom of the press shall specifically include the following elements; (a) prohibition of any form of censorship, (a) access to information of public interest.

The Constitution has also enshrined laws on how the Ethiopian people can participate in development. For instance, Recognizing the importance of citizens' right to participate in the affairs of government and its development endeavours the following articles.

Article 43, The Right to Development stipulates that (1) The peoples of Ethiopia as a whole, and each Nation, Nationality and People in Ethiopia in particular have the right to improved living standards and to sustainable development.(2) Nationals have the right to participate in national development and, in particular, to be consulted with respect to policies and projects affecting their community.

Article 89, Economic Objectives, sub article (6) Government shall at all times promote the participation of the people in the formulation of national development policies and programs; it shall also have the duty to support the initiatives of the people in their development endeavors.

Inaccessibility of social services were the problem of the Ethiopian people specially, the poor, women and other marginalized groups, therefore, The Consultation guaranty these services as enshrined in the following articles:

Article 90, Social Objective, (1) To the extent the country's resources permit, policies shall aim to provide all Ethiopians access to public health and education, clean water, housing, food and social security. (2), Education shall be provided in a manner that is free from any religious influence, political partisanship or cultural prejudices.

In addition to those articles that apply to both men and women, the Constitution has also addressed the issues of women as never before. The Constitution of 1995 not only addressed the problem as enshrined in the following articles but also entitled women to affirmative action to correct the age-old marginalization of women in Ethiopian society.

In this regard, the most important Article that explicitly recognizes the various rights of women is Article 35. It is reproduced here for clarity purposes.

(1) Women shall, in the enjoyment of rights and protections provided for by this Constitution, have equal rights with men.
(2) Women have equal rights with men in marriage as prescribed by this Constitution. However, the Constitution permits the wedding parties to elect the religious or customary law such as Sharia to settle disputes.
(3) The historical legacy of inequality and discrimination suffered by women in Ethiopia has taken into account that women, in order to remedy this legacy, are entitled to affirmative measures. The purpose of such measures shall be to provide special attention to women so as to enable them to compete and participate on the basis of equality with men in political, social and economic life as well as in public and private institutions.
(4) The State shall enforce the right of women to eliminate the influence of harmful customs. Laws, customs and practices that oppress or cause bodily or mental harm to women are prohibited.
(5) (a) Women have the right to maternity leave with full pay. The duration of maternity leave shall be determined by law taking into account the nature of the work, the health of the mother and the wellbeing of the child and family. (b) Maternity leave may, in accordance with the provisions of the law, include prenatal leave with full pay.
(6) Women have the right to full consultation in the formulation of national development policies, the designing and execution of projects, and particularity in the case of projects affecting the interests of women.
(7) Women have the right to acquire, administer, control, use

and transfer property. In particular, they have equal rights with men with respect to use, transfer, administration and control of land. They shall also enjoy equal treatment in the inheritance of property.

(8) Women shall have the right to equality in employment, promotion, pay and transfer of pension entitlement.

(9) To prevent harm arising from pregnancy and childbearing and in order to safeguard their health, women have the right of access to family planning education, information and capacity.

One of the most important elements of the Constitution is the adoption of affirmative action in favour of women. The Constitution recognized the historical marginalization of women; therefore, it adopted affirmative action to redress the discriminatory legacy. Law that grants formal equality to men and women based on the liberal principle of the 'sameness' model fails to address the reality that women's lives are different from men's; therefore, in order to achieve real equality it is important to have protective legislation dealing with the special needs of women (Daniel 2004). The Constitution recognized the effect of past discrimination against women and made such provisions.

A working woman's pension, including her own contributions to the pension fund, was not transferable to her husband when they die unlike a working man's pension which was transferable to his wife. The assumption in this ruling was based on the traditional value that it is the man rather than the woman who is the bread winner; therefore, her husband does not get the pension of his wife.

Both the new labour and the civil service proclamation No. 262/2002 address the concerns of women in employment. Thus the labour proclamation outlaws discrimination against women on the grounds of sex and also protects women from working in conditions harmful to their health. Furthermore, Article 87(3) and (4) of the labour proclamation prohibits assignment of pregnant women in the night shift of 10 p.m. to 6 a.m. or their dismissal from work. The civil service proclamation also provides many provisions in regard to the equality of women. Among these are prohibition of discrimination against women and preference to be given to women candidates in employment where they have equal or close scores to that of men.

By addressing most of the issues, the Constitution has become an excellent basis for the amendment of the criminal codes and the civil law. However, some of the articles were put into practice without waiting for the revision of the civil and criminal codes. For instance sub-Article (8) of the Constitution which allows women to transfer their pension entitlement was put into practice right away. In line with the patriarchal ideology that considers only men as the breadwinners, a widower in Ethiopia was not entitled to his wife's pension funds.

The Family Law of 2000

Subsequent to the ratification of the Constitution, it became necessary to draft a new Family Law in order to change the old discriminatory practices that had marginalized women in marriage, family, property ownership and government etc.

Drafting of the family law was beset with many hurdles despite the fact that women's equality was recognized by the Constitution and a democratic government was at the helm. It started with the bureaucracy in the Ministry of Justice which was reluctant to do it until it was challenged by the Women's Committee of the Parliament. Once the draft was prepared, it was widely debated in various forums organized by women's associations, government, and the parliament. The debate took place in every part of the country especially in cities and towns where every segment of the society from religious leader to professionals such as lawyers, university professors and more importantly women participated. The debate itself was a historic one in the struggle of Ethiopian women for equality. Every idea that reflected the patriarchal values about women was disseminated in every forum. The various forums were battlegrounds between traditionalists and progressives; those who wanted to curtail the equality of women and those who wanted to advance it. Many were against women having equal say in family matters, property ownership and control, and equal rights for marriage and divorce. 'Preserving culture' and 'saving the family' etc. were the *mantras* of the traditionalists. As the debate was being televised and broadcast through radio programs, women's equality became the topic of discussion for that brief period.

Women both organized and unorganized stood their ground in making sure that their concerns were addressed and their voices heard. However, it is important to note that not all women were advancing the equality issues of women. There were a few who were adamant that the old Civil Code should not be changed altogether suggesting some reforms here and there. For instance, many wanted that the law makes it explicit for a husband to leave the house at the time of separation (until property ownership between the spouses is settled); however, others including women insisted that the law cannot be partial thus it should be left to the conscious decision of the judge who reviews the case. Socialized in patriarchal values these women could not realize its impact on their lives. Thus the family law was ratified by the Parliament addressing most of the concerns of women if not all.

In the case of the Criminal Code, the situation was a bit different. Though it was discussed among the stakeholders, it did not go through public scrutiny with the same vigor that the Family Law went through. As most of the views of the progressive groups had been popularized through the debates of the Family Law, it did not need much of a debate to make those undignified harmful traditional practices and violence inflicted on women punishable crimes.

As discussed earlier, discrimination against women was expressed in the social, economic, political and cultural spheres both private and public. One essential legal document where the superiority of men was explicitly stated was the 1960 Civil Code of Ethiopia. Suffice it to quote just a few of the articles which demonstrate the discrimination of women in public affairs:

> "The husband is the head of the family and the wife owes him obedience in all lawful things which he orders (*Art. 635*) The common residence is chosen by the husband who also watches over her relations and guides her in her conduct (*Art. 641*).

Where the husband cannot afford servants, the wife is bound to take care of household duties (*Art. 646*).
A married woman takes the domicile of her husband for the duration of the marriage (*Art. 189*)
The spouses shall cooperate, under the guidance of the husband, in the interest of the family, to ensure the moral and material direction of the family, to bring up the children and to prepare for their establishment (*Art. 637*).
Common property other than the earnings, salaries and income of the wife, shall be administered by the husband (*Art. 656 (l)*).

The preceding articles indicate how Ethiopian women were not equal citizens with men and the state does not provide them with necessary protection. After almost a half century of struggle the Constitution of 1995 has made the discrimination of women illegal hence, a new Family law and Criminal Act based on its principles has been enacted. The Family Law of 2000 and The Penal Act of 2004 are discussed below.

In Section 2 of Chapter One the law deals with "Essential Conditions of Marriage". It provides that "A valid marriage shall take place only when the spouses have given their free and full consent"—Article (6). If the consent of both or either of the spouses may have been obtained through misinformation, fraud or/and duress (an act of violence). Article 6 is also important in that it doesn't recognize parents or guardians as appropriate persons to give consent on behalf of any of the spouses. Article 7 stipulates that neither a man nor a woman who has not attained the full age of 18 years shall conclude marriage. Matrimonial property should be shared and the husband must consult with his wife when making decisions concerning property.

The Family Law of 2000 redefined betrothal from being a familial affair to a personal matter of the spouses. The law also changed matrimonial property and the household from being administered by the husband to a joint administration of the spouses. It provides legal provisions for protecting women whose views or interests are not given adequate consideration.

The Criminal Code of 2004

The Constitution of 1995 created the setting for radical social, political and economic changes in the country. Among the major changes is the prohibition of harmful "cultural" practices that were inimical to women by rendering many of them illegal. As declared in the preface to the new Criminal Code of 2004.

Another point that should not be overlooked is the Penal Code's failure to acknowledge the grave sufferings caused to women and children by reason of harmful traditional practices. Surely the Constitution guarantees respect of the culture of people, but it does not buttress up those practices scientifically proven to be harmful. It is also futile to issue a law that does not have the trust and support of the people for it usually remains impracticable. But it is well recognized in the philosophy of criminal legislation that the legislature should, by adopting progressive laws at times, educate and guide the public to dissociate itself from harmful traditional practices.

Thus the Criminal Code made most of the harmful traditional practices that were inflicted on women punishable acts. One of these practices was rape, which is now broadened to include a wide range of setting and forms in which it manifest itself. The penalty for rape has been raised from five to fifteen years.

Rape is said to be committed wherever coercion is used on a woman either in the form of actual physical violence or force or in the form of serious threat or intimidation, real or implied.

The most significant change made in the criminal code was the declaration of abduction as an illegal act punishable by rigorous imprisonment of three to ten years. In the past abduction was not considered a crime especially if it was followed by marriage. But according to the new penal code, the subsequent conclusion of a marriage between the abductor and the abducted shall not preclude criminal liability.

In the case of abduction where women are forced by violence to submit to marriage against their will and free consent, the Criminal Code has provided the following:

The areas of family law such as property, marriage and divorce are well covered. However, there are areas that are not exhaustively dealt within the law. This ambiguity goes against women. For instance domestic violence and sexual harassment that are inflicted on women day by day both at home and at work place are not clearly addressed. Women very often do not dare to take the sexual harassment and domestic violence offenders to court as they would be accused of instigating the act through "unwomanly" behaviours as well as the stigma that follows. Thus, the victim is considered the criminal. The justice system is by and large manned by men all the way from police officers to judges, hence; there is a high possibility and room for the legal system to be manipulated by chauvinistic attitude of men in handling sexual harassment cases. Therefore, there should be directives or mechanisms that take all these factors into consideration to tackle the problem seriously.

The strength of any constitution is in its fair implementation. For this, citizens must be aware about the Constitution and their legal rights. Often marginalized groups like women and other minorities cannot use the law the same way as the privileged ones and men. Many women are not also aware of their right guaranteed by the family law and the criminal law. Serious campaigns and advocacies are required at great length by the justice system.

CHAPTER X
Women in the New Democratic Ethiopia

Introduction

The present government has committed itself to eradicate poverty, establish a democratic system and maintain peace and stability in the country. In order to achieve these lofty goals a number of social, economic and political policies and strategies have been formulated. The strategies used not only entail broad based participation but also strives for inclusive growth. More importantly the policies are pro poor in order to uplift the lives of the majority of the people including women from abject poverty.

As a developmental state, the government builds infrastructure, provides energy; creates access to education, health services, safe and potable water etc. which all have far reaching impact in improving the lives of women and thereby empowering them.

Moreover, there is a deliberate effort to ensure that women benefit from economic growth and social development that is underway in the country. Measure to be taken to encourage women to participate and benefit from different social, economic and political policies have been clearly identified.

Institutional Set-ups

Right after the establishment of the Transitional Government, a Women's Affairs Office was opened in 1992 under the supervision of the Prime Minister's Office. Its purpose was to promote gender equality. Shortly afterwards, in 1993, a National Policy on Ethiopian Women (NPEW) was introduced. This new policy was an important first step towards mainstreaming gender. The objectives were stated as follows:

To facilitate conditions conducive to the speeding up of equality between the sexes so that women can participate in the political, social and economic life of their country on equal terms with men, ensuring that their right to own property as well as other human rights are respected and that they are not excluded from the enjoyment of the fruits of their labour or from performing public functions and being decision makers;

To facilitate the necessary conditions thereby rural women can have access to basic social services and to find ways and means of lightening their work load.

To eliminate, step by step, prejudices as well as customary and other practices, that are based on the idea of male supremacy and to enable women to hold public office and participate in the decision making process at all levels.

Women's Affairs Offices were also set up in 16 sectorial ministries and in all regional states, responsible for monitoring and following up as well as designing ways of implementing women's policies and strategies. However, these departments were not adequately staffed and lacked the necessary support from the ministers, indicating that the importance of women's equality has not been internalized even by higher officials who were leading the democratic changes in the country. In some ministries, the departments were staffed with people who had neither gender sensitivity, commitment nor the skills. Where committed women are diligently trying to advance the work, they were either ridiculed or blatantly attacked.

In 2005, the Women's Affair's Office was reorganized and upgraded to a ministerial level, with decentralized structure up to *wereda* administration. A Women's Development and Change Package was released as framework document in which various economic, social and political measures to be taken by the various institutions were articulated (MOWA, 2005).

The package identified five major areas of interventions:

(a) Ensuring women's access to productive assets,
(b) Fostering changes in attitudes towards women with respect to traditional and customary practices,
(c) Improving women's effective access to health and education,
(d) Promoting women's participation in social, political and economic spheres,
(e) Strengthening the legal protection of women.

Throughout the world, women's contribution to their households and national economies is significant yet, they are the poorest of the poor, constituting 70 per cent of the world poor (PMO 2004). The fate of women in Ethiopia is also similar. Access to land, credit, and other productive resources was unavailable to the majority of women. As the main focus of the Government is poverty eradication and democratization of the society as articulated in many of its policy and strategy documents, gender equality has been emphasized in PRSP that encompasses a two-phased program. The first is the Sustainable Development and Poverty Reduction Programmes (SDPRP) that was implemented during the 2002-05 period. The second one is a Plan for Accelerated and Sustained Development to End Poverty (PASDEP) implemented up to 2010. These programme documents proposed measures that addressed gender inequalities in areas such as food security, agriculture, education, health and politics. PASDEP aims to mainstream gender through the implementation of the National Action Plan for Gender Equality which identified the following four priority areas:

(a) Enhancing rapid economic growth, including priorities for enhancing women's and girls' economic empowerment,
(b) Enhancing women's important role in society,.
(c) Democratization and governance, including reducing violence against women and girls and improving their human rights; and increasing women's access to all levels of decision making in the political and public spheres,
(d) Improving performance of public institutions in the areas of gender equality including implementing a gender-based

analysis and approach in all government departments and supporting institutional mechanisms for gender mainstreaming (MOWA 2006).

Access to Social Service

As Ethiopia is an agrarian country, where 85 per cent of the population's livelihood is based on farming and animal husbandry, an Agriculture Led Industrialization economic policy is being implemented by the Ethiopian Government. The prime concerns and objectives of the economic policy are to irradiate poverty and improve living standards through achieving broad-based and pro-poor growth (MOFED 1995).

Hence, to eradicate poverty and stimulate economic growth the highest priority is given to pro- poor economic and social sectors such as education, health, road construction and water as evidenced in the budget allocation between 1995 and 2003 EC (*see* Table 10.1).

Excluded from access to property, and means of livelihood, women are the poorest of the poor in any society like Ethiopia where poverty is rampant. Before 1991, more than half of the population was living below the poverty line with less than 20 per cent of school age children enrolled in education and many children dying before they reached the age of five.

Table 10.1: Budget Allocated for Different Sectors (Between 1995 and 2003 EC)

(In Millions of *Birr*)

Sector	*1995*	*1997*	*1998*	*1999*	*2000*	*2001*	*2002*	*2003*
Education	16.1	19.7	21.7	23.7	21.3	22.1	23.6	24.9
Health	4.9	4.8	4.6	6.6	7.3	6.7	6.4	6.7
Agriculture	8.1	16.3	15.1	12.9	11.7	11.7	8.8	7.9
Water	2.9	4.5	6.1	5.7	6.1	6.1	6.6	6.6
Road cons.	9.9	11.2	12.4	14.1	17.9	17.9	20.8	20.2
Total	**42.0**	**57.0**	**59.9**	**62.9**	**64.2**	**64.2**	**66.1**	**66.2**

Source: Constitution and Development in Ethiopia (an Amharic paper), 2004 E.C.

Now, 30 per cent of women in the rural areas have benefited from the agricultural extension programme generating income by participating in activities such as poultry, animal fattening, dairy farming, and beekeeping. Micro credit is expanding in the rural areas and women have started benefiting from it. Likewise, women in the urban areas are actively participating in micro and small scale industries that are designed as employment generation endeavors.

Provision of water for the family is the main responsibility of woman in Ethiopian society which has a clear sexual division of labor within a family. Inaccessibility of potable water in one's vicinity poses multifaceted problems for women who walk long distances carrying heavy clay pots or plastic jerrycans to fetch water. In the process, women become susceptible to all kinds of hazards, including sexual harassment, rape and abduction as they walk through woods. On top of all these problems, the water that they fetch from springs or rivers is mostly infested with waterborne diseases that endanger the health of their families. Provision of clean drinking water to both rural and urban populations is the plan of the government that is under implementation. As a result, the percentage of people who are provided with potable water is increasing. For instance, in 1983 E.C., only 11 per cent of the rural areas and 36 per cent of the urban areas had access to potable water but in 2003 E.C., 71.3 per cent and 92.5 per cent respectively have access to clean drinking water. When potable water becomes available in their vicinities, the vulnerability of women, as well as health related problems of their families will be minimized. Thus providing access to drinking water for the population is also addressing one of the main concerns of women.

There is no question that infrastructure building is essential for the development of a country's economy. The lack of roads in many areas means people have no means of transportation. But, in a society where women have to walk miles and miles to procure food and other provisions for the household, road transport provides advantage to them. Because of lack of transport, women have to walk many hours to go to health stations either to give birth or to seek medical services for themselves and/or for members of their family and many of them die during pregnancy and delivery for lack of transportation to health centers. It is in view of such problems, that road construction becames an essential infrastrasture that the Government has engaged itself intensively for the last fifteen years. For instance, in 1984 EC there were only 19,020 km of roads throughout the country. By 2003 EC, it has reached to 53,143 km.

Like water, energy and appropriate technology are areas that have far reaching benefits for women. The strategy of electrifying rural Ethiopia by 2015 is a measure that will relieve women from many household burdens. In 1984 EC, the country generated only 407 mwts electricity; in 2003 EC it has grown to 2049 mwts. Three big dams under construction are expected to expand the energy generating capacity to 10,000 mwts. Provision of rural appropriate technology and energy are important time saving mechanisms for women who spend 15-18 hours a day on household chores of fetching firewood, water, grinding and pounding grains, cooking, washing, etc. With such technologies, women will have time to be engaged in income generating activities. Their health also can be improved when they are spared from physical exhaustion.

Collective Voices

The Constitution recognizes the rights of the Ethiopian people to organize themselves in any manner, be it politically, economically, socially, and/or professionally. In this regard, many independent women's organizations were formed and will hopefully be formed in the future too. Organizations such as Forum for Women's Education, Ethiopian Women Lawyers' Association, Ethiopian Teachers' Association, Women's Coalition Against HIV and Aids, Nurses' Association, The EPRDF Women's League, Regional Women's Association, Women Entrepreneurs, Women in Mass Media, Women Writers Association; Women Painters Association, etc. are actively working to advance women's causes in one manner or another.

Women members of the EPRDF are also organized under the name of EPRDF's Women's League whose purpose is to encourage women to participate in politics and political leadership. NGO like Ethiopian Women Lawyers' Association and Coalition of Women against HIV and Aids, and Forum for African Women Educationalists' Ethiopian-Chapter are some of the organizations that have achieved exemplary results in their respective areas.

Women in each regional state as well as the two administrative councils are organized in which large numbers of women are members. Some of these organizations have memberships of one-half to one million. Examples are Oromia, Amhara, Tigray and Addis Abeba Women's Associations. The objectives of these regional women's associations are: (1) to work towards the economic and political empowerment of women, (2) to eliminate traditional harmful practices from their respective regions, (3) to assist women participate in education and skills training, (4) to help women access credit, gainful employment, land and other property etc. In order to achieve these objectives, the organizations sensitize the population about women's equality, create awareness against traditional harmful practices, make sure that regional governments incorporate women's issues in their development agendas, oppose and protest injustices inflicted on women. For example women in Dire Dawa and Addis Ababa organized big demonstrations against the rape of a child by an elderly man and the defacing of a young lady by her boyfriend respectively.

When the media censorship rule was lifted by the Transitional Government of Ethiopia, it paved the way for many private newspapers to mushroom. While most of the newspapers were of a political and ideological nature, *Aphrodite, yefeker chewata, were* pornographic ones, with most of their articles and pictures focused on sexuality. Women of Addis Ababa saw the danger of pornographic magazines and kept on protesting until they were shut by the government.

The readership of these papers mainly targeted the youth. Their contents and pictures became a cause for concern especially for mothers who saw the danger of their young boys and girls led into unwanted actions. More importantly, most mothers were indignant that the papers portrayed women as sex objects, devalued and belittled them, therefore, the protesters resolved not to rest until the paper were discontinued. Thus in Addis Ababa, women set up a committee that would tackle the problem and through it they met in Menilike II School (the oldest school) and discussed the action that they would take. Many pertinent points about the dangerous messages that the magazines transmitted along with pictures, especially in the light of HIV and AIDS, were raised and thoroughly discussed. The women then resolved to stage a protest demonstration against the magazines and appeal to the Prime Minister's Office. Finally on August 22, 1985 (E.C.) thousands of women in Addis Ababa went into the streets, marched to the Prime Minister's Office demanding and appealing for action and closure of the papers. Their pleas were heard and the papers were discontinued. The action of the women of Addis Ababa is a very good example in fighting against devaluing women.

Significant progress has been made in advancing women's equality so far, and in all of it the organized voices of women have made big impacts. For example, the role women played to have their concerns addressed in the Constitution of 1995 as well as the efforts made by regional women's organizations to encourage girls' education are but a few of the examples. Similarly, women's organizations in each region initiated the ratification of the revised Family Law by each Regional State, after it was ratified by the Federal Parliament in 2000. The consultative meetings that were organized by regional women's groups and women parliamentarians were held for almost a year throughout the country where the articles of the Family law discussed were of how women challenged patriarchal values. The heated debates between those who upheld the patriarchal views and those who opposed them were very stimulating and educational. As the old family law was the bastion of patriarchy, the new one ushered in a democratic order by redressing many of the traditional values against the equality of women that were sanctioned by the Ethiopian Civil Law of 1960. In fact both the Constitution of 1995 and the Family Law of 2000 recognized women as full and equal citizens with rights to participate in economic, social and political spheres of the country.

In 2009, some of the women's organizations federated themselves under one umbrella organization known as Ethiopian Women's Federation. About twenty one associations that are both regional and national in nature become members of the Federation. The vision of the Federation is "to see to it that Ethiopian women achieve their equality and actively participate in development of Ethiopia, through their organized participation" (2009). The Federation has a little over three million members. Even though in comparison with the number of women in the country, this number is very insignificant, however, in the light of the short life span of its existence, it is not discouraging.

The Federation campaign of "healthy motherhood' and the sensitization programme that it undertook in areas of human rights violation and violence against women were exemplary activities that are worth mentioning. The Federation has also worked to minimize the dropout rates of female students in collaboration with teachers' associations and educational institutions.

In many of the higher education institutions and universities, female students have formed associations for the purpose of redressing female students' educational, social, and economical problems as well as to voice grievances to the authorities in an organized manner.

Conclusion

As the government has a clear direction of poverty alleviation, its focus is on providing pro poor social services such as water, road and energy. The government's provision of such services is a very enabling factor for women's empowerment as these services relieve women from being overburdened by workloads. Reluctance to take collective actions in the face of challenges are slowly changing. Though very few, there are cases where women as a group complain when one of them face injustice such as sexual harassment or gender discrimination (Gennet, 2010). For instance, Female Students Association of Addis Ababa University campaigned against the placement of female students in colleges that do not provide dormitory facilities since female students who live outside the campus encounter sexual harassment and even rape. The campaign was highly successful.

Part Four

*T*he following chapters discuss the opportunities and challenges of the Ethiopian women in accessing social services like health and education; their participation in the public domain as expressed in their political and economic empowerment and the unchanged roles of women in the household. A few suggestions on how to finish the unfinished business of women's equality are finally discussed.

CHAPTER XI

Access to Education

Education develops the personality of individuals, qualifies them to participate meaningfully in certain political and economic functions and assists their social mobility as well. Educating women means educating the whole family. But many economical, social, cultural and political factors such as sexism in school, the societal values that are reflected in the structure of the school, its administration, the "hidden" curriculum, teachers' behaviour and attitude, all have adverse effects on women's education. Women are perceived as intellectually incapable of pursuing fields of study like the sciences, engineering and technology which are viewed as tough subjects to be understood by them.

As noted earlier, Ethiopian society is predominantly Christian and Islamic and both religions have a profound impact in shaping the culture of the people of Ethiopia. In fact Christianity and Islam had played important roles in providing traditional education in different parts of the country from which women were excluded (Yeshimeberat 2008).

Traditional Ethiopian education has a rich history of literature and philosophy. In fact, the church and the mosque were the sole providers of traditional education in Ethiopia until the end of the nineteenth century. Women were not allowed to attend these traditional schools and go beyond reading and writing.

When modern education was finally introduced at the end of the nineteenth century, girls were also allowed to attend schools; however, separate and different curricula for boys and girls were designed as discussed earlier. When comprehensive high schools were introduced in the country along the model of American schools system in the early 60s, admission to the academic and industrial streams was allowed only for boys. Girls were channeled either to the secretarial or home economics streams. The practice of confining girls to "women area" persisted until a new education policy was put into practice.

The cultural context in which the girls receive their education influences their ability to use what they have learned. Where traditional cultural patterns exclude women from the control of resources and participation in the public sphere, only access to education becomes necessary for them to earn an independent income, increase their status and have social impact. However, the social impact of women's education would be limited not only if access to education and economic opportunities is limited, but also if traditional and cultural patterns limit them to domestic activities.

Studies indicate that women in Ethiopia face several constraints not only accessing education at all levels but also in successfully completing their courses of study (Gennet 1991). Cultural division of labour which overburdens girls at home as well as other factors such as early marriage, parents' illiteracy, unequal treatment in the class rooms, school distance from home are constraints for girls' education. In Ethiopia, girls spend much of their time on non-marketable activities at home while their brothers are allowed time to work on their schooling. Girls are responsible for every type of household chores many times over their brothers, and are called to substitute for their mother's labour two to three times more often than boys. In most cases, it is a female child that is kept from school to help with household chores. According to Legovini (2005), in any weekday, 42 per cent of boys and 36 per cent of girls spend time on school work; while 11 per cent of boys and 63 per cent of girls spend time on housework.

Girls' participation in higher education in Ethiopia was even worse. Until recently only 8 per cent of those enrolled in higher education were women (EMIS 1995). Access to higher education is strongly dependent on class, location and income, but even those from privileged classes who have access to higher education fail to be successful in the best paid professions. Because Ethiopian women are channeled into certain subjects that are identified as 'women's' such as social work, nursing and secretarial sciences, courses such as medicine, law and engineering (that lead to the best paid jobs) are still dominated by men. Because of lack of education in the sciences and mathematics, women did not benefit from the advancement of science and technology as well as from securing professional occupations.

The New Education and Training Policy (NETP) of 1994

As discussed earlier, Government of Ethiopia pursues a democratic developmental political economy that is inclusive and participatory, where men and women equally benefit and involve as well in the development pursued. Furthermore, giving the highest priority to education as it is the engine of development, it developed a New Education and Training Policy (NETP), that adddresses political, social and economic problems of the country. One of the goals of NETP is, therefore, to provide universal primary education to all school-aged children through establishing schools in rural areas and marginalized communities in line with the Government's poverty alleviation program. These commitments of the government created a favourable situation for girls' education. However, since school provision alone is not sufficient, special support schemes and compensatory measures are proposed in the policy to encourage girls' education. A review of various interventions and programmes used by developing countries to encourage girls' education indicated that interventions that address issues at both the demand and supply side are more effective than traditional ones (USAID 1991). The non traditional programmes that target not just one obstacle of girls' participation in education but several of them were addressed in order to make schools accessible to girls. The review identified proximity of schools to the community, using effective teachers, relevant curricula, friendly school environment for girls, free education at least till primary level and, community participation as the most effective interventions that encourage girls' to attend and perform well in school (USAID 1991).

In order to encourage girls' education many of the interventions had been put in place. Thus, Article 3.9.5 of the NETP states that the Government provides financial support to raise the participation of women in education (1994). Moreover, providing free education up to general secondary education and a cost sharing scheme thereafter were also conditions that favour girls. This is because one of the barriers that hinder them from attending school is cost of education. The fact that such enabling conditions were put in the policy was an important first step in promoting girls education. Similar important factors of the policy which are favourable to girls' education were the utilization of nationality languages as medium of instruction in the primary schools, the provision of secular education, and the use of continuous assessment with automatic promotion. The policy of automatic promotion with continuous assessment that is being implemented in grades one to four has helped girls not to remain (unnecessarily of course) in one class from year to year and which encouraged both the parents and the girls (MoE 2004). The medium of instruction in the Ethiopian school system was Amharic which was not the mother tongue of the majority of the Ethiopian people. As a result many of the children who had access to education would drop out of schools for lack of understanding of what was being taught in the classroom. Thus, adoption of the mother tongue as medium of instruction encouraged girls to stay in schools.

Secularism in education, that is, the non-interference of religious institutions has encouraged girls' attendance and participation in schools. In the past civic education was given as moral education based on the Orthodox Christian morality which propagates the importance of sexual division of labour that discourages girls' education. In the new civic education curriculum, however, democratic values that enhance the equality of women are stressed. For instances, issues such as democratic and human rights, rule of law, equality and justice are a few of the values in which issues about women's empowerment are embedded. Civic education is an important tool to bring about changes not only among students but also in the larger society. As every school age child in the country that passes through eight years of primary education is being exposed to these values, it is hoped that he/she is able to question if not counteract, the traditional values that are associated with women's subjugation. Today, there are close to nineteen million students in primary and secondary school system (this number will increase in the future) who have been exposed to civic education. And these young men and women who are the future mothers, fathers, workers, policy makers etc. will be in positions to hasten the empowerment of women. Though, anecdotal, we hear stories where young men and women today who are in schools, universities and other institutes have started challenging the traditional values.

While civic education, instructions in local languages, proper educational finance, access to primary education for all, are measures that apply to both boys and girls, special measures that ease the barriers of girls education are also put in place in implementing the new education policy. NETP states that education will be geared towards reorienting society's attitude towards the important role women play in the society and their contributions to development (1994). The Policy further states that attention would be given to gender issues in the design and preparation of curricula and textbooks, in the recruitment and assignment of women in teacher training institutes. Affirmative action is also put in place. It gives priority to women when recruiting teachers. Thus, a guide entitled Gender Mainstreaming Guidelines and Checklist was prepared in 2004. Capacity building training was given for curriculum designers, educational personnel and teacher training institute instructors on how to prepare gender sensitive curricula and address women's issues. Manuals on girls' education were prepared and disseminated to regions, institutions, teacher training institutions and colleges as well as schools. Furthermore, one of the criteria that was used to evaluate school textbooks is the neutrality of the content from gender biases. Guidelines on the evaluation of text books on gender sensitivity were prepared by the Ministry of Education and distributed to the relevant departments (MoE 2004).

To encourage girls' education, the first ESDP I program that ran from 1997-98 to 2001-2002 was designed shortly after the 1994 policy was formulated; its focus was on the provision of access to primary education to girls. Therefore, the program called for the increment of girls' participation in primary education through sensitizing the community, specially parents, about the importance of girls' education (ESDP Action Plan 1999). While the first program targeted the demand side of education, the second ESDP II (which ran from 2002-03 to 2004-05) addressed both the supply and demand sides of education. Therefore the following actions were taken: (a) attempts were made to provide safe environment, gender sensitive curriculum, textbooks and teachers; (b) awareness was created within the education community and those outside in order to change the negative attitudes, values and practices about women's education; (c) attempts were made to increase the number of female teachers, head teachers and managers; and (d) affirmative action for female students in both tertiary education and technical vocational education were implemented. Based on the assessment of the implementation of ESDP II, a third one (ESDP III) which was under implementation till 2010-11 is designed with further and more specific measures to minimize the challenges faced by girls. These are:

- To build schools nearer to communities,
- Increase parents' awareness about the benefits of girls' education,
- Hold teachers and head teachers accountable,
- Celebrate girls' day in schools,
- Entitlement of at least one year of TVET for girls who complete grade 10,
- Counseling services for female students,
- Tutorial services and advice for female students,
- Special support for female students in higher education institutions,
- Gender training as part of the pre- and in-service teacher training,
- Strengthen the Female Education Forum, and
- In-service capacity building for women leaders (p. 63).

In the implementation of the ESDPs many measures have

been put in place to encourage girls' participation. The expansion of primary, secondary, technical/vocational as well as tertiary education, the provision of free education up to the end of general secondary education and the cost sharing schemes for paying school fees after grade 10, have all expanded women's educational opportunities. The new family law of 2000, the revised penal and civil codes of 2005 that were enacted to protect girls from early marriage, abduction and rape also encourage parents to send their daughters to school without fear. In addition mechanisms that help increase enrollment of girls in school as well as improve their academic performance are put in place at National, Regional, District and Kebele Levels of the education system. Educational committees, girls' clubs and associations organized in almost all schools and school districts that are involved encourage girls' education one way or another. The most important institutional set-up is the establishment of Parent Teacher Associations (PTA) in every school. One of the main tasks of the associations is to see to it that girls in the school community attend and at least complete primary education.

Educational boards organized at district and kebele level, PTAs as well as school communities, continuously campaign about the importance of girl's education for the purpose of creating awareness within the society. Sensitization takes place wherever the community gathers for social or political meetings. Moreover, formal meetings and workshops are also held for the purpose of creating awareness about the importance of girls' education by the school, PTAs, and committees set up in schools. In those cases where it is suspected that parents still keep their school age children at home, the committee members move from house to house to convince the parents about the importance of girls' education. In most districts, schools register all children who are in the 7-14 age group residing in their respective areas in order to identify those children who are out of school (UNICEF 2004).

As a result of the decentralization of the education system, each district, kebele and school initiates its own strategies by which it encourages girls' education. Some of the outcomes of these initiatives are:

(a) girls are given priority of admission in places where space is limited;
(b) those parents who send all their daughters to school are rewarded and/acknowledged; and
(c) Girls are encouraged to be assertive and inform their homeroom teachers and seek their assistance in the event of problems.

District and Kebele boards of education as well as PTAs campaign against early marriage which is a compelling factor for girls to drop out of school. In some communities strong partnership is forged among women's organizations and Kebele leaders to jointly campaign against early marriage Some schools have given homeroom teachers responsibility to identifying and following up those students who become frequently absent from school or dropout.

In most schools female teachers as well as female students' groups are organized under the name of girls clubs, girls' education committees or female teachers' clubs, in order to help girls stay at school and improve their academic performance. In some schools teachers make home visits to persuade mothers so household chores that female students perform are minimized as much as possible in order to have time to their studies. The various committees sensitize the community about the importance of girls' education, visits houses and discuss with parents whose daughters have dropped out of school. Parents who try to marry off their children before they reach the legal age of 18, without the consent of the girls are reported to district courts. Thousands of girls have been saved from early marriage by these girls' education committees. Significant numbers of female students have been retained in schools through the efforts of these groups. For instance, in the Amhara region where early marriage is widely practiced, 31,053 girls were spared the practice during the years between 2005 to 2008. A UNICEF study undertaken in 2004 states that female groups organized in schools not only assisted girls coming from poor households but also stood with them when they are subjected to harmful practices such as sexual harassment, abduction and physical violence (p. 36).

Almost all schools provide tutorial services to female students after school and during weekends. The tutorial services mainly focus on mathematics and the English language. Both female and male teachers are required to give these services. Peer coaching is also widely used (UNICF 2004). In cases where there is shortage, priority is given to girls in the distribution of books. Recognizing or giving prizes for high achievers to encourage others, using continuous student competition are few of the measures used to improve the performance of female students.

To create conducive environments for female students gender units are established in almost all higher education institutions. The purposes of these units are to work towards assisting students so that they become academically successful. The Gender Unit has also helped to tackle sexual harassment inflicted on female students. Discussion forums are organized mostly by the Gender Unit on such topics as assertiveness, gender and leadership, gender and academic achievement to both male and female students and the staff to sensitize the community about women's equality.

At Addis Ababa University, the nation's oldest institution, there are courses in gender issues in the faculty of law and in the department of philosophy. In addition, some female instructors voluntarily include topics on women's empowerment which usually generate a heated debate among female and male students. There are sensitization programmes as well as courses in the faculty of law, department of philosophy and in the Institute of Gender Studies, which have contributed to making the university community more gender sensitive than it was earlier.

Affirmative Action

Affirmative action is a measure that is used to redress discriminatory practices that have been inflicted on minorities like women, physically impaired, African Americans in the case of the US etc. Affirmative action has been introduced during the Military Government where quotas were reserved in higher education for ex soldiers, and for both male and female students from rural areas. However, a constitutionally backed policy of affirmative action for female students was sanctioned in the new education policy. As is the case in many places, where affirmative action is implemented (for example USA), it has generated a heated debate in Ethiopia too. Those proponents of affirmative action argue that (a) affirmative action is needed to compensate minorities for centuries of oppression; (b) diversity is desirable and won't always occur if left to chance; (c) students starting with a disadvantage need a boost; (d) affirmative action draws people to areas of study and work they may never consider otherwise; and (e) some stereotypes may never be broken without affirmative action. On the other hand, those who oppose affirmative action point out that: (a) affirmative action leads to reverse discrimination; (b) Affirmative action lowers standards of accountability needed to push students or employees to perform better; (c) students admitted on this basis are often ill-equipped to handle the schools to which they've been admitted and; (d) it is condescending to minorities to say they need affirmative action to succeed since it demeans true minority achievement; i.e. success is labeled a as result of affirmative action rather than hard work and ability (www.balancedpolitics.org/affirmative_action.ht.)

Positive discrimination or affirmative action is used in Ethiopia to enhance women's participation particularly beyond secondary education. To create female role models in schools and encourage women to the teaching profession, 30 per cent seats are reserved for female students in teacher training institutions and colleges. In the same light, affirmative action is also put in place to enhance the enrollment of women in tertiary education.

Because of the controversy around the importance of affirmative action and also since many felt that affirmative action did not help female students but contributed to their drop out from higher education institutions, a study was commissioned by MoE in 2008 to analyze the situation. The study indicated that retention and university success of girls were adversely affected more by gender biased institutional roles, traditional academic expectations about girls etc. that are prevalent in the institution rather than by affirmative action (Yeshimebrat, Alemayehu *et al.*, 2009). Furthermore, the same study indicated that both higher institution instructors and students have a favourable attitude towards affirmative action (p. 49).

The policy has doubtless provided opportunities for women to enroll in undergraduate and graduate programs thereby increasing the chance of employment and therefore of their economic independence, political empowerment, greater self confidence and self esteem.

Female students today are more assertive than before in protecting their rights, equalities and interests. What is different today from the past is that women are exposed to gender issues through the media and through awareness creation programs undertaken by both government and non government organizations.

A better opportunity to attend higher education institutions is created and there is a visible difference in the enrollment and the quality of academic performance between the female students of ten years ago and the current ones. Female students are increasingly involved in academic endeavors; their participation is qualitatively improving and has become more assertive (Gennet 2010). There used to be discrimination in assigning fields of study where women were put in "soft courses" and men in science. Some used to justify the discrimination by attributing it to so called biological differences in capabilities. In the U.K. girls have been known to excel in math and science leaving the authorities to devise schemes to encourage boys to enter the science stream. Women do equally well as men in all programs and the traditionally accepted wisdom that women are not academically capable does not hold water now. Female students are enrolled in all areas. Most of them also successfully complete their studies even in those 'men only fields' such as engineering, hard sciences and technology.

However, the number of female students in higher education in general and in some areas in particular is still much lower than that of male students. This is because of the conditions under which they are socialized. Hopefully, the situation will change as the gap between boys and girls is closing at primary and secondary levels.

Enrollment and Participation in All Levels of Education

In order to compare the progress of girls' enrollment in every level of education before and after the implementation of NETP, a table showing the number of students and schools in 1991 and

Table 11.1: The Number of Students Enrolled in Education in the Years 1990-91 and 2010-11

Level of Education	*Number of Students, Schools and Institutes*							
	1990-91				*2010-11*			
	School/ Institutes	*Boys*	*Girls*	*Total*	*School/ Institutes*	*Boys*	*Girls*	*Total*
Primary	8,256	1,200,393	863,242	2,063,635	28,349	8,196,498	7,356.644	16,718,111
Secondary	275	264, 783	189,202	453,985	1,500	976,822	777,321	1,750,134
Technical / Vocation	17	NA	NA	2,506	505	197,463	169,150	366,613
Higher Education*	2	15942	1953	17,895	86	344,137	123,706	467,843

Source: EMIS, 2010/11.

2006-07 is shown in Table 11.1. The table depicts the number of students in primary, secondary, technical/vocational and tertiary education in 1991, right before the NETP was formulated and in 2010-11.

Note that the 1991 data for technical/vocational education is not aggregated by gender. Therefore, it is impossible to know the exact number of female students at the time. Nevertheless, one can only assume that the participation of female students would be much less than 50 per cent of the total number of students given the social, cultural and political environment within which girls' education was viewed.

The comparison of the number of educational institutions indicates that educational facilities were very few in 1991 indicating the fact that the majority of school age children did not have access to education. In situations where there are limited educational facilities, male rather than female students tend to be sent to school. However, the 2010-11 data reveals a huge increase in the number of educational institutions. This is because of the commitment of the government to provide universal primary education as well as due to the human resource development programs under way in the country. As a result, school facilities, institutions and universities were built all over the country. Addressing the issue of access of education at all levels is a favorable condition that is created for girls to participate in primary, secondary, technical/vocational and tertiary education in the process of implementation of the NETP. The number of girls who are enrolled in education is growing as depicted in the tables and included here. Though the policy has been implemented since 1994, the data in the following tables show only the ones for the last five years.

Table 11.2 depicts the gross enrollment trend of both boys and girls in primary first and second cycles.

Table 11.2 shows that within sixteen years of the implementation of NETP, the trend in terms of girls' enrollment is showing tremendous progress and the gap between boys and girls is closing specially in the first cycle of primary education, grades 1-4.

A study done in 2008 by the World Bank on Ethiopia's

Table 11.2: Gross Enrollment Trends at Primary Level

Year	*Primary 1st Cycle (1-4) (%)*			*Primary 2nd Cycle (5-8) (%)*			*Primary (1-8) (%)*		
	Boys	*Girls*	*Total*	*Boys*	*Girls*	*Total*	*Boys*	*Girls*	*Total*
2006-07	122.9	111.2	117.1	68.3	53.7	61.1	98.0	85.1	91.7
2007-08	133.0	122.5	127.8	64.8	55.5	60.2	100.5	90.5	95.6
2008-09	126.7	118.4	122.6	65.6	60.6	63.1	97.6	90.7	94.4
2009-10	1232.9	114.3	118.8	67.4	63.5	65.5	96.6	90.1	93.4
2010-11	128.8	119.1	124.0	67.4	64.8	66.1	99.5	93.2	96.4

Source: MoE, Education Statistics Annual Abstract (2010-11).

performance on gender equality acknowledges that not only has school enrollment shown progress, Ethiopia's progress in primary education has also brought the country much closer to the SSA average in regard to girls' participation in primary education. Furthermore, the same study acknowledges that on some dimensions such as political representation, it is ahead of both SSA and Low Income Countries (World Bank 2008).

In secondary education also, enrollment of girls is steadily growing every year. Moreover, the five years average of annual growth rate for both first and second cycles is higher for girls (9.0% and 19.5% respectively) than for boys, indicating that the gender gap is closing as depicted in Table 11.3.

Table 11.4 depicts the enrollment of students in TVET. Here again, the enrollment of female students has increased manifold compared to what it was before the implementation of NETP.

Table 11.3: Total Enrollment at Secondary Education

Year	*First Cycle*			*Second Cycle*		
	Enrollment			*Enrollment*		
	Boys	*Girls*	*Total*	*Boys*	*Girls*	*Total*
2006/07	760,674	462,988	1,223,662	117,000	52,219	175,219
2007/08	793,228	514,691	1,307,919	130,533	62,911	193,444
2008/09	803,389	578,936	1,382,325	146,547	58,713	205,260
2009/10	818,280	634,570	1,452,850	156,194	86,886	243.080
2010/11	807,251	654,667	1,461,918	169,571	118,645	288.216
Average Annual Growth Rate	1.5%	9.0%	4.5%	9.7%	19.5%	13.2.0%

Source: Education Statistics Annual Abstract, 2010-2011.

The expansion of TVET centers has created opportunities for female students. This is the area where women get skills training to be gainfully employed even if they drop out of school without completing a level due to many challenges that female students face. As the table indicates, the gap between female and male students is gradually closing. However, the majority of girls are still being enrolled in textile, commercial and service sectors which are traditionally known as women's areas.

Table 11.4: Student Enrollment in Technical/Vocational Programmes (Between 2006-7 and 2010/11)

Year	*Male*	*Female*	*Total*	*% of Female*
2006/7	107,327	83,824	191,151	43.9
2007/8	119,123	110,129	229,252	48.0
2008/9	165,910	142,591	308,501	46.2
2009/10	196,937	156,483	353,420	44.3
2010/11	199,799	171,548	371,347	46.2

Source: MoE, Education Statistics Annual Abstract (2010/11).

In regard to female students' participation in tertiary education, similar progress is demonstrated. Even though the percentage of female students is still low when compared to the participation rate of male students, there is unmistakable progress over the last five years. Table 11.4 indicates a steady growth when compared to the number of female students in 2006-07.

Table 11.5: Student Enrollment in Undergraduate Programs in Higher Education (Between the Years 2006/7 and 2010/11)

Year	*Male*	*Female*	*Total*	*Female %*
2006/7	150,530	52,869	203,399	26
2007/8	199,684	63,317	263.001	24
2008/9	220,510	90,192	310,702	29
2009/10	306,758	113,629	420,387	27
2010/11	326,769	120,924	447,693	27

Source: EMIS, 2010-11.

Table 11.5 shows the consistent increase in undergraduate degree enrollment of both male and female students. The increase in the number of female students from 52,869 to 120,924 within a span of five years is progress that is unprecedented in the history of female education in Ethiopia. Likewise, progress made in the enrollment of female students in post graduate programmes. The number of female students in post graduate programmes jumped from 708 to 2,782 in a span of five years according to the Table 11.6 above. The opportunity to participate in higher education, of course, will have an unparalleled impact on the economic, political and social empowerment of women.

Table 11.6: Student Enrollment in Post Graduate Programmes (Between 2006/7 and 2010/11)

Year	*Male*	*Female*	*Total*	*Female %*
2006/7	6,349	708	7,057	10.0
2007/8	6,652	703	7,355	9.6
2008/9	8,979	1,146	10,125	11.3
2009/10	12,569	1,703	14,272	11.9
2010/11	17,368	2,782	20,150	13.8

Source: MoE: Education Statistics Annual Abstract (2010-11).

The expansion of education has created employment opportunity for women; however, in any of the levels, the 50 per cent is not reached. Given the condition that women did not have much access to education about 20 years ago, the unequal number of female teachers in every level is understandable. An affirmative action used to reserve 30 per cent seat at teacher training institutes has served its purpose in primary but not in secondary education. However, as education at every level has expanded and women have access to them, 50 per cent of women teachers at least at primary and secondary school can be targeted.

Table 11.7: Number of Teaching Staff in the Education System by Level (in 2011)

Level	*No. of Men*	*No. of Female*	*Total*	*% of Female*
Primary	193,599	114,683	308,282	37.20
Secondary	43,041	9,690	52,731	18.37
Teacher Edu.	1,792	165	1,957	8.43
TVET	10,758	2,132	12,890	16.53
Higher Edu.	15,798	1,604	17,402	9.21

Source: MoE: Education Information Annual Statistics Information (2010/11).

The role of the State in provision of social services is indispensable if marginalized groups like women have to access education. The Ethiopian government has given the highest priority to expand education as it is demonstrated by the budget allocation for the last 20 years; hence, about twenty million (almost one-fourth of the population) are being educated at different levels. If it were not for the Education policy's objectives of creating access, equity, quality and decentralized education, girls would not have been able to access the service. The provision of free and secular education along with the measures used to encourage girls' education had enabled girls to access education. Today, there are a little over 7 million female students accounting for about 45.9 per cent of the number of total primary students attend schools. Participation of girls in secondary, technical/vocational education and tertiary education has also increased from what it was.

Ethiopia's efforts at educating women have already shown positive results in its economic progress. The Gender Parity Index (GPI), which is an index designed to measure the relative access of males and females in education, indicates that the gender gap especially at primary levels, is closing. The GPI for the levels of 1-4, 5-8, 9-10 and 11-12 are 0.90, 0.96, 0.83 and 0.71 respectively (EMTS 2010-11). An increase in girls education has many benefits as many studies of the World Bank and UNESCO indicate. A woman with primary education is most likely to educate her children, raise healthier children being aware of immunization, hygiene and sanitation moreover, an educated woman will contribute better to the overall economic development and democratization. However, there are areas where women's participation has to further improve, for example their participation in higher education is still skewed. Measures that help make the education system gender friendly such as having women teachers, directors and supervisors are still lagging behind. If women have to play an important role the transformation of the economy from agriculture to industry women's education beyond primary level is essential.

CHAPTER XII

Access to Health Services

Poverty and gender inequality are the main causes of women's health problems in Ethiopia. Because of poverty, women and their children used to die of diseases caused by lack of nutritious food or communicable and water borne diseases that could have been easily prevented. Non-availability of mother and child health services killed hundreds of mothers and children. The maternal mortality rate was 358 per 1000 while under-five mortality rate per 1000 people was 190 and the percentage of the population that had access to safe water was only 19 (MOFED and WDI, 2000). Gender inequality makes women more vulnerable to sexually transmitted diseases such as HIV/AIDS, as well as complications that result from unsafe abortions. Six percent of all maternal deaths were attributable to complications from unsafe abortions. According to the Ministry of Health Report of 2010, the major causes of maternal mortality are prolonged labour, ruptured uterus and malaria. Children's deaths are caused by pneumonia, diarrhea, malaria, neonatal problems, malnutrition and HIV/AIDS.

Early marriage and female genital mutilation further complicated the health problems of women. Many young women, especially those in the Amhara Regional State suffer from Fistula which inflicts psychological, mental, physical and social problems on the victims. Most of the Ethiopian people live in the rural areas where there were only handful of health services, thus women had deliveries at home using untrained traditional birth attendants. Whenever the traditional health attendant is unable to assist, the women in labour are carried to the nearest health center which might take more than a full day's walk. Early marriage and female genital mutilation, sexual harassment including rape are still prevalent despite the laws prohibiting them.

Unsafe abortion has killed and/or has resulted in lifelong complications for many women. That is because abortion is illegal unless the pregnancy is life threatening. Many hospital beds are occupied by women who have health problems due to illegal abortion. Saba Kidane Mariam whose organization I.P.A.S. collaborated with the Government and other non governmental organizations in a study done in 1990 (E.C.) noted that 53 per cent of the government health center beds were occupied by women who had health complications associated with unsafe abortions (interview with Saba, in 2011).

Therefore, it was necessary to initiate the process of revising the old law that did not address many of the issues that were related to unsafe abortions. Hence Article 551, of the revised Criminal Code of 2004, has made abortion legal if the pregnancy is the result of:

(a) rape or incest; or
(b) the continuance of the pregnancy endangers the life of the mother or the child or the health of the mother or where the birth of the child is a risk to the life or health of the mother; or
(c) where the child has an incurable and serious deformity; or
(d) where the pregnant woman, owing to a physical or mental deficiency, is physically as well as mentally unfit to bring up the child.

In the case of grave and imminent danger which can be averted only by an immediate intervention, an act of termination of pregnancy in accordance with the provision of Article 75 of this Code is not punishable.

To revise the law was no easy task for those who campaigned for its revision. It was very challenging to convince the Ethiopian society into accepting the legality of abortion due to the factors raised above. The society being predominately Christian and Muslim, the question of abortion is filtered through religious eyes. Saba and her colleagues had held discussion forums with religious leaders explaining the gravity of the issue in terms of women's health, life and government expenditure (interview with Saba, 2011).

The government and non-government organizations are mobilizing society in order to eradicate both poverty and associated adversities like harmful traditional practices and HIV/AIDS. This mobilization has sometimes taken the form of an organization. One such organization which has achieved tremendous results is the National Coalition for Women against HIV/AIDS known as the Coalition for short. The Coalition was established in June 2003 to combat HIV/AIDS by a group of committed, prominent and professional Ethiopian women at all levels in order to create a national movement against HIV/AIDS (Report of the Coalition 2008-9). Believing that women's involvement in the fight against HIV/AIDS is crucial, charters of the Coalition are organized in all the nine regional states and in Addis Ababa and Dire Dawa cities.

It is the vision of the Coalition not only to combat HIV/AIDS but also poverty and gender inequity; it is therefore actively involved in the campaign combating violence against women and their equality. The Coalition operates through education/communication; organizing forums in various regions of the country to educate women about their legal rights. It uses advocacy, campaigning and lobbying to involve the community at large including religious and community leaders, about the impact of violence against women for the spread of HIV/AIDS and the underdevelopment of the country. Moreover, it promotes women's leadership through training that focuses on how women leaders can significantly contribute not only to the betterment of their families but also to the entire community (Report of the Coalition 2008/09). Through intensive community mobilization and under the slogan of "Save the Unborn Child" and "Treat Every Child as Your Own" it promoted PMCT ART and provision of care and support for orphans and vulnerable children.

The Coalition's most successful campaign that resulted in

unprecedented effects was its campaign against early marriage and female genital mutilation; the two major health problems of Ethiopian women. Regarding its achievement, the Coalition Report of 2008/09 states:

(a) In the Afar Region, the tradition of Female Genital Mutilation was considered as *HARAM (Haram* means something forbidden) by all the participants who included women, men, religious leaders, and youth.
(b) In Somalia Region, forums were held and religious leaders also talked about the harmful effects of the practice.
(c) In Tigray and Amhara where early marriage is the norm, the Coalition went beyond advocacy and social mobilization but recruited community sensitizers and zonal and woreda level coordinators in order to ensure that girls are not married before they are ready for it. It also identified women with fistula (as a result of early marriage) and referred them to hospitals.

Additionally, those who were economically vulnerable as a result of early marriage were provided access to some economic activities so that they would be productive and self-sufficient.

The coalition is a voluntary membership organization that is chaired by a former freedom fighter Azeb Mesfin who joined the armed struggle while she was in her teens. Azeb had given birth during the struggle (Bush) marrying the late Mr. Melese Zenawi, one of the leaders in the struggle who became the President during the Transitional Government and later on the Prime Minister of Ehiopia. Azeb now heads EFFORT, one of the endowment organizations.

As in the case of education, the Transitional Government produced a Health Policy in 1993. which was very comprehensive. It touched upon many economic and social issues related to the health problems of the country. Health issues that are pertinent to women's problems have been adequately addressed in the implementation strategies of the health policy. Thus, there are strategies such as making pregnancy safer and improving reproductive health such as Reproductive Health (2006),

Adolescent and Youth Reproductive Health (2006) and the Revised Abortion Law (2005). Moreover, in order to make health services accessible to poor women, a health care financing strategy is in place where maternal and child health services are rendered free for the needy (Health Care Financing Strategy).

In order to implement these strategies, the health extension package envisages that the community, especially the mother and child would receive health services in their respective communities/homes without having to go to the health service centers. The health extension package has two parts: one deals with family oriented health while another deals with community health problems. One important initiative taken by the government towards improving the health situation is the training and deployment of the new health workforce.

The health Extension programme was introduced in 2002/03 with a view of dissemination of the right health knowledge and skills would enable households to take responsibility for maintaining their own health. The package encompasses the following areas:

Personal Hygiene and Environmental Sanitation: Excreta disposal, proper and safe solid and liquid waste management; water supply safety measures; Food hygiene and safety measures; healthy home environment; arthropods and rodent control and personal hygiene.

Communicable Disease Prevention and Control: HIV and Aids prevention and control; TB prevention and control; Malaria Prevention and Control; First Aid.

Health Education and Communication: Provision of information; social mobilization; behavioral change communication (IEC/BCC);

Family Health Services: Maternal and Child Health; Family Planning; Immunization; Adolescent Reproductive Health: Nutrition.

As a result of the activities of these extension workers, the awareness in the community about health issues has improved and access to health services has increased. The number of children who get immunization, women who receive family planning services, mothers who have pre-maternity services as well as HIV and Aids counseling has increased.

The extension package is implemented by EHWs, who are

all women who have taken one year's training after completing the 10th grade. The deployment of women extension health workers in the community has multifaceted advantages. As the health services and advocacy are being done in and around the domicile of the women, the health workers can develop easy rapport with the women of the community. The women health workers can also easily understand and appreciate the problems of women better than men health workers. The practice has also an added positive impact on the society about women's ability to perform important tasks such as health work. Needless to say that the health extension program has also created employment and training opportunities for women.

As a result of the activities undertaken in the country, the health situation of women has improved, though the ultimate goal is not reached yet. According to the Ministry of Health report of 2010, the number of women who benefited from household latrines is about 72 per cent, and those with clean drinking water are 58.7 per cent; the time to fetch drinking water has also decreased: what used to take about two to three hours now it takes women 30 minutes or less. Unlike in the past, the awareness of women about family planning and child immunization has improved; thus, the percentage of women who use contraceptives grew from 15 per cent in 2005 to 40 per cent in 2010. Likewise the number of children immunized in 2010 reached to 52 per cent from 22 per cent in 2005. The following tables and graphs tell the rest of the story (*see* Graphs 12.1 and 12.2).

Table 12.1: Health Facilities Constructed for the Last 10 Years

Facility	*1996/97*	*2003/2004*	*2010*
HP	76	2,899	14,416
HC	412	519	2689
Hospitals	87	126	195

Source: Ministry of Health, Ethopia.

With the expansion of health facilities, 98 per cent of the population can access health services within two hours of walking distance which is a great improvement compared to 2004 where only 63 per cent of the population had access at this distance.

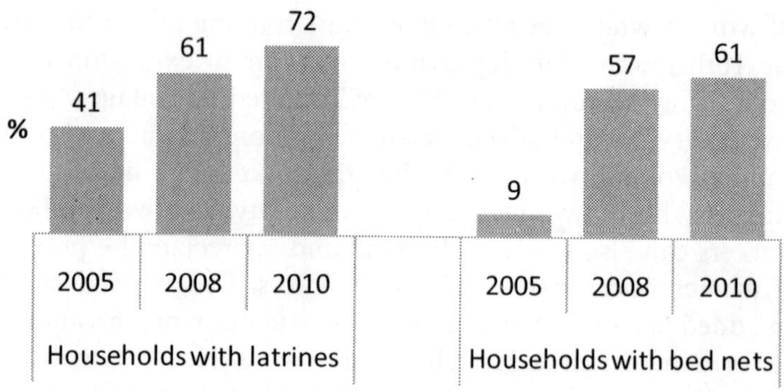

Graph 12.1: Trend in Household Health Practices

Source: Ministry of Health (Ethopia) (2010).

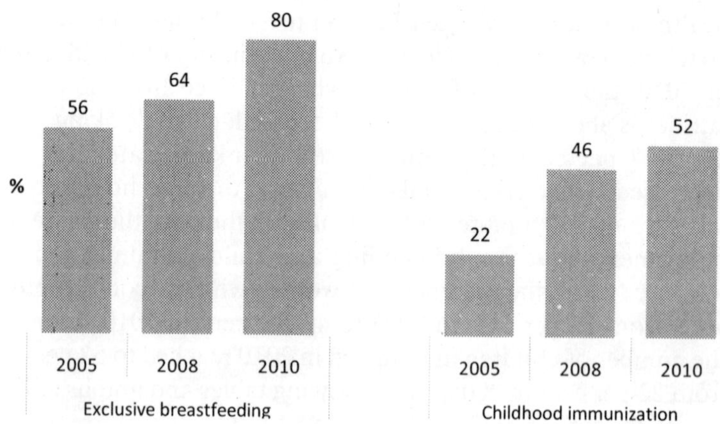

Graph 12.2: Trend in Childhood Immunization and Exclusive Breastfeeding

Source: Ministry of Health (Ethopia) (2010).

A tremendous improvement has been registered in the area of health during the PASDEP period where women have benefited; hence, the number of women of child bearing age using contraceptives increased from 15 per cent to 32 per cent, prenatal service coverage increased from 46 per cent to 63 per cent; postnatal service coverage increased from 15 per cent to 30 per cent; and trained birth assisted delivery increased from 13 per cent to 25 per cent — although the target was to reach 32 per cent. In general the number of deaths of mothers which were related to delivery decreased from 871/100,000 in 2005 to 590/

100,000 in 2010. The under-five mortality rate decreased from 123/1000 to 101/1000. By 2009/10 about 10 million households living in malaria infested areas had received two mosquito bed nets each and by this means the coverage of mosquito net usage has increased from 1 per cent to 100 per cent in the plan period. Also during the PASDEP period, the cure rate for TB increased from 65 per cent to 67 per cent and the incidence of HIV decreased from 0.68 to 0.28.

Before I conclude this chapter, I would like to narrate the conversation I had with Dr. Kesete Birhane, Minister of Health, about the contribution of the Policy for women's empowerment, in 2012. Dr. Kesete was a state minister at the time of our conversation.

According to him, the health policy is a revolutionary one as it does not follow the provider and receiver model unlike the conventional health services. The policy is based on a principle that every family can produce its own health like it produces its own food in farming. Thus, extension health workers move from house to house and teach each family about health skills. In the process, women become beneficiaries since the training, information and the service about family planning, hygiene, child care, nutrition etc. comes to their doorsteps.

As statistics show, addressing women as an important element in improving the health of the family has borne fruits. Dr. Kessete (2011) explained how women have become serious players in the provision of family health by giving examples of unique situations in Tigraye. As statistics shows, addressing women as key players in improving the health of the family has borne fruits. Dr. Kessete describes how this has worked in the northern region of Tigray:

> "Rural women in Tigray preferred to deliver their babies at home rather than in hospital or health stations; that is because at home people can pray for their safety and they can sprinkle holy water and make genfo (porridge) immediately after delivery to ward off evil spirits and welcome the new born. In order to encourage delivery at health stations community women came around the cultural constraints by being creative: they brought holy water to the health stations and also began to make genfo

> there! The other reason for expectant women's reluctance to go to health stations was the fact that they would have to be carried on a stretcher, something that many considered to be a bad omen since it is often the terminally ill or the dead were carried on stretchers. In view of this, the enterprising women of Tigray came up with a new idea: in place of the stretchers they decided that young and strong men should carry the expectant women to the health services!"

The country has made impressive progress in health where child mortality has decreased by about 30 per cent according to the World Bank and the country is on track to meet its Millennium Development Goals in health, including those of child survival, HIV/Aids and malaria. Surely the progress wills women's empowerment as one of their concerns is their children's health.

CHAPTER XIII
Access to Economic and Political Power

Economic Empowerment Access to Productive Resources*

In rural Ethiopia where eighty three percent of the population live, women spend many hours in domestic chores such as fetching of water and fire wood, cooking for the family, agricultural work like farming and animal rearing as well as off farm employment (Women's Affairs Office 1992). In southern Ethiopia, women's role in agriculture ranges from preparation of organic fertilizer for tree plants like Ensete (false banana) to the laborious task of processing food. In many places they play significant roles in animal rearing. Similarly in the north, women are engaged in agricultural tasks of weeding, transporting the harvest, storing the grain and in animal husbandry.

As land is a crucial factor in an agrarian economy like Ethiopia, access to land is an empowering factor. As pointed out earlier, the 1975 Rural Land Proclamation (RLP) of Ethiopia that was implemented under the Derg did not grant women land either though they had been denied land ownership in the past. Before the proclamation, the land tenure arrangements in Imperial Ethiopia excluded women's ownership as discussed above. According to the criteria, women were not entitled to possess land

* In writing this chapter, I have used information that I have gathered for my study on the "Impact of the New Education Policy on the Empowerment of Women" (Unpublished Dissertation 2010).

since they were excluded from the political and military activities which merited land grant. It was only in the northern part of Ethiopia that women could be entitled to land ownership. Therefore, in both rural and urban areas, most women did not own land.

Thus, in addressing gender inequality, one of the priority areas of the Ethiopian Government is providing land to women. The Constitution as well as the Federal Proclamation on Rural Land Administration of 1997 asserted that women were entitled to land. Equal rights between women and men with respect to use, transfer, administration, control and inheritance have been established, and the legal presumption of joint property by spouses has been recognized (The World Bank, 2008). In the Amhara region, about 110,000 landless women were given land by the regional government. Moreover, in a land certification program that was undertaken in four of the biggest regions, the names and pictures of the wives as co-owners was included which strengthened the land rights of women. A World Bank (2008) study indicated that there was quantitative evidence to the effect that women were developing a strong sense of ownership, and they felt that in cases of divorce their rights would be more secured than in the past (p. 42). Furthermore a nation-wide survey indicates that more than 80 per cent of households expected rural land certification to improve women's position; and the women who have received the certification have pointed out that there has been improvement in their economic and social status (The World Bank 2008). Women also receive extension services to improve their skill in increasing productivity of their lands, for instance 2003 EC, 27.5 per cent of women farmers had the service and 114 women farmers have been awarded national medal given for model farmers who build assets.

In cases where women cannot make a living out of agriculture, they become wage earners in non-agricultural small and micro enterprises that do not require high startup capital that is encouraged by the Government through various incentives. In the last 10 years microfinance institutions that give credit to the poor in the rural areas have been established. Since these institutions are established to help the poor women have benefited from them. According to Wolday, (2008) out of 1.73 million clients of the microfinance institutions, 38 per cent were women furthermore, despite the fact that women take smaller loans to avoid indebtedness, lack entrepreneurial skills and dropout more frequently than men, microfinance has improved their income.

The pattern of wage employment of women shows that they were mostly engaged in contractual, temporary and seasonal jobs that require low skills. Ethiopian women's participation in the formal paid sector is very limited. Women have less income than men because of disparities in different employment patterns.

Table 13.1: Nature and Terms of Wage Employment in Total Wage Employment (For the Year 2005)

Types of Employment	*All*	*Male %*	*Female %*
Wage Employment			
Public formal wage employment	43	47	38
Private formal wage employment	35	40	28
Private informal wage employment	22	13	34
Permanent/Temporary Employment			
Permanent employment	43	48	36
Temporary employment	39	33	47
Contract employment	9	10	8
Casual or other employment	9	9	9

Source: LFS, 2005.

According to Legovini (2005) most women, 71 per cent of government employees are working as cleaners, messengers and typists. Women are also concentrating in those jobs that are flexible and offer less money and security as shown in Table 13.1. The table shows that among those who are engaged in temporary employment work, the majority (47%) are women.

According to a survey conducted in 501 manufacturing and electricity industries by the Central Statistical Authority (1996 EC) to compare the income of men and women, it was found that the per capita income of male workers was 433 Eth Birr (Ehopian currency) while the per capita income of the female workers was 363 or 83 per cent of the income of men. Another survey undertaken by the Authority covering large and medium scale manufacturing and electricity industries showed similar differences. Per capita income of male workers was Eth. Birr 510.49; while that of the female workers stood at birr 405.12 or 79.35 per cent of the male workers (Daniel 2004).

The reasons for this disparity in the formal labour markets include time constraints that women face because of child rearing, preoccupation with household chores, lack of vocational training, unfair hiring practices, and occupational discrimination by employers (Daniel 2004). In a study conducted by Daniel (2004) about women's status in the formal labour market, it was found that 31.9 per cent of the employers consider women to be less productive and less efficient; 48.9 per cent consider them to be less endowed with supervisory skills, while 44.7 per cent and 57.4 per cent consider them to be more prone to lateness and absenteeism respectively.

Of course women are reluctant to take up jobs with multiple, responsibilities as the schedules of activities interfere with their domestic work. Women have the habit of being absent from their work more frequently than men because of childbearing or other reasons connected with their domestic responsibilities. There are no support mechanisms and systems in many work places to alleviate the problems faced by women because of their dual responsibilities, thus they do not excel and advance in their professions. For instance, University communities tend not to support the nomination of women to responsible positions of deanship, department headship, in the case of higher education. In rare cases, women with extraordinary credentials who are far better than men may get nominated; though being nominated does not necessarily ensure getting the job. They are not even given leadership position in committee work than being minute secretaries, bursars (records) and event organizers. The exclusion of women from working in responsible places and positions lead to lack of self confidence and self respect in themselves.

However, the recent statistical data reproduced in Table 13.2 indicates that the situation is changing and women are securing employment in almost all areas. As shown in Table 13.2, the number of women entering professional occupations such as legislators' senior officials and managers has increased at a higher rate than the numbers of men, between 1994 and 2005. As professional occupations require knowledge and skill, the increased involvement of women in these areas could be attributed to the expansion of educational opportunities for women. As shown above, women's participation in technical/vocational and higher education has increased tremendously between 2005/06 and 2010/11.

Representation in High Paying Jobs

One of the measures of women's economic empowerment is that they are represented in high paying jobs. Thus Table 13.1 indicates those who are employed in professional and semi professional occupations that are relatively high paying compared to non-professional jobs.

As revealed in Table 13.2, the percentage increase in the employment of women in professional jobs between 1994 and 2005 is much higher for women than for men though their total number is lower than men's. This indicates that more women have access to education that leads to their entry into high paying jobs.

Table 13.2: Employed Population by Major Occupation and Gender (In 1994 and 2005)

Occupation	*1994*		*2005*		*Increase between 1994 – 2005 (in %age)*	
	Male	*Female*	*Male*	*Female*	*Male*	*Female*
Legislator senior officials & Managers	43,451	6,984	80,438	20,227	85.12	189.61
Professionals	37,932	7,577	113,017	45,653	197.94	502.52
Technicians and Associate Professionals	166,503	58,207	216,389	94,308	29.96	62.02

Source: CSA 2006.

Ownership and Control of Assets. Access to material resources such as land, houses, and cars, bank accounts or credit facilities are very important indicators of women's economic empowerment. However, even if the wife earns an income, the husband controls it and whatever property is acquired by the family is still registered in the name of the husband in many households, though there is a slight change recently. This is despite the fact that the Family Law of 2000 requires that common property be registered in the name of the couples. In fact, married respondents in my study (Gennet 2010) remarked that they were not aware that a couple's common property must be registered in both names according to the Law.

The economic situation of women has improved as they are benefiting from microfinance, micro and small scale industries that are promoted by the government. There are women role models who come out of being dependent either on their husbands or male relatives by earning their living through the help of microfinance and other services. The perception of women being physically weak is changing since many women work on construction sites and other places where they never ventured earlier. Women have also started having their own savings by opening bank accounts as opposed to the past when they used to keep their money in the house somethimes hiding it from their husbands. In a CSA of Ethiopia and ICF International of USA study in 2012, women's ownership of property and participating in decision making in the household has improved. Thus, 60 per cent, and 66 per cent of rural women own land and house respectively either alone or jointly with their husbands. Similarly about 30 per cent and 18 per cent of women have houses and land respectively. The family property is also being controlled by the couple. In fact some 40 per cent urban and 35 per cent of the rural married women respondents in the same study indicated that they make independent decision in how to spend their personal income. Such progress is a move forward towards women's empowerment.

Access to Political Power

As it has been discussed earlier women have been discriminated against participation in political discourse. Historically, women have been excluded from politics and power as women were regarded as incompetent to make political decisions. Even women themselves do not consider politics as something complex that they comprehend nor have the competence to deal with. Thus, socialized in an ideology that marginalizes women, they too shy away and distance themselves from political participation. For instance, in district or community (kebele) meetings which were mostly held to discuss economic, social and political issues of the district or a particular community, the attendance of women were minimal. And, when they attended, it is very rear to find many women express their views; letting the men make decisions in matters concerning their lives and the lives of their children. In cases where women do participate it becomes controversial even in western democracies let alone in Ethiopian society as if they are in the wrong places. Cultural attitude and low level of awareness in the society played a significant role in this respect. Society perceives women as 'weak and emotional', unable to shoulder political responsibilities.

Furthermore, their responsibility of the household and also child rearing is a hindrance for women to ponder about politics as it is the case with excelling in their careers and/or profession. As a result of long exclusion from the political process, women have not developed the experience to involve themselves in political discourse.

A look at the participation of women in the executive branch of Government reveals that women's number is very insignificant. For the first time in the history of the country, three women were appointed to cabinet ministerial posts (education, health and social and labour affairs during the Transitional Government of 1993; and one cabinet minister thereafter until 2005. After the 2005 elections, there were only two women, one of them being the minister for women's affairs and the other the minister of Sports and Youth. Subsequent to the 2010 elections there are three women ministers with portfolios of Women's and Children's Affairs, Minister of Mining and Government Representative in the Parliament.

Women's participation in political parties can ensure the inclusion of gender friendly policies not only in the political platform of the parties but also in the wider society. Though their numbers were few, Ethiopian women have joined political parties and movements since the inception of such organizations in the country. During the rule of the military government, women joined both the ruling and opposition parties and movements. Women are also members of the ruling party of EPRDF and other regional and opposition parties.

Despite the fact that women have struggled against tyranny and have fought for democracy and equality participating in political parties, mass organizations and in the armed struggle their accession to leadership positions is still alarmingly low. Table 13.3 shows the leadership positions of women in the EPRDF the largest and the governing political organization. There was only one woman in the Executive Committee, however, in the Ninth Congress of the Organization one more woman has been elected to the Executive Committee.

Table 13.3: Composition of EPRDF Political Leaders at All Levels

No.	*Level of Leadership*	*Total*	*Male*	*Female*	*Percentage*
1.	EPRDF Executive comm.	36	35	1	2.77
2.	EPRDF Council	180	154	26	14.44
3.	Higher Leadership	2154	1961	193	8.96
4.	Middle Leadership	23568	19974	3594	17.99
5.	Lower Leadership	195528	150337	45191	23.11

Source: Compiled from the data gathered from the office of EPRDF in 2009.

Often times, reasons such as low level of women's education, poverty, unfavorable agenda, burden of house work, illiteracy and low level of education are cited as causes for lack of women's active participation in the political parties (Tigist 2007). Though most of the reasons cited above may discourage women from political participation, I believe that political agenda should not. As political parties are organized in any one country to manage the political, economic and social affairs of a particular country, their agendas must be pertinent to the lives of women. If it is not the case, then it should be the responsibility of women through political participation to make things corrected. Women relate to political agendas especially the ones that concern safety, security, economic development, health, education etc. as they are also the agendas of women. The history of women in the armed struggle revealed that women are apt in politics and political participation despite the common view that they are apolitical.

Women's Representation in Regional and National Councils

According to the 1993 Electoral Law of Ethiopia, any Ethiopian whose electoral right is not legally restricted is eligible to elect or be elected. Hence in such light, women are legally entitled both to vote and be elected.

Since 1992, four national and regional elections have taken place for Federal and Regional parliaments. These are institutions where important issues are debated, policies, budgets, laws and proclamations are legislated. The degree of women's participation is also one indicator of women's empowerment as where they voice their issues, concerns and interests. Therefore, it is important that women participate in such important institution where destiny of their families and themselves are determined.

In the first multiparty election of 1995, women representatives were only 15 (or 2.56%) out of 547 seats. In the second, third and fourth elections held in 2000, 2005 and 2010 their numbers increased to 42 and 117 and 152 respectively. Though the number of women who were elected to the Federal Parliament increased from time to time, their representation is still low compared to the 30 per cent minimum that is said to be required for women to have strong voices. The representation of women in Regional Councils is much better than their representation at the Federal level. Even better is the women's participation at the *woreda* and the *kebele* levels which are the lowest level of administration and whose act is decisive to the lives of the people where budget allocation to different sectors, administering schools, health posts even social courts are handled.

As noted earlier, some countries (for instance. Uganda, Rwanda) instituted an electoral system that sets aside a women's quota or seat reservations. Although the benefit of allocating quotas is significant in terms of making women visible in parliament, a closer scrutiny is needed to gauge the contributions of these women in influencing policies, programs, laws etc. There are cases where family members of authorities or ineffective women are handpicked and put in parliament just to full fill the requirment in some countries where quotas are implemented. In other words, the concrete gains that are made in achieving gender equality through quota system have to be assessed (Goetz and Hassim 2003; Byanyima 2004).

The Ethiopian Electoral Law does not provide affirmative action by way of quota allocation of seats for women. In spite of this, however, the Ethiopian People's Revolutionary Democratic Front (EPRDF), had a party based quota of 30 per cent and 30-40 per cent of its candidates to be women for the National and Regional Assemblies respectively since 2005 election. Since EPRDF lost all the seats in many urban centers including Addis Ababa in the 2005 election, the number of women's seats in the House of People's Representative is only 21 per cent. Likewise in the four regions where EPRDF contested, (Tigray, Amhara, Oromiya SNNP), the women's seats are between 26 and 49 per cent. The front had again pledged to have 30 per cent of its candidates to be women in 2010 election; but, in some electoral places where it contested, the measure was not implemented for allegedly lack of "eligible" women candidates.

Tables 13.4 and 13.5 indicate the number of seats secured by women in both regional and national parliaments in the last three elections. The comparison of the number of women's seats between the 2000 and 2010 elections indicate that the number of women, who were elected to the Federal Parliament in 2010, especially from those regions which have larger representation, has increased tremendously. More importantly, the representation of women in Regional Councils is much better than their representation at the National level, *woreda* and *kebele* levels. The increase of women's participation at the regional levels is a positive move since greater participation and influence at the local government structure, where decisions that directly affect the lives of the poor are made is relevant for women.

Table 13.4 shows the percentage of women's participation in the four Region and two City Administrative Councils where EPRDF administers. A closer look into the table indicates that though the party pledged to have a 50 per cent participation of women in 2013 Woreda and Kebele elections, not all but only one Region and one City Administrative Council have met the target and many of them are very close.

Table 13.4: Women's Seats in Woreda and Kebele Councils where EPRDF Administers (In 2013 Election)

Region	*Woreda*	*Kebele*
Addis Ababa	50%	50%
Amahra	48%	47%
Dire Dawa	NA*	43%
Oromiya	48%	47%
Southern People	39.2%	46.4%
Tigraye	50%	50%

Source: Office of EPRDF, May 2013.

Table 13.5 shows the number of seats for women in the Regional Councils in the second· third and fourth elections. Note that the number has increased tremendously between the elections of 200 and 2010. In fact, in one of the regions, namely Tigray women representatives account for 50 per cent of the members of the Regional Council. It was also in Tigray that Aregash Adane, who was a veteran fighter and member of the Central Committee of EPRDF, became the first woman General Secretary of the Regional Government which was the third highest position of the Government at the time.

As lack of education limits women's participation in politics, the expansion of women's education since the implementation

Table 13.5: Seats Women secured in the House of People's Representatives by Region in 2000, 2005 and 2010 Elections

Region		*Years*					
		2000		*2005*		*2010*	
		No. of seats	*%*	*No. of seats*	*%*	*No. of Seats*	*%*
Tigray	38	3	7.9	14	36.8	13	34
Afar	8	1	12.5	1	12.5		
Amhara	138	14	10.1	29	21	46	33.3
Oromiya	177	10	5.7	39	22	47	26
Somali	23	0	0	1	4.3		
Benishangul-gumuze	9	1	11.1	0	—		
S.n.n.p.	123	6	4.9	29	23.6	36	29
Gambella	3	0	—	0	—		
Diredawa	2	0	—		—		
Harari	2	0	—	0	—		
Addis Ababa	23	4	17.4	2	8.8	7	30
Total	**546**	**39**	**7.3**	**105**	**21.20**	**152**	**27.7**

of NETP has contributed to the participation of women in parliaments as most of the parties gave preference to those who had at least high school diplomas when they selected the candidates from among their members.

Table 13.6: Seats secured by Women in Regional Councils (2000, 2005 and 2010)

Region	*Total no. of Seats*	*Years*					
		2000		*2005*		*2010*	
		Women's seats	*%*	*Women's seats*	*%*	*Women's seats*	*%*
Tigray	152	42	27.6	75	49.3	64	42.1
Afar	87	2	2.3	7	8.1	9	9.63
Amhara	294	43	14.6	84	28.6	89	30.27
Oromiya	537	68	12.7	196	36.5	157	29.24
Somalia	183	2	1.1	4	2.2	5	2.69
Benshangule	99	11	11.1	11	11.1	14	14.14
SNNP	348	44	12.6	91	26.2	110	31.61
Gambela	82	0		12	14.6	55	35.26
Diredawa	—	—	NA	—	NA		
Harare	36	6	16.7	12	33.3	12	33.33
Addis Ababa	138	22	15.9	19	13.8	NA	NA*

* Did not have regional elections in 2010.

Source: Office of the House of Peoples' Representatives.

Hopefully, the women members of these legislative bodies play key roles by participating in all standing committees For instance in the House of People's Representatives, women parliamentarians are members in each of the 13 standing committees, of which two of them are chaired by women. A woman member is also a deputy chair in a Legal Affairs Committee. In addition, there is a women's parliamentarian committee which oversees that women's issues are mainstreamed in all work programmes of the executive. Moreover, the Deputy Speaker of the House of Peoples' Representatives and also the Speaker of one of the Regional Councils (Amhara) are women.*

* Honourable Mrs. Shitaye Minale is the Deputy Speaker of the House of Peoples Representative since 2000 election. H.E. Dr. Misrak Mekonnen was the Speaker of Amhara Regional Council between 2005-2010 until she was appointed State Minister of Civil Service Ministry.

As women's awareness in participating in the political processes increased, they began involving themselves in politics as can be seen by the participation in all the four elections that were held in the country since Ethiopia became a Federal Democratic Republic. Women not only voted in all the elections but also ran for parliamentary seats representing both the ruling and the opposition parties of both the Federal and Regional Councils. His Excellency, Prime Minister Meles Zenawi, the late Prime Minister of Ethiopia, singled out women and appreciated them for the decisive role that they played during the 2010 national elections.

The late Prime Minister Melese was a gender sensitive political leader who firmly believed and advocated that any development effort can not succeed without equal participation of women. It is because of the political, social and economic policies that were crafted by PM Melese that women are benefiting at present.

Unlike in the past, women have also shown interest in participating in professional or social organizations as members. Most educated women that I had discussed with regarding this issue expressed that they had no problem in involving themselves in politics and joining political parties. According to my study (Gennet 2010), the expansion of education in general and the introduction of civic education, a subject that deals with democratic and human rights, women's rights, the Constitution, family law and so on offered in primary/secondary schools as well as in the university, has helped in enhancing women's political involvement.

Women's access to property and their participation in political process has increased for the last ten years. Slowly but sure they are determining their own destiny as they have started to make decisions and choices. However, women in Ethiopia still have to go a long way to achieve their full political and economic equality to be empowered. Women still do not have equal recruitment and promotional opportunities in their work; all participants involved in my study indicated that men and women with the same qualification have unequal opportunities for jobs and promotions. Though the government has issued a directive that gives priority in the recruitment of women in the civil services at the federal and regional levels, women employed in the civil service slightly increased from 29 per cent in 1994/95 to 32 per cent in 2005 (EC) according to a study by Mohammed Musa (2005 EC). Patriarchal thinking still prevails when women aspire to higher political leadership, higher posts in government and private sectors. Women's reproductive role is considered as a liability that hinders women's participation in the public sphere, rather than a virtue. Society should not punish women for their role as mothers rather accommodate their needs through various measures so that they can comfortably play their roles in both the private and the public arena. It is obvious that women's reproductive role is very important to the society and as such should be recognized in facilitating women's work at the public arena. This is possible with state subsidized child care facilities and inculcating men with sharing household responsibilities.

CHAPTER XIV

Women in the Household

As women play multiple roles, the level of their empowerment differs depending on their roles. Women may be empowered at societal level but may be not so at the household level and vice versa. For instance, a woman medical doctor makes decisions daily concerning the health of her patients; however, she may not be empowered to do so in her personal life depending on the cultural values of her community. Therefore, assessments of women's empowerment should look into their position not only at societal but also at household levels.

Ethiopian women's achievement in having the rights to political, economic power as well as access to social services like education and health is praiseworthy, however; the rights have not brought them as much change in the private lives of women as they do in their public lives. The cultural attitude in regard to the sexually determined gender based role of men and women is far from being reversed, though change is being observed. Women are now appointed, ministers, chief engineers, and construction workers, though their numbers are small. The perception that women are incompetent for high decision making position is being challenged day by day.

A look into the household, shows that most of the chores are still the responsibility of the women and most husbands do not share domestic work with their wives. In countries like Ethiopia, women gather firewood, walk many kilometers to fetch water, reach the market, work on the farm, and prepare food and so on. However, the hours spent with the children; in the market selling or buying family provision; fetching water or fire wood is not considered as time spent at work; even though it is evident that the tasks are not done in leisure.

As the universal "division of labour' between the sexes has apportioned the daily drudgery work, to women, men can indulge in sport, entertainment, artistic expression and so on which helps them develop their mental capacity. Girls learn about work at a tender age, they are kept at home to do housework while their siblings are told to play outside or study. And yet women's work is not recognized. For instance when a person is asked if his/her mother is working or if his wife is working, he or she would say no if the mother or the wife was not an employee.

Household chores take up much time especially in countries like Ethiopia where there are not many time saving technologies. Moreover, since they are routine and mundane, they don't contribute much to intellectual development. Household chores adversely affect their efforts to develop their career, advance in their education and take responsible positions outside the home. One of the reasons, that girls do not do well in school is because of lack of time, burdened as they are with household chores. Working women also have little time for self-development since they have to juggle their time between family responsibilities and work. Employers consider time spent on child bearing, taking care of children, the sick and the elderly as time wasted not contributed to the wellbeing of the society. It is never adequately acknowledged let alone appreciated that it is because of women's contribution in taking care of the social obligations of the family that men are able to execute their work without problems and interruption.

Married female graduate students in my study indicated the fact that while they were pursuing their studies and working full time, their husbands expected them to be solely responsible for the household too (Gennet, 2010). Even in the cases where families hire a domestic help, the wife will not be totally relieved from household chores as she has to supervise and administer the whole household.

It is cause for concern that mothers are not training their sons to be gender sensitive and share the household chores. In a household where there are boys and girls, the mothers want their daughters to do much of the work than equally share it with the sons. Here I would like to say a few things about the experience of the *Awra-Amba* community which is a small collective village in north Ethiopia. This is a community which has challenged patriarchal values in practice, thus, there is no gender based division of labour. Both husband and wife share the household work; men cook *wote* (stew) and make *enjera,* do spinning and baby-sit. In the same manner women do every job that men do including ploughing. Both husband and wife take joint decisions in every family and property matter with equal participation. Moreover, it is the community rule and regulation that there is no gender discrimination against women and the rules are applied to the letter. The *Awra-Amba* community's approach to the division of household chores could be used as a model.

Furthermore, there is one school in Baher Dare which has established a kitchen in school just to train male students on how to cook. I asked why and how the owner of the school came up with the idea as it was the first of its kind in the country, and here is why:

> In the survey that I conducted, I found out that 85 per cent of the boys in the school are either not allowed to go into the kitchen or do not have to do housework, while the girls, (they all come from relatively well to do families), in the same school were demanded to do housework before coming to school. In fact to my dismay I found out from all the girls in the school that they prefer to be boys as the boys have all the privileges in life and also they were not obliged to do housework. Thus after having a lengthy discussion with the parents, we set up where both boys and girls are taught how to cook, of course the kitchen is set up not to teach the techniques of cooking but to change the mindset (Mrs. Frealem Shibabaw 2012).

Another innovative idea of the same school is the setting up of a mothers' room in the school. This is a place where mothers can bring their young children with their nannies to work so that the babies are breast fed and mothers can also execute their work without worrying about their babies. Such provision of crèches, day care centers around the work place helps women to juggle between career and motherhood.

The legal rights to make a decision on the property of the family, access and control of resources such as land, house, cars and bank accounts has been won. However, because of traditions, the majority of women still don't practise control over the joint property of a household. They look up to their husbands and/ or sons for their livelihood. Societal values rather than the formal law still dictate that property has to be owned and controlled only by men since they are considered as breadwinners and heads of the family. Women themselves do not aspire to have property on their own. Thus, whatever joint property is acquired by the family is still registered in the name of the husband as they have been socialized as such.

Many women still feel uncomfortable about openly arguing with their husbands even if the issues at hand were decisions that concern their wellbeing and those of their children. Most of the participants in my study believe that women who are known to be effective decision makers in their work place tend not to be so in their personal lives and often depend on their family members, particularly their husbands and/or sons.

I remember a story told to me by a woman in a prominent position whose daughter always listens to her talking about women's rights on radio or TV. One day the daughter heard the prominent woman giving a lame excuse for turning down a request by a neighbor who wanted to borrow a video camera. The real reason for not giving the camera was that she was afraid her husband would disapprove. The daughter questioned her mother's public declarations if she was unable to apply them to her private life!

Wife beating is the most common violence inflicted on women today throughout the world. Ethiopia is not an exception for that matter. Obviously, given patriarchal ideology, societies (including women themselves) do not believe that wife beating is a crime, though it has become a criminal act in the Criminal Code of 2004 (see Art. 564). It is justified as though a married man has power over his wife including shaping her character with a stick. Wife beating is a practice that is not limited to a certain section or class of society, this is an act which is prevalent among the rich, the poor, the rural and urban areas. It is practiced in all classes without exception. The crime is committed even within educated households where the wives try to deny it instead of seeking help. Husbands and "lovers" not only beat but every so often mutilate, and kill their wives and friends as illustrated by the horrible stories, such as poking the eyes of the wife; mutilating with acid etc. that we hear on Ethipoian television programmes of the police on Sunday mornings.

Thus, the old saying that "Women and donkeys need the stick" is still alive and well. A study undertaken by USAID (2006) sadly confirms this fact. The study done in collaboration with CSO and the Ministry of Health, has included questions about attitudes towards wife beating [or battering]. The findings laid out in the following tables are quite revealing.

As depicted in Table 14.1, women accept to be beaten or hit by their husbands if they go out of the house without their husband's permission, argue with him, neglect the children, refuse to have sex or burn the food. These reasons should not have warranted violence against women had there been equality between men and women in decision making in the family. A look into the table also indicates that even younger women (77%) agree that physical punishment of wives by their husbands might be justified. Despite the fact that their numbers are smaller than the number of elderly women, it is hard to avoid the conclusion that the younger generation of women is still influenced by age-old beliefs about women's inferiority.

If this is what women believe about wife beating, it might not be surprising that men believe that they have the right, in fact a duty, to beat their wives. It is interesting, however, as shown in Table 14.2, that only about half of the young men in the study believed that wives should be beaten. But then, both older and younger men believe equally that women need to be shaped or disciplined by their husbands.

As in the case with women, men (not surprisingly) too believe that they have the right to beat their wives for the reasons mentioned earlier as revealed in Table 14.2. However, unlike the women only roughly half of the men in the study believed that

Table 14.1: Attitude of Women towards Wife Beating

Background characteristic	*Husband is justified in hitting or beating his wife if she:*						
	Burns the food	*Argues with him*	*Goes out without telling him*	*Neglects the children*	*Refuses to have sex with him*	*Agrees with at least one specified reason*	*Number of women*
Age							
15-19	57.4	55.6	59.9	59.9	36.3	77.3	3,266
20-24	59.3	56.4	61.9	63.5	42.0	78.4	2,547
25-29	61.2	58.8	66.3	66.5	45.4	81.8	2,517
30-34	64.4	61.7	66.0	66.8	49.2	83.9	1,808
35-39	62.7	62.3	68.1	67.3	49.1	83.5	1,602
40-44	62.9	59.8	66.4	66.9	47.0	83.5	1,187
45-49	65.3	61.5	66.0	66.2	52.7	84.9	1,143

Source: Ministry of Health (Ethopia), 2005.

the wife should be beaten for one reason or another. But there is no difference in the response between the older and the younger respondents as both believe that women should be shaped.

A woman who is always treated like a minor loses her self-esteem and self confidence rendering her useless to perform anything. In regard to the harm made on the self confidence of battered women the same study states those women who believe that a husband is justified in hitting or beating his wife for any of the five specified reasons may believe themselves to be low in status (2005). Such self-perception of course acts as a deterrent for women to stand up for their rights, equalities and more importantly would not render them useful for themselves, the family and the nation.

Wife beating has also a very profound negative impact on children as well. It has been acknowledged that children who have been exposed to domestic violence during their upbringing will suffer in their developmental and psychological welfare demonstrating aggressiveness, anxiety, and changes in how they socialize with friends, family and authorities (Dodd, L.W. 2009). Thus wife beating is a harmful practice that has to be seriously tackled as it affects the family and the society as a whole.

Table 14.2: Attitude of Men towards Wife Beating

Background characteristic	*Husband is justified in hitting or beating his wife if she:*						
	Burns the food	*Argues with him*	*Goes out with-out telling him*	*Neglects the children*	*Refuses to have sex with him*	*Agrees with at least one specified reason*	*Number of men*
Age							
15-19	27.5	32.4	36.6	32.6	26.6	53.3	1,335
20-24	24.3	29.9	36.5	29.9	23.2	50.6	1,064
25-29	23.0	29.3	36.3	29.4	21.6	50.0	741
30-34	22.6	31.2	35.2	30.8	20.9	50.9	754
35-39	21.2	26.4	32.7	26.6	21.5	48.9	651
40-44	24.6	32.0	37.9	35.6	26.3	53.2	497
45-49	22.6	27.8	36.2	27.4	20.7	50.2	422
50-54	21.7	32.0	37.1	36.0	19.7	53.0	335
55-59	24.7	34.9	39.7	34.4	27.5	55.6	235

Source: Ministry of Health (Ethopia), 2005.

As mentioned earlier, wife beating has become a criminal act by the law, but as it is considered an accepted practice to tame a woman, it is sanctioned by tradition and custom which is more powerful than the law. Therefore, women's groups as well as democratic men have to bring it out of the private domain into the public so that it becomes an agenda that is talked about, discussed and remedied.

Ethiopia is on the path to fast economic development with the goal of material and non-material betterment of its people. However, if the household, where all individuals including women and children live, take part in decisions as equal partners, the country's aspiration of achieving sustainable development where all citizens become beneficiaries would be hampered if not curtailed. It is, therefore, essential to work towards change in the mindset of the society about the crime inflicted on women in the name of shaping their characters and blaming victims. The silence about domestic violence on account of culture should be broken. This is possible through both state and civil society proactive intervention.

CHAPTER XV

The Unfinished Business

The patriarchal structure of Ethiopian society as elsewhere, has restrained women from access to economic, political and social participation. As a result women have been subjected to a life of despicable dependency on men (fathers, husbands and sons), with no voice, agency and dignity. The country also lost the active and meaningful contributions of women in its development efforts.

Progress in the lives of women worldwide has been attained in many places though it varies from region to region. While some countries in the west such as Scandinavia has greatly advanced in women's empowerment, others such as in Sub-Saharan Africa and Asia lag behind. The progress that has been recorded in women's attainment of certain rights and degree of freedom in leading their own lives was the result of women's rights movements at the beginning of the nineteeth century. These movements called for women's right to vote, for education as both political participation and education are empowering tools. True enough it is in those countries where women have access to all levels of education that they are able to meaningfully participate in politics, attain economic power and social status.

In Ethiopia too, women have participated and fought against national subjugation, had joined in the liberation wars against foreign aggression, to keep Ethiopia independent; have participated in the student movements against the monarchy and the Derg. Women have also joined the 17 years of armed struggle that was waged against tyranny, for democracy and economic development; that shaped the present political and economic landscape of the country. Unfortunately, their contributions have been unrecognized like those of their counterparts because it is assumed that women do not make "history". I urge Ethiopians to write about the women, their contributions to our rich history, social fabric, our development agenda and so on, so that it is woven into the national narratives.

The armed struggle, where women sacrificed their lives and youth, not only liberated Ethiopian society from the shackles of dictatorship and national oppression but also shattered patriarchy. Patriarchal thinking that sanctioned the oppression of Ethiopian women in every sphere of their lives had been challenged and in the process women developed self-esteem and confidence. This was because the women fighters in the struggle demonstrated not only unprecedented gallantry in the military assignments that they undertook, competence in political leadership and capability in administration in the work that they were assigned. Unlike some armed struggles that were waged for national liberation against colonialism; the armed struggle in Ethiopia had addressed women's equality as a democratic issue that had to be reckoned within the struggle. Hence, the struggle waged for women's equality within the organization has surely created gender sensitivity among its members and ultimately paved the way to women's empowerment within the Ethiopian society.

Taking Stock: How Empowered are Women?

Today women are entitled to their legal political and economic rights as enshrined in the Constitution. The civil and democratic rights that are enshrined in the 1995 Constitution with the recognition of both the individual and group rights have a special meaning for women as they enable them to demand and seek their rightful place as equal citizens in the society. Furthermore the right to property as well as equality in the family are stipulated in Article 35 of the Constitution. The recognition of women's rights for the first time in Ethiopian history is the biggest victory of the Ethiopian women's struggle.

Women's issues (which are economic, political, social) have become important developmental issues to be dealt with. Those laws that subordinate women to men in family matters; in property ownership and the like have been abolished, and in their places, new and progressive ones that protect and advance women's equality are enacted. To protect women from harmful traditional practices and violence such as, rape, abduction, early marriage and sexual harassment that were deemed as either normal or necessary by society have become criminal acts. Women now have the legal right to participate in the political sphere, have option to education; options to work and determine their own destiny.

The number of women in parliament is growing from one election to another (elections are held every five years) though the percentage of women in parliament is not at the 30 per cent, mark yet as proposed by the United Nations to be a critical mass to impact policies, legislation and debates in Parliament with women's interests and concerns; but it is far better than the participation of women in Africa, given the fact that Ethiopia's elector system does not allow a quota system. As discussed in Chapter II, those countries which have reached the 30 per cent are mostly the ones which have used the quota system. However women have fared better, justifiably, in the regional and local Woreda and Kebele Councils where their membership has reached almost 50 per cent and these are councils where problems and concerns such as schools, health issues, water, rural roads, safety etc. are addressed at grassroots level.

As the Constitution recognizes not only individual but group rights, organized women take steps to address the various cultural barriers that limit their empowerment. This is evident in the case of women in Tigray Region where organized women challenged the values and norms of society and brought about changes in their legal, social and political rights. For instance, even before the Federal Government of Ethiopia revised the Civil Code of 1960, the women in Tigray had fought and won to have a new family law passed by the Regional Government despite the reluctance of the then regional government (Interview with Kiddusan 2011). In the same manner the Women's Coalition against HIV/Aids (the Coalition) campaigns against harmful practices such as FGM, early marriage, fistula and HIV/Aids. Because of the campaign of the Coalition against FGM in the two most widely practiced regions, it has been considered as HARAM in Afar and religious leaders have joined the campaign in Somalia. The organization's work against early marriage in Amhara and Tigray where the practice is prevalent has contributed to the decrease of the practice, and also in getting medical assistance for those women with the fistula problem. Though there are women's organizations which are working to uplift the plight of women, their number is not as much as it should have been given the size of the population and the problems women face. One cause of concern is the educated elite women seldom involve themselves to fight for the equality of women; may be an aware that an individual woman can not be truly equal and empowered unless the women as a group are. Hopefully, all women, including the elites will organize themselves in different ways and contribute to the empowerment of women.

There are about twenty million students (almost one-fourth of the population) in the education system (in 2013). Of the 20 million slightly less than 50 per cent of them are women which is another milestone in the progress of women towards their empowerment. The provision of free and secular education along with the measures used to encourage girls' education had enabled girls to access education. As demonstrated earlier, female students today are pursuing their education not only at primary and secondary levels, but also in higher educational institutions. Those discriminatory practices based on the assumption that women are not capable of understanding certain fields have been challenged. Science and engineering are not off limit for women and they are doing well in these areas. In fact, Ethiopia has achieved much better than some of the developed countries within a span of just twenty years, the trend indicates that the country will achieve the MDG in education by the year 2015. Though options for education have opened for women in Ethiopia, there are still hurdles that are not surmounted. For instance, the policy direction of having equal numbers of teachers at primary and secondary levels, the promotion of women to director and supervisory positions in order to create gender friendly environment in school has not been implemented. Moreover, the participation of women in secondary and higher education has not reached the targeted goal yet.

The country has also made progress in health and if we look into health concerns and issues of women, we can see that problems are being tackled. The child mortality rate has decreased by 30 per cent, and pregnancy and child delivery associated death of mothers has also decreased from 871 per 100,000 in 2005 to 590 per 100,000 in 2010. The incidence of HIV has decreased from 0.68 to 0.28. Surely these progresses advance women's empowerment. Here too women's aim should be that no child and mother should die because of lack of health services.

Women's access to property and control is being practiced too. As land is in the hands of the Government, landless women have been allotted land and married women's right to land has been recognized in the land registration process where the land use certificate is issued in both the names of the couple, which is an empowering factor. Similarly, in urban areas women have access to micro and small enterprises and get assistance in finance, working space, and some entrepreneurship skill training. But only about 30 per cent who received the services are women. In housing development projects that are underway in the urban areas, 20-30 per cent of the houses, particularly in Addis Ababa, are reserved for women applicants in addition to competing for the remaining 70 per cent of houses, equally with men. It is hoped that such afermative action would be applied in other parts of the country as well.

Overall, the status of women within Ethiopian society has shown signs of progress given the fact that the democratization process is only a few years old. In 1974, I was denied the right to bail out a friend, who was accused of a petty offence and detained in a Police Station, on account of my sex. I was denied this right even though as a salaried person, I was qualified to be a guarantor. In 1987 or 1989, I remember a discussion at a meeting of the Academic Commission of the Faculty of Education, where I was a member, as to whether or not a kebele letter produced by a student who wanted to sit for re-examination should be accepted. According to the regulation of AAU then, students should produce evidence of a reasonable cause for missing exams, so the said student produced a letter from his kebele indicating that he was sick and sought traditional "Holy Water" treatment rather than going to a doctor. The point of contention was that all the three witnesses to the sickness of the student were women. To my dismay and disbelief a member of the commission insisted that the women's words should not be trusted.

I also vividly remember a question posed to me by a visiting professor from the UK when he found me having lunch with male faculty members of a department of AAU. The Professor asked me if I was the secretary of the department, and I replied I was not. Then he asked again if I was a student to which I replied in the negative. Again, "You must be a graduate student", he asserted. At this point, one of the instructors intervened and told him that I was a faculty member too!

Today, a trend has begun where not only words but also judgments, decisions and directives of women are taken seriously. As the career options for women have expanded beyond secretarial and clerical work, they are found in every field (though in small numbers) including the ones that are considered "men's". For instance, about 20 per cent of the judges in Ethiopia currently are women; they are working as engineers leading big projects, heading ministries, government and non-government organizations, companies and banks etc.

Ethiopian women should not be complacent of the progress made as there are still many challenges that they have to surmount. There are still areas where women are discriminated against. Needless to say that the attitudes, behaviour and values about women that have been in place for centuries cannot be removed totally within a span of a short twenty years. Cultural values and attitudes linger even when the political economy that caused them disappears.

There are still economic, political and social issues that concern women. One of the problems of women is poverty; though tackled, but not completely eradicated yet. In situations where poverty is prevalent women become the poorest of the poor. There are still concerns in social services such as health and education. In education women's participation in secondary and higher education is not equal yet. The death of children at birth as well as mothers', because of pregnancy related complications, are unacceptable.

Women suffer from sexual harassment at work places, offices, schools, and higher education institutions. There are many stories we hear in whispers about sexual harassment. Women often do not report or talk in the open about sexual harassment that they encounter at work as they are afraid that it might backfire against them and jeopardize their education, families or jobs. As people often blame the women for being "provocative" and in cases where they are reported, they are hushed, thus it is rarely that justice against the victim is served. Cases are cited where women who seek justice for sexual harassment were viewed as trouble makers, unruly, and indecent, (Gennet 2010). In some countries where sexual harassment is a crime by law, like in Ethiopia, organizations both Government and non-Government are required to have a policy on the issue with the clear guidelines on how it is reported, how and what actions are taken against the offender. Ethiopia might require to have such policies and also monitor their applications.

Working women are overburdened by the dual responsibility of work outside and household chores what Acker (1982) calls the 'greedy institutions'. Some countries consciously use energy and time saving technologies in order to relieve women from the burden. The household chores are also shared by all members of the family including the husband, moreover; nurseries, crèches are provided at work places, near condominiums etc. so that mothers peacefully execute their responsibilities at work.

There are still chauvinistic attitudes regarding women's access to leadership position, including political, as it entails sharing resources and powers. For instance, in some of the regions, the political cadres (gate keepers) could not nominate women candidates on account of the non-availability of "eligible" women to leadership positions in their respective constituencies, therefore, it is extremely rear to find women heading bureaus or administering zones and *woredas* unless it has to deal with women's affairs bureaus. A look into women's position into the EPRDF's (the leading party) leadership also affirms the fact that male chauvinism is still lingering. Granted, women do not have experience in the political process due to long exclusion and some women are reluctant to participate in politics because of the burden of child rearing and household chores. However, these problems should be and can be tackled with. It is not rational to deny women the opportunity of economic and political participation on account of lack of experience and yet claim that they are not fit. Women's participation in political leadership is very essential to address the concerns of women.

The stumbling block that hinders women from achieving equality is not conscious and systematic discrimination by the state. It is, rather from the deeply-rooted views and attitudes that assert female inferiority. These views and attitudes are persistent in the minds of women too. Unless unrelenting struggle is undertaken against them by both women and men, even those gained rights can be revised as was the case in China and Russia.

China and Russia had favourable policies and programmes that encouraged women to participate in social, political and economic activities of their respective societies as discussed earlier. However, since the equality of women and its importance had not become the dominant view of the society; the gains of women were curtailed when the economy was not progressing and when the ideology changed indicating its susceptibility. In China, enhancing equal opportunity between men and women had been the principal policy of the Communist Party and women's participation in all spheres was accelerated. The situation changed for a while when China adapted a socialist economy with market characteristics in 1987, where employers were given the opportunity to hire and fire workers, they openly opposed the employment of women in certain areas stating that women were not as strong as men, and that they would marry and have children. Therefore, women's employability was affected until affirmative action was reinstated in 1990 (Zhang, Yongnian, Guo Xiajuan & Zhao Litao, 2009). Similarly, in Soviet Russia where women gained many rights and played active roles, the first programs that were sacrificed on account of economic hardship were kindergartens, nurseries and the like that were organized to help women; therefore, they were unable to focus on their work like men.

Thus women's equality can only be achieved by changing the

tradition that gives males and females distinct rights resulting in the inequality of the sexes. And change of the culture can be effected only through the collective action of the society.

Family has no substitute in imparting positive values. Hence the present practice of discriminating between sons and daughters along the lines of traditional values requires changing. It is my view that mothers can play an important role in teaching in their children about the equality of men and women in all aspects including the household.

The education system can be used to bring about cultural change in the society and counteract the inequality of the sexes that is built in the minds of people through the socialization process. As almost every child passes at least through primary education, as access to education is expanding, it would be an effective entry point of socializing young minds about the importance of women's equality. The present experience of teaching civic education where democratic values are being instilled in our children needs further strengthening. However, not only through civic education but also with other subjects the issues of gender must be incorporated.

Popular culture including the media is a very powerful tool that can transmit values and attitudes in any given society. The media powerful as it is can be utilized as an effective tool to impart a new democratic culture that enhances the equality of women. Therefore, dramas, poems, songs should be encouraged in fact sponsored so that they change the culture through subtle presentation of the new realities about women. Thus, the government, women's organizations and others have to strive to make the media democratic and play an appropriate role in presenting women's views. It will be very helpful if associations of popular culture (artists, singers, and mass-media) adopt in their rules and regulations a Code of Conduct not portraying women either negatively or as sex objects.

However, the key elements in changing the mind-set of the society are the organized voices of women. As the country is in a transformational process where multiple projects, programmes and policies are being implemented nationwide, women will be left behind unless they actively pursue their interests and concerns through participation as both beneficiaries and actors. This is the time when they have to make great strides in making the new Ethiopia not only free of poverty but also free of discrimination against women.

In a struggle for equality, women have no better substitute mechanism than using their collective voices. Through their organizations, women can assess and evaluate government programmes and policies from the point of view of advancing women's empowerment during consultations held while the policies are formulated (as discussed earlier, the government has to consult people at the time of policy formulation). Likewise, women's organizations can ensure that discriminatory measures, strategies and laws are replaced with appropriate ones. Once policies are formulated and the law are enacted, the women's organizations ensure that the implementers (the government offices and organizations as well as the justice system) are accountable for their actions. In a society like Ethiopia where some individuals pay "lip service" to women's equality for many reasons, one of them being male chauvinism, not policy formulation but implementation becomes the stumbling block. This is why women's organizations have to be very vigilant in monitoring the implementation of policies.

Women's organizations can also help in creating awareness in the society about the new and emerging roles that women play in the new democratic Ethiopia. Values and attitudes that discourage women from engaging in economic and political activities have to be addressed so that women become independent and develop self-confidence. So it is the primary responsibility of women and their organizations to change the mind set of both men and women as they did during the armed struggle.

Finally, women's struggle has come a long way and women have progressed in many ways. This is because of the organized struggle that they waged using different ways and methods, be it peaceful or otherwise. The same spirit of fighting for women's rightful place in society has to be revived because there still is discrimination against them. There are so many experiences and success stories that should inspire women to get organized and finish the unfinished business of women's empowerment. Let me conclude by quoting from a book entitled *Women's Renaissance of the Seventies* (Kimball, 1981), "It is going to take arm twisting in the back rooms of legislatures, it is going to take getting out on the streets again, it is going to take arrests, it is going to take its own form of real confrontation. It is after all, a battle about power". Well, let women take all the avenues that their sisters, mothers and the democratic men have taken to bring us to the finishing line of the unfinished business of women's equality.

Bibliography

Note: Ethiopian authors are used here with their first given names in accordance with the Ethiopian academic tradition.

Abaninesh Birru: "Women and Mass Media" an Amharic Paper presented at Ministry of Information Symposium 1985 E.C.

Abdella, Gebeyehu (1999), "Major Academic Problems of Female Students, The Case of Higher 12 Comprehensive Secondary School", Addis Ababa University, Department of Education and Psychology, Addis Ababa.

Addis Alem, Balema (2003), Economic Development and Democracy in Ethiopia, Erasmus University, Rotterdam.

Acker, S. (1982), "Women and Education", in *World Yearbook of Education*, 1984.

——(1980), "Women, the Other Academics", *British Journal of Sociology of Education*; 1, 1, pp. 81-91.

Ackerly A. (1995),"Testing the Tools of Development: Credit Programs, Loans, Investment and Women Empowerment": *IDS Bulletin*, 26.

——(2000), Political Theory and Feminist Social Criticism: Cambridge University Press.

Adeleye-Fayemi, Bisi (2004), "Creating a New World with New Visions: African Feminism and Trends in the Global Women's Movement", Joanna Kerr, Ellen Sprenger and Alison Symington (eds.), in *The Future of Women's Rights: Global Visions and Strategies*, London, Zed Books Ltd.

Adjetey, Fitnat Naa-Adjeley (1995). "Religious and Cultural Rights: Reclaiming the African Woman's Individuality: The Struggle Between Women's Reproductive Autonomy and African Society and Culture", *American University Law Review*, 44:1351.

Afro-Asian Rural Development Organization (2006). "Empowerment of Women through Rural Enterprise": (AARDO) New Delhi.

Allasebu, Gebresellasie (1988), "A Situation of Women in Ethiopia—A Review", Report to the U.N. Inter-Agency Group on WID.

Alem Desta (2008). Candace: Invincible women of Ethiopia, Ethiopian Millennium Foundation (SEM), Amsterdam.

Abreham Alemu, "Oral narrative as ideological weapon for subordination women: The case of Jimma Oromo", *Journal of African Cultural Studies* in 2007.

Alemtsehay, Tesfaye (1997), "Comparative Study between Men and Women Teachers in Their Managerial Skills in Two High Schools", Addis Ababa University, Addis Ababa (Unpublished paper)

Alemtsehay, Zeleke (1985), "A Critical Analysis of The Problems of Women's Education in Ethiopia", Institute of Social Studies, Hague.

Alemayehu, Debebe (2004), "Determinants of Female Participation and Its Implications to Universalize Primary Education in SNNPRG" Centre for Research Training and Information for Women (CERTWID), Addis Ababa, (Unpublished paper).

Alidou. H. and Rock-Utne, B, (2005). Teaching in a Familiar Language, UNESCO.

Amanuel Gebru (1996). "Gender Differences in Participation in Group Discussions in Freshman English Classes at Addis Ababa University" Addis Ababa University, Centre for Research Training and Information for Women (CERTWID), Addis Ababa.

Goetz, Anna Maria and Hassim, Shireen, (eds.) (2003), *No Short Cut to Power: African Women in Politics and Policy Making*, Amzon Books.

Anker, R. (1998), Gender and Jobs: Sex Segregation of Occupations in the World, Geneva: ILO.

Anker, R., Chernyshev, I. Egger, P. Mehran F. and Ritter, J. (2002), "Measuring Decent Work with Statistical Indicator." Policy Integration Paper No. 1. Geneva: ILO.

Appiah, E.N. and McMahon, W. (2002), "The Social Outcomes of Education and Feedbacks on Growth in Africa", *Journal of Developments Studies*, 38: pp. 27-68.

Arnot, M. (1981), Culture and Political Economy: Dual perspectives in Sociology of Women's Education, *Educational Analysis*, 3.1.

Auret and Barrientos (2004), "Participatory Social Auditing: A Practice Guide to Developing a Gender Sensitive Approach".

Awura Amba: "Where men make Injera: Culture and Change: Ethiopian Women Challenging the future", International Institute of Rural Reconstruction in 2003.

Background Paper of the Task Force on Education and Gender Equality, Promises to Keep: Achieving Gender Equality and the Empowerment of Women, April 2003, www.idrc.ca/en/ev-42962-201-1-DO_TOPIC.html

Bahru Zewde (2010). (ed.), Documenting the Ethiopian Student Movement: An Exercise in Oral History, Forum for Social Studies, Addis Ababa.

Ball, S.J. (1993b), "What is policy? Texts, Trajectories and Toolboxes", *Discourse*, 13(2), pp. 10-17.

Ball, S.J. and Bowe, R. (1991), "Micro Politics of Radical Change" in Blais, J.

(ed), *The Politics of Life in Schools, Power, Conflict and Cooperation*, Newbury Park: CA, Saga Publications, pp. 19-45.

Benavot, Aaron (1985) "Education, Gender and Economic Development: A Cross-National Analysis", in Julia Wrigly (ed), Education and Gender Equality, Routledge Publishers.

Banerji, Amita and Kumar, Sen, Raj, (ed.), (2000), *Women and Economic Development*: Deep and Deep Publications Pvt. Ltd, New Delhi.

Bardwick, Judith M. (1980). *Women in Transition*, The Harvester Press Ltd., Brighton, Sussex.

Barro, R. and Lee J., (1996), "International Data on Educational Attainment", *American Economic Review*, 86 pp. 218-223.

Barwell, Richard (1996), "Bilingual Identity and Empowerment in School Mathematics", in Gillborne, D. and Lipps, C. (eds), *Recent Research on the Achievement of Ethnic Minority Pupil*, London: HMSO/OFSTED.

Batliwala, S. (2004), "Putting Power Back into Empowerment", www.opendemocracy.net.

Bernstien, B. (1972), "On the Classification and Framing of Educational Knowledge", Class, *Codes and Control*, Volume, 3, 1st edition, Rutledge and Kegan Paul.

Berman, Paul (1978), "The Study of Macro- and Micro-Implementation", Public Policy 26:2, pp, 157-84.

Betre Adom: "The Staff of Adam", Culture and Change: Ethiopian Women Challenging the future", *International Institute of Rural Reconstruction in 2003.*

Biraimah, Karen Coffyn (1980), "Different Knowledge for Different Folks: Knowledge Distribution in a Togolese Secondary School", In Philip G. Altbock, Robert F. Arnove and Gail P. Kelly (Eds.) Comparative Education: Macmillan Publishing Co., New York.

Black Feminist Thought in the Matrix of Domination, Boston 1990, http://www.hartford-hwp.com/archives/45a/252.html

Bower, R. *et al.* (1992). Reforming Education and Changing Schools. London: Routledge, Brewer and Deleon.

Bowman, Cynthia Grant and Akua Kuenyehia (2003), Women and Law in Sub-Saharan Africa, Accra, Sedco Publishing Ltd.

Brabeck, M. and Brown, L. (1997), "Feminist Theory and Psychological Practice, In J. Worell and N. Johnson (Eds.), Shaping the Future of Feminist Psychology: Education, Research and Practice, pp. 15-35. Washington, D.C.: American Psychological Association, http://en.wikipedia.org/wiki/Feminism

Bremer, Johana (2006), Women and the Politics of Class: AAKAR Books, Delhi.

Brinda Karat (2005). Foreword by Aijaz Ahmad, Survival and Emancipation: Notes from Indian Women's Struggles, Three Essays Collective, Gurgaon (India)

Bridgman, P. and Davis, G. (2004), *The Australian Policy Handbook* (3rd ed.). Sydney: Allen & Unwin.

Brock-Utne (ed) (2005), Languages of Instruction for African Emancipation Focus on Postcolonial Contexts and Considerations, Rudney, Kofi Hopson, Mukuki na Nyot Publishers: Tanzania.

Bruns, B. and A. Mingat (2002), The Chance for Every Child Achieving Universal Primary Education by 2015, Washington, D.C.: The Word Bank.

Bryson, Walerie (1992), Feminist Political Theory: An Introduction: Paragon House Publisher, New York.

Byanyima, Winnie (2004), "Perils and Promises: Living Feminist Politics in Uganda", Africa Gender Institute, Panel Discussion on International Woman's Day, www.gwsafrica.org.

Butegwa, Florence (1990), 'Challenges of Creating Legal Awareness among Grassroots Women in Uganda', in Margaret Schuler, (ed.), *Women, Law and Development in Africa-WILDAF: Origins and Issues*, Washington D.C., OEF International.

Byren, E. (ed), (1996), *Women and Education*, New York: Academic Press London: Tavisfock.

Canian, Frances (1989 "'Love and the Rise of Capitalism", in Barbara, J. Risman and Schwartz, P. (Eds), *Gender in Intimate Relationship*, Belmont, CA: Wadsworth, pp. 12-25.

Campbell, R.F., and Mazzoni, T.L. (1976), *State Policy-making for Public Schools*. Berkeley: CA, McCutchan.

Carely, M. (1980), *Rational Techniques in Policy Analysis*,. London: Heinemann Educational Books.

Carmer, Lassain (2005). "Gender Sensitive and Pro-Poor Indicators of Good Governance", Indian Council for Social Science Research (ICSSR): New Delhi.

Cibulka, J.G. (1994), "Policy Analysis and the Study of the Politics of Education", Politics of Education Association Yearbook, pp. 105-125.

Collins, Patricia Hill (1989), "The Social Construction of Black Feminist Thought", Signs 14: pp. 745-73.

——, (1990), Black Feminist Thought: Knowledge, Consciousness and the Politics of Empowerment, Boston: http://en.wikipedia.org/wiki/feminism

Collins *et al.* (1993). "Toward an Integrated Theory of Gender Stratification", Sociology Perspective, 36: pp. 185-216.

Coomb, R.H. (1988), "Surgeons' Personalities: The Influence of Medical School', *Journal of Medical Education*, Vol. 27, Issue 4, pp. 337-343.

Cornwall, A. (2000), "Making a Difference? Gender and Participatory Development", IDS Discussion Paper 378.

COVAW (2002), "In Pursuit of Justice: A Research Report on Service Providers, "Response to Cases of Violence Against Women in Nairobi Province", Nairobi, Kenya, COVAW.

Daniel Haile, "The Legal Status of Ethiopian Women at the Workplace", Ewia Sponsored Research in October 2004.

Deble, Isabelle (1980), The School Education of Girls: UNESCO, Paris.

Dawson, J., and A. Jeans (1997). "Looking Beyond Credit: Business Development Services and the Promotion of Innovation among Small Producers", Working Paper, London: Intermediate Technology Publications Ltd.

De Beavoir, S. (1972), The Second Sex, Translated by H.M. Parshley, London, Penguin.

Deere, C.D., and M. Leon (2001). "Disjuncture in Law and Practice: Women's Inheritance of Land in Latin America." In KIT (Royal Tropical Institute), Gender Perspectives on Property and Inheritance. A Global Source Book, Amsterdam: KIT Publishers and Oxfam GB.

Delamonica, E., S. Mehrotra, and J. Vandemoortele (2001), "Is EFA Affordable? Estimating the Global Minimum Cost of 'Education for All", Innocenti Working Paper No. 87. Florence: UNICEF, Innocenti Research Center.

Delmont, S. (1980), Sex Role and School, London, Methauen.

Deem, R. (1978), Women and Schooling, London: Routledge and Kegan Paul.

Desjardins, Richanr (2004). "Learning for Well Being": Institute of International Education, Stockholm University, Stockholm.

Dessalegn, Rahmato (1993), "Rural Women in Ethiopia: Problems and Prospects", Institution of Development Research, Addis Ababa University.

Deutsch, R., *et al.* (2001), "Working Within Confines: Occupational Segregation by Gender for Three Latin American Countries", Presented at the Seminar "Women at Work: A Challenge for Development", March, Santiago, Chile.

Devarajan, S.W. Easterly, and Pack, H. (2001), "Is Investment in Africa Too High Or Too Low? Macro- and Micro-Evidence": *Journal of African Economies* 10, Supplement 2, pp. 81-108.

Dollar, D. and Gatti, R. (1999), "Gender Inequality, Income, and Growth: Are Good Times Good for Women?", Mimeographed, Washington DC.

Dorsey, R. (1978), "Challenges Faced by Female Primary School Heads: The Zimbabwe Experience", www.emasa.co.za

Drèze, J. and A. Sen. (1989), *Hunger and Public Action*, Clarendon Press, New York.

Duncan, Wendy (1989), Engendering School Learning, Institute of International Education, University of Stockholm: Stockholm. Sweden.

Dunsire, Andrew (1978), Implementation in a Bureaucracy, Oxford: Martin Robertson. Dye, T. (1972). Understanding Public Policy, Eaglewood Cliffs, N.J.: Prentice-Hall.

Dupont, Beatrice (1981), "Unequal Education—A Study of Sex Differences in Secondary School Curricula", UNESCO, Paris.

Dureyea, S., A. Cox, and M. Ureta (2001), "Women in the Latin American Labour Market: The Remarkable 1990's.", Washington, D.C.: IADB.

Dworkin, Ronald and Savereign, Vistue (2000), The Theory and Practice of Equality: Harvard University Press, London.

Dwasi (1999), "Human Rights and Legal Dimensions to HIV/AIDS", www.wafnet.co.ke.

Eisenstein, Zillah R. (1994), The Colour of Gender: Re-imaging Democracy: University of California Press, London.

Echols, Alice (1989), Daring To Be Bad: Radical Feminism in America, Minneapolis: University of Minnesota Press.

Economic Commission for Latin America and the Caribbean (1999), 'Gender Indicators for Follow-up and Evaluation of the Regional Programme of Action for the Women of Latin America and the Caribbean, 1995-2001; and the Beijing Platform for Action. Santiago, Chile.

Emebet, Gelan (1996), "Factors Affecting the Attainment of Girls' Education in Addis Ababa", Addis Ababa University, Addis Ababa (unpuplished Paper)

Emebet, Mulugeta (2000). "Some Problems and Coping Strategies of Female Students in Addis Ababa High School", CERTWID, Addis Ababa (Unpuplished paper).

Engels, Friedrich (1972). The Origin of the Family, Private Property, and the State, in the light of the researches of Lewis H. Morgan. New York: International Publishers. http://en.wikipedia.org/wiki/Feminism.

Equality (2007), http://plato.stanford.edu/entries/equality

Etsegennet, Wondimagegnehu (2003)."Gender and Education: Policies, Targets and Practices/Implementations", Paper Prepared by Ethiopian Women's Lawyers Association, Ethiopia, Addis Ababa.

Faludi, Susan (1991). Backlash: The Undeclared War Against American Women: Crown Publishers, Inc., New York

Feng Yang (2009). Studies on Contemporary: Chinese Women Development, People's Publishing House, China.

Feminism, http://en.wikipedia.org/wiki/feminism

Feminist Perspectives on Power, http://plato.standord.edu/entries/feminist-power

Feminist Social Theory, http://uregina/ca/~gingrich/319m1703.htm

Feminist Theorists, http://womenshistory.about.com/od/feminism/tp/feminist_theory.

Foucault, M. (1978), The History of Sexuality: Random House Inc.

Floro, Maria and Wolf, Joyce M.(1990), The Economic and Social Impacts of Girls' Primary Education in Developing Countries, Creative Associates International, Inc. Washington D.C.

Forbes, K. (2000), "A Reassessment of the Relationship between Inequality and Growth": American Economic Review, 90: 869-887.

Frealem Shibabaw, "Development Dialogue on Gender Empowerment in the World Development Report 2012", Nov 11, 2012 Addis Ababa Ethiopia.

Freeman, Jo (1975), The Politics of Women's Liberation: Case Study of an Emerging Social Movement and its Relation to the Policy Process, New York: McKay. http://en.wikipedia.org/wiki/feminism

Friedan, Betty (1962), The Feminine Mystique, W. Norton & Co. Inc.

Gaidzanwa, Rudo (1995), "Land and the Economic Empowerment of Women: A Gendered Analysis" Vol. 1 Southern African Feminist Review, 1:1.

Garlor, O. and Weil, D.N. (1996), "The Gender Gap, Fertility, and Growth", American Economic Review, 86: pp. 374-387.

Gaventa, J. (2002), "Introduction: Exploring Citizenship, Participation and Accountability", IDS Bulletin, 33(2).

Gelawdious Ararya: *Ethiopia: The Political Economy of Transitions* University Press of America, 1995.

Geller, H.A. and Johnston, A.P. (1990), "Policy as Linear and Non-Linear Science", *Journal of Education Policy*, 5(1), 49-65.

Gender Forum, Genderisation (2002).

www.genderforum.unikoeln.de/genderealisations/weedon.html.

Gender Inequality and Theories of Patriarch, http://www.planetpapers.com/assets/2190.

Gender Issues Research Report Series No. 13 Organizations for Social Science Research in Eastern and Southern Africa, 2001.

"Gender, Poverty and Micro-Enterprise Service in Ethiopia: Why Only Few Women are Joining?" by Getaneh Gobezia.

Gennet, Zewide,(1998). *Women Education: A Study of the Academic Performance and Participation of Female Students in the High Schools of Addis Ababa region*, IER Flambeau, Vol. 6: pp. 26-54.

——, (2009), The Impact of the New Ethopian Education Policy on the empowerment of Women (1994-2006), Ph.d Dissertation.

Goetz, A.M. (2002), "Voice, Accountability and Human Development: The Emergence of a New Agenda", Human Development Report Office, Occasional Paper.

Goetz, A.M. and R. Sengupta, (1996), "Who Takes the Credit? Gender, Power and Control over Loan Use in Rural Credit Programmes in Bangladesh", World Development, 24:45-63.

Goetz, A.M. and Jenkins, R. (2001), "Hybrid Forms of Accountability: Citizen Engagement in Institutions of Public Sector Oversight in India", Public Management Review, 3(3)

Government of Ethiopia (1994), Federal Civil Service Commission of Ethiopia Personnel Statistics of the Federal Civil Service Commission,(in Amharic).

——(1994), The Education and Training policy, Prime Minister's Office, Addis Ababa.

——(1995), The Constitution of the Federal Democratic Republic of Ethiopia, People Proclamation No. 1.

——(1999), Women in Ethiopia, National Office of Population, Ministry of Finance and Economic Development, Ethiopia, Addis Ababa.

——(2000), Revised Family Law of Ethiopia, Federal Democratic Republic of Ethiopia, People's Council, Proclamation No. 213, Addis Ababa.

——(2000), Ethiopian sustainable Development strategies and policies and instruments, Ministry of Finance and Economic Development, Addis Ababa (in Amharic)

——(2001), "Education as key, Instrument for Development" Prime Minister's Office, Addis Ababa (in Amharic).

——(2000), Capacity Building Strategy Program, Ministry of Capacity Building, Addis Ababa, (in Amharic)

——(2002), Civic Value "A Document on Civic Education, Ministry of Education, Addis Ababa, (in Amharic).

——(2002), Education and Training Policy and Its implementation, Ministry of Education, Addis Ababa.

——(2002), The Education and Training Policy and Its Implementation, of Education, Ministry of Education, Ethiopia, Addis Ababa.

——2002/03, Household Income Consumption and Expenditure Survey of Ethiopia, Ministry of Finance and Economic Development, Addis Ababa.

——2004, Enhancing Civil Society Organizations and Women's Participation in Ethiopia, A Programme Designed for Civil Society and Women's Empowerment.

——2004, Five Year Strategic Framework for Enhancing Women's Participation in Tertiary Education in Ethiopia, Ministry of Education, Ethiopia, Addis Ababa.

——2004, Gender Mainstreaming Guidelines and Checklists, Ministry of Education, Ethiopia, Addis Ababa.

——2005, Educational Statistics Annual Abstract (2004-2005), Ministry of Education, Addis Ababa,

——2006, Ethiopian Women's Development Strategy, Ministry of Women's Affairs, Addis Ababa, (in Amharic).

——2006, Year Book, Ethiopia Government of Ethiopia, Ministry of Information, Press and Audio-Visual department, Addis Ababa.

——2006, Decentralized Management of Education in Ethiopia: A Reference Manual, Ministry of Education, Ethiopia, Addis Ababa.

——2006, Profile on Ethiopian Women, Ministry of Education, Women's Affairs Department, Ethiopia, Addis Ababa.

——2007, Comprehensive Education Quality Improvement Package, Ministry of Education, Ethiopia, Addis Ababa.

——2007, Population Census, Central Statistics Office, Addis Ababa (in Amharic)

——2003/04/05/06/07, Educational Management and Information System, Ministry of Education, Addis Ababa.

——2010, Ministry of Health Report.

——2006, A Study by Ministry of Health, USAID and CSO.

Govindasamy, Pavalavalli and Anju Malhotra (1996), 'Women's Position and Family Planning in Egypt', Studies in Family Planning, 27(6), 7328-7340.

Grown, Gupta and Khan, (2003), 'Achieving Gender Equality and the Empowerment of Women', paper presented at International Conference on Engendering Macroeconomics and International Economic, University of Utah, USA.

Gubta, E.G. (1984), The Effect of Definitions of Policy on the Nature and Outcomes of Policy Analysis, Educational Leadership, 42(2), pp. 63-71.

Guthrie and Kopopoich (1993), 'Feminist Inquiry and the Transformation' in the *Public*, http://en.wikipedia.org/wiki/feminisim.

Gwaunza *et al*. (2000), "The Socio-economic and Legal Implications of EPZs in Zimbabwe: Some Emerging Gender Concerns" in Tsikata and Kerr, (eds), *Demanding Dignity: Women Confronting Economic Reforms in Africa*, North-South Institute and Third World Network, Africa.

Habtamu, Hirut, Yusuf and Konjit (2009) Gender and Cross-Cultural Dynamics in Ethiopia: *The Case of Eleven Ethnic Groups*, Center for Research Training and Information on Women in Development.

Haider, A., October (2005), "Deconstructing Postmodernism and the Mainstream Developmental Discourse of Women's Empowerment in the (South) Asian Context.

Hence, P. (1991), *The Horn of Africa: From War to Peace*, London: Macmillan.

——(1998), "Is Ethiopia Democratic? A Political Success Story', *Journal of Democracy*, Vol. 9, No. 4, pp. 40-45.

Haddad and Demsky (1995), Education Policy Planning Process and Applied Framework, UNESCO.

Ham, C., and Hill, M. (1984). *The Policy Process in the Modern Capitalist State*, (2nd ed.). Brighton: Wheat Sheaf Books.

Harvey, D. (1990), The Condition of Post Modernity, Blackwell.

Hasan, Zoya and Manon, Ritu, (2004). Unequal citizens, A Study of Women in India: Oxford University Press, New Delhi.

Hashemi, S., S. Schuler, and A. Riley (1996), "Rural Credit Programmes and Women's Empowerment in Bangladesh." *World Development*. 24(4). Oxford: Elsevier Science Ltd.

Held, Verginia (1993), Feminist Moral Inquiry: The Role of Experience, http://en.wikipedia.org/wiki/Feminism

Hill, A., and E. King (1995), "Women's Education and Economic Well-being", *Feminist Economics*, 1(2): 1-26.

History, http://en.wikipedia.org/wiki/Feminism

Hochschild, Arlie Russell (2001), *The Time Bind: When Work Becomes Home and Home Becomes Work*. New York: Henry Holt & Co.

Horton, S. (1999), "Marginalization Revisited: Women's Market Work and Pay, and Economic Development", *World Development*, 27:571-582.

Howlett, M. and Ramesh, M. (1995), *Studying Public Policy: Policy Cycles and Policy Sub-systems*, Toronto: Oxford University Press.

Hudson and Sullivan (1990), A Social Organization of Work. Belmont, CA: Wadsworth.

IGAD's Strategic Policy Seminar, Violence Against Women (2007), Ethiopia, Addis Ababa.

Spelman Elizabeth, (1988), Inessential Woman: Problems of Exclusion in Feminist Thought, Beacon Press, Boston, www.etext.org/politics/MIM/bookstore/books/gender/spelman.html

Ishengoma, Christine G. (2002), "Accessibility of Resources by Gender: The Case of Morogoro Region in Tanzania", paper presented at CODESRIA conference on 'African Gender in the New Millennium, Cairo, April 2002.

Jaggar, Allison (1983), *Feminist Politics and Human Nature*, New Jersey: Rowman and Allan held.

Jaggar, Allison and Young. Iris Morgan, (ed.), (2000), *A Companion to Feminist* Philosophy: Blackwell Publishing.

Jacobs, Susie (1988), "State, Class and Gendered Models of Land Resettlement", Working Paper, No. 172: Michigan State University,

Jenny Hammond (1989). *Sweeter than Honey: Testimonies of Tigrayan Women*, Link Publication.

Judith Lorber (2010). *Gender Inequality: Feminist Theories and Politics*, Oxford University Press, New York.

Judith Squires: "Gender Quotas in Briton: A Fast Track to Equality, Working Paper Series 2004.

Jenda: A Journal and African Women Studies (2001). www.jendajournal.com/voll.2/nako.html

Kabeer, N. (1991), 'The Quest for National Identity: Women, Islam and the State in Bangladesh", in Denis Kandiyotti, (ed.) Women, Islam and the State, London, Macmillan.

——(1999), "The Conditions and Consequences of Choice: Reflections on the Measurement of Women's Empowerment", Discussion Paper No. 108. Geneva: UNRISD (United Nations Research Institute for Social Development).

——(1999) "Resource, Agency, Achievement: Reflections on the Measurement of Women's Empowerment", *Development and Change*, 30: 435-64.

——(2000), *The Power to Choose: Bangladeshi Women and Labour Market Decisions in London and Dhaka*, London and New York: Verso.

——(2002, "Citizenship, Affiliation and Exclusion: Perspectives from the South", IDS Bulletin, 23(2).

Kagia, R. (1985), "Gender Differences in Public and Private Universities Enrollment in Kenya, What do they Mask?", *Journal of Black Political Economy*: Springer, New, Vol. 30, No. 1.

Kanbur, R. (2002), *Education, Empowerment and Gender Inequalities*, Ithaca, NY: Cornell University.

Kantar, A. (1997), *Men and Women of the Corporation*, New York: Basic Books, Inc.

Karat, Brinda (2005), *Survival and Emancipation: Notes from Indian Women's Struggle*, Glorious Printers, New Delhi.

Karan, Azza M. (1999), "Women's Political Participation". paper presented to a meeting on Women and Political Participation 21st Century Challenges, United Nations Development Program, New Delhi.

Karen Oppenheim Mason (2006), "Measuring Women's Empowerment: Learning from Gross-National Research" in Deepa Narayan (Ed.) *Measuring Empowerment Gross Disciplinary Perspective*: Oxford University Press, New Delhi.

Kenefe, Abreha (1998), "An Educational Intervention Model of Secondary School Female Students", *IER Flambeau*, Vol. 6: pp. 54-59, Addis Ababa University, Addis Ababa.

Kenewane and Erayee:"Women's Activities in the 20th Century", Prime Minister's Office; Woman's Affairs Department: 1993 E.C. Amharic Book.

Kenny, Sally J (1990), *For Whose Protection? Reproductive Hazards and Exclusionary Policies in the US and Britain*, University of Michigan Press.

Kess, Joannia, Springes, Ellen and Others (eds), (2004), *The Future of Women's Rights: Global Visions and Strategies*, Zed Books, London.

King, Elizabeth (1978) "Does Education Pay in the Labour Market? The Labour Force Participation, Occupation and Earning of Peruvian Women". *Living Standards Measurement Study*. Working Paper 67. Washington, D.C. World Bank.

King, Elizabeth M. and Hill, M. Anne, (eds), (1993) Women's Education in Developing Countries, Barriers, Benefits and Policies: The Johns Hopkins Press, Baltimore and London.

Khadiagala Lym S. (2001), "Justice and Power in the Adjudication of Women's Property Rights in Uganda", *Africa Today*, Vol. 49, Number 2, pp. 101-121.

Kishor, Sunita (2000), "Women's Contraceptive Use in Egypt: What do Direct Measures of Empowerment Tell Us", paper presented at the 2000 Annual meeting of The Population Association of America, Los Angeles, California.

Klasen, S. and Lamanna F. (2003), "The Impact of Gender Inequality in Education and Employment on Economic Growth in the Middle East and North Africa", mimeographed, University of Gottingen.

Klansen S. and Wink C. (2002), "Is there a Turning Point in Gender Bias in Mortality? An Update on the Number of 'Missing Women'", *Population and Development Review*.

Knowles, S., Lorgelly P.K., and Owen P.D. (2002), "Are Educational Gender Gaps a Brake on Economic Development? Some Cross-Country Empirical Evidence", Oxford Economic Papers, 54:118-149.

Konjit, Kefetew (1995), "Female Education in Ethiopia Past and Present Trend: An Overview", Addis Ababa University, Centre for Research Training and Information for Women (CERTWID), Ethiopia, Addis Ababa.

Kuenyehia, Akua (1990), "In Ghana: Legal Aid Services for Women", in Margaret Schuler, (ed.) Women, *Law and Development—Action for Change, Washington*, D.C., OEF International.

Kum-Kum Bhavnani, Foran, John, and Priya Kurian (2003). (eds), *Feminist* Futures.

Re-imagining Women, Culture and Development: Zed Books Ltd., London.

Kum-Kum Bhavnani, John Foran and Priya A. Kurian (2006). (ed.), *Feminist Futures: Re-Imagining Women, Culture and Development*, Zubaan (New Delhi) and Zed Books (UK)

Kuhn, A. and Wolpe, A. (1978), *Feminism and Materialism*,. Routledge Publishers: Kegan Paul Group.

Lagerl of, N. (1999), "Gender Inequality, Fertility, and Growth", Mimeographed, Department of Economics, University of Sydney.

Legovini, A. (2005), 'Measuring Women's Empowerment in Ethiopia' in Ruth Alsop, Metter Bertelson and Jeremy Holloand (eds), Empswerment in Practice: From Analysis to Implementation, World Bank.

Lin, Nan (1999), "Social Network and Status Attainment", Annual Review of Sociology, 25: pp. 467-87.

Len Ski *et al.* (1995), "Preparing Pre-Service Teachers in Diverse World", *Action in Teacher Education*, 27, (3), 1-12.

Levine, D. (1965), *Wax and Gold*, University of Chicago Press.

Living the Legacy: "The Women's Rights Movement 1848-1998", www.legacy98.org/move-hist.html

Lishan, Bekele (1974), 'The Status of Women in Ethiopia Before and After the Revolution of 1974", (unpublished paper).

Lobban, R. (1977), "Class and Kinship in Sudanese Urban Communities", Edinburgh University Press.

Lorgelly, P. (2000). "Are There Gender-Separate Human Capital Effects on Growth? A Review of the Recent Empirical Evidence", Research Paper 13, Nottingham: University of Nottingham.

Lorgelly, P.K. and Owen P.D. (1999), "The Effect of Female and Male Schooling on Economic Growth in the Barro-Lee Model", *Empirical Economics*, 24:537-557.

Lovell C.A. (2003), "Unit cost and Unit Labour Cost", Working Paper, Department of Economics, University of Georgia, Athens, GA, USA.

MacKinnon, C. (1982), "Feminism, Marxism, Method and the State: An Agenda for Theory", *Signs*, 7, 515-544.

Malhotra, Anju and Mark Mather (1997), "Do Schooling and Work Empower Women in Developing Countries? Gender and Domestic Decisions in Sri Lanka", *Sociological Forum*, 12(4), 1997, 599–630.

Malhotra, Anju, Sidney Ruth Schuler and Carol Boender (2002), "'Measuring Women's Empowerment as a Variable in International Development", Washington DC, World Bank.

Malhotra, A., S. Schuler, and C. Boender (2002), "Measuring Women's Empowerment as a Variable in International Development." http://www.icrw.org/docs/MeasuringEmpowerment_working paper_802.doc.

Mankiw, N.G., Roemer D., and Weil D. (1992), "A Contribution to the Empirics of Economic Growth", *Quarterly Journal of Economics*, 107: 407-437.

Mama, Amina (1996), "Women's Studies and Studies of Women in Africa During the 1990s", available at www.gwsafrica.org

——2002, "Gains and Challenges: Linking Theory and Practice", Keynote address at Women's World Congress, Makerere University.

Martin, John: Oksanen, Ritta and Takala, Tuomas (2000). Preparation of the Education Sector Development Programme in Ethiopia: Association for the Development of Education in Africa, (ADEA) Paris.

Mason Andrew (2005), "Economic Demography", in Hand Book on Population, Michael Micklin and Dudley Poston (eds), Klewer Academic Plenum Publishers.

Mason, Karen Oppenheim, (2005), "Measuring Women's Empowerment: Learning from Gross-National Research.", Measuring Empowerment: Cross Disciplinary Perspectives, Deep Narayan (ed), Washington DC: The World Bank, pp. 89-102.

Mayoux, L. (2000), "Micro-Finance and the Empowerment of Women", Geneva: ILO. http//www.ilo.org/public/English/employment/finance/download/wpap23.pdf

Mbaya, Sue (2001), "Land Issues in East and Southern Africa", *An Overview*, Volume 1: Southern Africa Harare, Mwengo.

Mbilinyi, M. (1991), Agribusiness and The Crises of Women's Empowerment in Tanzania: Dar es Salaam: Dare es Salaam University Press, Tanzania.

McDonnell, L., and Elmore, R. (1987), "Getting the Job Done: Alternative Policy Instruments", *Educational Evaluation and Policy Analysis*, 9(2), 133-152.

Meaza, Ashenafi (2007), Participation of Women in Politics and Public Decision Making in Ethiopia, Master Thesis.

Meaza Ashenafi (2009). *Participation of Women in Politics and Public Decision Making in Ethiopia*, Forum for Social Studies, Addis Ababa.

Meer, Shamim (1997), *Women, Land and Authority: Perspectives from South Africa*, Cape Town, David Philip.

Milne, Claudia (1982), Asanti Market Women, Video Recording, Granada Television International.http://www.therai.org.uk/film/catalogue-2/11-ashante.html.

Miller, F. (1991), *Latin American Women and the Search for Social Justice*, Hanover, University Press of New England.

Minale Adujna: "Women and Warfare in Ethiopia" A case study of their role during the campaign of Adwa, 1895/96 and the Italio-Ethiopian War, 1935-41.

Ministry of Women's Affair: Development and Change Package of Ethiopian Women, July 1998 E. C.

Misra, Greetanjali and Radhika, Chandiramoni, (eds), (2005), *Sexuality, Gender and Rights: Exploring Theory and Practice in South and South East Asia*: Sage Publications, New Delhi.

Mitchell, Juliet (1966), "*Women: The Longest Revolution*", New Left Review http://en.wikipedia.org/wiki/Feminism

Mitchell, J. (1971), Women's Estate. Reprint: New York: Vintage Books.

Mobanty, Jagarmath (2000), *Current Trends in Higher Education*, Deep and Deep Publications Pvt. Ltd., Delhi.

Mreforiate Kamel, "Women and their Constitutional Benefits" An Amharic Paper presented.

Mukhopadhyay, Swapna (1998), *In the Name of Justice: Women and Law In Society*, New Delhi, Manohar Publishers and Distributor.

Mukhopadhyay, *M. and S. Meer (2004), Creating Voice and Carving Space: Redefining Governance from a Gender Perspective*, Amsterdam: KIT.

Mulugeta, Yimam (2006). "Women's Empowerment in the Millennium", paper presented on April 20, 2006 at the seminar organized to evaluate Women's Development Institute Program (WDIP): Addis Ababa.

Murthi, M., Guio A. C., and Drèze J. (1995), "Mortality, Fertility, and Gender Bias in India: A District-Level Analysis": Population and Development Review 21:745-782.

Murthi, M. and Drèze J. (2001), "Fertility, Education, and Development: Evidence from India": *Population and Development Review*, 27:33-63.

Manuh, I. (1998), 'Women in Africa's Development', Briefing Paper No. 11, African Recovery, UN, Department of Public Information.

Namar Agrippimah, (2001), "The Invisible Workers: Paid Domestic Work in Kampala City, Uganda" Working Paper No. 74, Kampala, Centre for Basic Research.

Narayan, Deep (2006). *Measuring Empowerment-Cross Disciplinary Perspective*, Oxford University Press, New Delhi.

Narayan, D. *et al.*, ed. (2000), Voices of the Poor: Can Anyone Hear Us?, Washington, D.C., World Bank.

Narayan, D. and P. Petesch, ed. (2002), *Voices of the Poor: From Many Lands*, Washington, D.C., World Bank.

Ncube, Welshman (1998), "Defending and Protecting Gender Equality and the Family Under a Decidedly Undecided Constitution in Zimbabwe" in J. Eekelaar and R.T. Nhlapo, ed., *The Changing Family: International Perspectives on the Family and Family Law*, Oxford, Hart Publishing.

Netsanet Asfaw (2007), Women, Their Struggle and Achievement of May 28 (Amharic Paper presented to the 16th Anniversary of May 28 Victory), Addis Ababa, Ethiopia.

Netsanet Assefaw: "Women and the Media" an Amharic Paper presented 1998 E. C.

Nnoli, Okwudina (1994), Ethnicity and Democracy in Africa: Malthouse Press Ltd., Lagos.

Nussbaum, Martha C. (2000), *Women and Human Development: The Capabilities Approach*, Cambridge, Cambridge University Press: 238.

Nyamu-Musembi, Celestine (2002), "Are Local Norms and Practices Fences or Pathways? The Example of Women's Property Rights", in Abdullahu A. An-Na'im (ed), *Cultural Transformation and Human Rights in Africa*, New York, Zed Books Ltd.

Oakley, A. (1981), "Interviewing Women: A Contradiction in Terms", in H. Robers (Ed.), *Doing Feminist Research* (pp. 30-61), London: Routledge & Kegan Paul.

O'Neill, Onora (2000), "Justice, Gender and International Boundaries", in *Bounds of Justice*, Cambridge, Cambridge University Press.

——2000. "Women's Rights, Whose Obligations?", in *Bounds of Justice*, Cambridge, Cambridge University Press.

Okin, Susan Moller (1989), *Justice, Gender and the Family*, New York: Basic Books Inc.

Okoye, Ada (2002), "Sharing the Citizenship of Women: A Comparative Gendered Analysis of the Concept of "Legal Personhood in Africa"", www.gwsafrica.org.

Oxaal, Zoe and Baden, Sally (1997) "Gender and Empowerment: Definitions, Approaches and Implications for Policy." Bridge Report 40. Briefing prepared for the Swedish International Development Cooperation Agency (SIDA), Institute of Development Studies, University of Sussex, Brighton, UK.

Pandey, V.C. (2001), *Education and Globalization*, Kalpoz Publication, Delhi.

Pankhurst, H. (2002), *Gender, Development and Identity*: Zed Books.

Pankhurst, R. (1976), 'The Ethiopian Women in Former Times'. *An Anthology*.

Pankhurst, S. (ed), (1958) 'History of Ethiopian Schools', *Ethiopian Observer*, Vol. 2, No. 4.

Peasle, (1965), "Primary School Enrollment and Comparative Education", *Economic Growth, Comparative Education*.

Parsons, W. (1995), Public Policy: An introduction to the Theory and Practice of Policy Analysis, Eduward Elgar: Aldershot, UK.

Pateman, Carole (1988), *The Sexual Contract*, Stanford University Press, California, Stanford.

Pereira, Charmaine (2002), "Understanding Experiences of Citizenship in Nigeria: From Advocacy to Research", paper presented at CODESRIA conference on 'African Gender in the New Millennium, Cairo', Egypt.

Pereira, Faustina (2002), *The Fractured Scales: The Search for a Uniform Personal Code*, Calcutta, India.

Petras, James and Veltmeyr, Henry (2001), *Globalization Unmasked*: Zed Books, London.

Phillips, Ann (ed), (1987), Feminism and Equality, New York University Press, www.etext.org/politics/MIM/bookstore/books/gender/spelman.html

——(ed), (1998), Feminism and Politics: Oxford University Press, New Delhi.

——(ed) (2001), "Feminism and Liberalism Revisited: Has Martha Nussbaum Got it Right?", Constellations 8/2.

Poluha, Eva (1987), "The Current Situation of Women in Ethiopia", Department of Social Anthropology, University of Stockholm, Sweden.

Pritchett, L. and L. Summers (1996), "Wealthier is Healthier." *Journal of Human Resources*, 31: 841-868.

Psychoropoulos, George (1985), "Return to Education: A Further International Update and Implications". *Journal of Human Resources* 20 (Fall): 583-604.

Psychoropoulos and Tzanotos (eds), (1992), "Case Studies on Women's Employment and Pay in Latin America", Washington D.C., World Bank.

Radical Feminism, www.questia.com/library/sociology-and-anthropology/radical-feminism.jsp

Raul Valdes Vivo (1977). Ethiopia the Unknown Revolution, Social Sciences Publishers, Cuba.

Rai, Shirin M. (2002), Gender and The Political Economy of Development, From Nationalism to Globalization: Blackwell Publishers, Cambridge.

Randi Ronning Balsvik (2007). The Quest for Expression: State and the University in Ethiopia Under Three Regimes, 1952-2005, Addis Ababa University Press, Ethiopia.

Rao, R.K. (ed) (2000), Women and Education: Kalpoz Publications, New Delhi.

Roman Gebreselassie (2000) Women Empowerment in Ethiopia: The Case of Tigray, Century University.

Ronit Lentin, http://ireland.iol.ie/~mazzoldi/toolsforchange/postmet/feminist.html

Reskin, Barbara and Padavic, Irene (1994), Women and Men at Work. Thousand Oaks, CA: Pine Fore Press.

Roman G. Sellassie and Gennet Taddesse, "The Role of Ethiopian Women in the Struggle for Equality, Democracy and Freedom" Amharic Paper presented at the Nation, Nationality Conference, Nov. 29, 2004 E. C.

Roger, D. (1980), "Education and The Capitalist State: Contributions and Contradictions?" in Apple, M.W. (ed), *Culture and Economic Reproduction in Education*. Essays on Class, Ideology and the State, Routledge and Kegan Paul, pp. 127-61.

Rowland, Jo (1995), 'Empowerment Examined', Development in Practice, 5 (2), pp. 101-7.

Rukata, Sara (2002), "La Problematique du Genre en Republique Demcoratique du Congo (RDC)/Zaire'epistemologies", paper presented at CODESRIA conference on African Gender in the New Millennium, Cairo, Egypt.

Sachs, J. and Warner M. (1995), "Natural Resource Abundance and Economic Growth", National Bureau of Economic Research Working Paper No. 5398, Cambridge, MA.

Sangari, Kumkum and Vaid Sudesh (eds), (1989), *Recasting Women*, Essays in Colonial History: Kali for Women, New Delhi.

Schultz, T.P. (1985) "Changing World Prices, Women's Wages, and the Fertility Transition in Sweden", Stockholm, pp. 1860-1910.

——(1994), "Human Capital, Family Planning and their Effects on Population Growth", American Economics Review 84, 255-260.

——(1997), "Demand for Children in Low Income Countries", in M. Rosenzweig and O. Stark (ed.), Handbook of Population and Family Economics, Amsterdam.

——(2002). "Why Governments should Invest More to Educate Girls." World Development, 30(2): 207-225. Oxford: Elsevier Science Ltd.

Schoeman, Maxi (2004), "Where are the Women and How are They Today? An Overview of the SADC Region", Occasional Paper, Copenhagen, University of Copenhagen, Center of African Studies.

Schwartz, H. and J. Jacobs (1979), Qualitative Sociology: A Method to the Madness. New York: Free Press.

Seidman, Gay W. (1989), "Women in Zimbabwe: Post Independence Struggle". *Feminist Studies*, No. 3.

Seltene Seyoem: "A History of Ethiopian Women and the Resistance: 1935-1941", Research Report to the Organization for Social Science Research in Eastern Africa, Addis Ababa, Ethiopia. (Dec. 1994).

Seguino, S. (1997), "Source of Slow Growth in American Economies", *Journal of African Economies*, 6:335-76.

——(2000), "Gender Inequality and Economic Growth: A Cross-Country Analysis", *World Development*, 28: 1211-1230.

Sen, Amartya (1995), *Inequality Reexamined*: Oxford University Press, New Delhi.

——(1999), *Development as Freedom*: Kalpoz, New York.

——(2004), *Social Exclusion, Concepts of Application Scrutiny Critical Quest*, New Delhi.

Smith, L. and L. Haddad (1999), "Explaining Child Malnutrition in Developing Countries", *International Food Policy Research Institute Research Report No. 111*, Washington DC.

Smith, L., U, Rama Krishnan, Haddad, L. and Others. (2001). "The Importance of Women's Status for Child Nutrition in Developing Countries", International Food Policy Research Institute, Draft Policy Report, Washington DC.

Srinivasan, Bina (2007), *Negotiating, Feminist Complexities — Collection of essays*: Promilla Publisher, New Delhi.

Tenesh, (Stand up) (1967 E.C). Amharic Paper of Ethiopian Women Coordinating Committee.

Tenesh Ethiopiawit, (Stand up Ethiopian Women), (1964 EC), *Journal of International Ethiopian Women Study Club*, Vol. 1, No. 2.

Steady, Filomina Chioma (2002), "An Investigative Framework for Gender Research in Africa in the New Millennium", Paper Presented at CODESRIA Conference on African Gender in the New Millennium, Cairo, Egypt.

Stiglitz, Joseph (2006), *Making Globalization Work*, Penguin Books Ltd., London.

Staudet, Kathelen (1984), "Women, Development and the State: On the Theoretical Impasse". *Development and Change*, 17, 2, 1986.

Subbarao, K. and Raney, L. (1995), "Social Gains from Female Education: A Cross-National Study." *Economic Development and Cultural Change*, 44 (1): 105-28.

Subrahmanian, R. (2002), "Gender and Education. A Review of Issues for Social Policy." Programme Paper No. 9 Geneva: UNRISD (United Nations Research Institute for Social Development).

Tamale, Sylvia (1998), *When Hens Begin to Crow: Gender and Parliamentary Politics in Uganda*, Boulder, West View Press.

Tanya Lyons, "Guns and Guerrilla Girls: Women in the Zimbabwean National Liberation Struggle" PhD thesis submitted to the Department of Politics, the University of Adelaide, South Australia in 1999.

——2002. "Gender Trauma in Africa: Enhancing Women's Links to Resources", paper presented at CODESRIA conference on 'African Gender in the New Millennium, Cairo, Egypt, April 2002.

Taylor, A. (1998), "On the Costs of Inward-looking Development", *Journal of Economic History*, 58:1-28.

Tesfaye, Demelash (1985), On Marxism and Ethiopian Student Radicalism in North America, http://findarticles.com/p/articles/mi_m1132/is_v35/ai_3115716/

Tesfaye Demmellash,"Marxism and Ethiopian Student Radicalism in North America", A Monthly Review.

Tekeste Negash (1990), The Crises of Ethiopian Education – Some Implication for Nation Building". Uppsala: Reprocentralen HSC.

——1996, *Rethinking Education in Ethiopia*, Uppsala: Nordiska Africa Institute.

Teshome Yzengaw (2006), "Implication of the Ethiopian Higher Education Expansion Strategy towards Quality, Equity and Reform", Unpublished paper.

Thakur, Ram Naresh (2000), "Education and Political Status of Indian Women – Key of Economic Development" in Anita Banerji, Raj Kumar Sen (eds), *Women and Economic Development*, Deep and Deep Publications Pvt. Ltd, Delhi.

Thankur, Devendra and Thankur, D.N. (2001). (eds), *Vocational and Technical Education*, Deep and Deep Publications Pvt. Ltd, Delhi.

"The Current Situation of Women in Ethiopia", A Report to the World Bank by Eva Poluna.

The Economic Equity Argument, www.idrc.ca/en/ev-42962-201-1-DO_TOPIC.html

The Federal Democratic Republic of Ethiopia's Constitution and Development", paper presented.

"The Portrayal of Women in Ethiopian Television Advertisement", A Thesis submitted to the School of Journalism and Communications, Addis Ababa in 2006.

Thomas, D. (1990), "Intrahousehold Resource Allocation: An Inferential Approach." *Journal of Human Resources*, 25:634-64.

Tietjen, Karen (1991), Educating Girls: Strategies to Increase Access, Persistence and Achievement, Creative Associates International, Inc. Washington D.C.

Tinker, I. (2002), "Many Paths to Power: Women in Contemporary Asia," Unpublished Paper.

——2002. "Quotas for Women in Elected Legislatures: Does This Really Empower Women?" Paper for WGGP Symposium 2002: Gender and Transnational Networks, October 17 – 19, University of Illinois Champaign/Urbana.

Tizeta, Mulugeta Yimam (2006). "Opportunities and Challenges focusing on Ethiopian Women and the Relevance of Women Development", Women's Development Institute Program, Addis Ababa.

Touré, Marema (2002), La recherche sur le genre en Afrique: quelques aspects épistémologiques, théoriques et culturels', paper presented at CODESRIA Conference on African Gender in the New Millennium, Cairo, Egypt, April 2002.

Transitional Government of Ethiopia (1992), "A Proclamation to Provide for the Establishment of National/Regional Self Government" Negarit Gazetta, 51st No. 2.

Trufat, Bekele (1998), "Women and Men in Ethiopia" OXFAM, Great Britain, Ethiopia, Addis Ababa.

Tsehai, Berhane Selassie (1984), "In Search of Ethiopian Women", CERTWID, (Unpublished Paper)

Tsehai Berhane Sellassie (1991) (ed.) Gender Issues in Ethiopia, Institute of Ethiopian Studies, Addis Ababa University.

Tsigereda, Tafesse (1999), "Factors Affecting the Involvement of Female Students in Higher Education and the Contribution of Affirmative Action" Addis Ababa University, Department of Sociology and Social Administration, Addis Ababa.

Tylor, Charles (1994), "The Politics of Recognition", in Gutmann A. (Ed.), Multiculturalism: Princeton University Press, Princeton.

Tzannatos, Z. (1999), "Women and Labour Market Changes in the Global Economy: Growth Helps, Inequalities Hurt and Public Policy Matters", World Development, 27(3): 551-569. Oxford: Elsevier Science Ltd.

UNICEF (2003), Gender Disparity in Ethiopian Primary Education, Ethiopia, Addis Ababa.

——(2005), Taking Stock of Girls' Education in Ethiopia, Preparing for Ethiopian Sector Development Program III (ESDP III), Ethiopia, Addis Ababa.

——(2007), Gender Disparities in Primary Education in Ethiopia: Challenges, Prospects and Best Practices, Ethiopia, Addis Ababa.

UNESCO, (2000), Right to Education, Scope and Implementation.

UNESCO, (2001), National Education Policies and Programmes and International Cooperation, What Role for UNESCO.

——, (2004), Taking Stock of Girls' Education in Ethiopia: Preparing for ESDP III.

United Nations (1993), Human Development Report. New York, Oxford University Press.

——(1980), Deble, Isabelle, The School Education of Girls: UNESCO, Paris.

——(1985), Bisraria, Sarojini "Identification and Elimination of Sex Stereotypes in and from Education programmes and School Textbooks": Mimeographed, UNESCO, Paris.

——(1988), Allasebu Gebresellasie "A Situation of Women in Ethiopia – A Review" Report to the U.N. Inter-Agency Group on W.I.D.

——(1992), Psacharopoulos, G., and Z. Tzannatos, eds. Case Studies on Women's Employment and Pay in Latin America, Washington D.C., World Bank.

——(1995), Women, Changing Global Economy – 1994 World Survey on the Role of Women in Development: Department for Policy Coordination and Sustainable Development, New York.

——(1994), "Human Capital, Family Planning and their Effects on Population Growth", *American Economies Review* 84, 255-260.

——(1995), Women: Looking Beyond 2000: United Nations Publication, New York.

——(1995), "Report of the Fourth World Conference on Women", New York. http://www.un.org/esa/gopher-data/conf/fwcw/off/a—20.en

——(1995), Haddad, W.D.; Demsky T. Education Policy—Planning Process: An Applied Framework. UNESCO, Paris.

——(1996 – 1999), Agreed Conclusions on the Critical Areas of Concern of the Beijing Platform for Action.

——(1997), IPU "Convention on the Elimination of All Forms of Discrimination against Women (CEDAW) and its protocol, "Women's Right in the Public and Political Life", No. 36, New Delhi.

——(1997), "Source of Slow Growth in American Economies", *Journal of African Economies*. 6:335-76.

——(1998), "Women in Africa's Development": African Recovery Briefing Paper. United Nations Publications, New York.

——(1998), "National Machineries for Gender Equality", Presented at the Expert Group Meeting August 31 – September 4, 1998, Santiago, Chile.

——(1999). CEDAW The Optional Protocol to the Convention on the Elimination of All Forms of Discrimination against Women: Text and Materials, Article 4.

——2000,. "Millennium Declaration", Department of Economic and Social Affairs Commission for Status of Women, New York.

——(2000). The World's Women 2000. Trends and Statistics. New York.

——2001. "Empowerment of Women throughout the Life Cycle as a Transformative Strategy in Poverty Eradication": Report of the expert group meeting Division for the Advancement of Women (DAW) 26-29.

——. 2001. "World Development Report 2000/2001 – Attacking Poverty": Oxford University Press.

United Nations (2002). "Education for All. Is the World on Track?" Paris.

——2002. Benschop, M. "Rights and Reality. Are Women's Equal Rights to Land, Housing and Property Implemented in East Africa?" Nairobi, Kenya: United Nations Human Settlements Programme (UN-HABITAT)

——2002. Cheston, S., and L. Kuhn "Empowering Women Through Microfinance", New York: UNIFEM.

——2002. Human Development Report 2002. New York and Oxford: Oxford University Press.

——2004. Ethiopia, A National Report on Progress Made in the Implementation of the Beijing Platform for Action.

——2006. Breines, Ingeborg and D'Orville, Hans, Sixty Women Contributing to the Sixty Years of UNESCO: UNESCO, Paris.

——2007. Promoting Gender Equality and Women's Empowerment, Global Monitoring Report.

——. 2008. Land Registration in Ethiopia: Early Impacts on Women.

United States International Development (1991). Educating Girls: Strategies to increase access, persistence and achievement, Washington DC.

——2007. Review of the Ethiopian Education Training Policy and its Implementation, Addis Ababa.

——2002. "Women's Property and Inheritance Rights: Improving Lives in Changing Times." Washington D.C.

Van de Moortele, J. (2002). "Are the MDGs Feasible?" New York: UNDP.

Valerie Bryson Foreword by Elizabeth Meehan (1992). Feminist Political Theory, Paragon House (New York)

Yeshi H. Mariam, "Ethiopian Women in the Period of Socialist Transformation" in 1994.

Vijfhuizen, Carin (2001). Losing Control: Gender and Land in Massaca Irrigation Scheme, Maputo Province', in Rachel Waterhouse and Carin Vijfhuizen, (ed.), Strategic Women,

Gainful Men: Gender, Land and Natural Resources in Different Rural Contexts in Mozambique,

Maputo, Nucleo de Estudos de Terra, Faculty of Agronomy and Forestry Engineering, University of Eduardo Mondlane and Action Aid-Mozambique.

Walby, S. (1990), Theorizing Patriarchy. Oxford: Basil Blackwell.

Walleligne, Mekonnen (1969), 'On the Question of Nationalities in Ethiopia', Struggle, Vol. V. No. 1, Nov. 17, by the University Students Union of Addis Ababa University.

Walker, Stephen and Bolton, Len (1983), (eds), Gender, Class and Education: The Palmer Press, Sussex.

Wharton, Amy. S., (1996), "Human Development Report", New York, Oxford University Press.

——(2006), The Sociology of Gender: An Introduction to Theory and Research: Blackwell Publishing, Oxford.

Wolpe, Anna Maria (1997), "Education and the Sexual Division of Labour in Feminism and Materialism", Routledge and Kegan Paul.

Wolpe and Oslen (1977), "Some Process in Sexist Education", London, Women's Research and Resource Center.

Becky Ellis, March (2007), Why Feminism isn't for Everybody www.newsocialist.org/index.php.

WLSA, Botswana (1999), Chasing the Mirage: Women and the Administration of Justice, Gaborone, WLSA.

WLSA Mozambique (2001), Power and Violence: Homicide and Femicide in Mozambique, Maputo, WLSA.

WLSA Zambia (1999), Justice in Zambia: Myth or Reality? Women and the Administration of Justice, Lusaka, WLSA.

"Women in Ethiopia: Problems and Prospects" by Almaz Eshete, Paper presented at the Seminar on Gender Issues in Ethiopia, January 1991 Addis Ababa University.

——(2001) Gender Violence: The Invisible Struggle: Responses of the Justice Delivery System in Zambia, Lusaka, WLSA.

WLSA Zimbabwe (2000) In the Shadow of the Law: Women and Justice Delivery in Zimbabwe, Harare, WLSA.

Women's Political Participation, Meeting on Women and Political Participation: 21st Century Challenges, www.idrc.ca/en/ev-42962-201-1-DO_TOPIC.html

——Summers, L. (1994), "Investing in All the People", Washington DC.

——(1997), "Demand for Children in Low Income Countries" in M. Rosenzweig and O. Stark (editors) Handbook of Population and Family Economics, Amsterdam.

——(1998),. Filmer, D., King, E. M., and Pritchett L. "Gender Disparity in South Asia: Comparison between and within Countries": Development and Research Group, Washington, D.C.

——(1998), Gaynor Cathy, Decentralization of Education, Teachers Management, Washington D.C.

——(1998), Implementing the Ethiopian National Policy for Women, Washington DC.

——(1999), Filmer, D. "The Structure of Social Disparities in Education: Gender and Wealth." Policy Research Report on Gender and Development, Working Paper Series, No. 5, Washington D.C.

——(1999), Standing, G. "Global Feminization Through Flexible Labour: A Theme Revisited": *World Development*, 27: 583-602.

——1999. Klasen, S. "Does Gender Inequality Reduce Growth and Development? Evidence from Cross-Country Regressions", World Bank Policy Research Report Working Paper No. 7, Washington DC.

——1999. Gatti, R. "A Cross-Country Analysis of Fertility Determinants": Mimeographed. Washington DC, The World Bank.

——2000. Mason, Andrew D: King, Elizabeth M: "Engendering Development Through Gender Equality in Rights, Resources and Voice" Policy Research Report Publication, Vol. I A.

——2001. Engendering Development: Through Gender Equality in Rights, Resources and Voice. Policy Research Report. Oxford: Oxford University Press.

——2002. Narayan, Deepa, Empowerment and Poverty Reduction: A Sourcebook. Washington DC.

——2004. Abu-Ghaida, Dina and Klasen Stephan, "The Economic and Human Development Cost of Missing the Millennium Development Goal and Gender Equity", Washington DC.

——2005. Alrop, R. and Heinsohn "Measuring Empowerment in Practice: Structuring and Framing Indicators", Policy Research Working Paper, Washington DC.

——2006. Gender Equality as Smart Economics. A World Bank Group Gender Action Plan, (Fiscal Years 2007-10)

——2007. "Ethiopia Accelerating Equitable Growth", A Country Economic Memorandum, Poverty Reduction and Economic Management Unit, Washington D.C.

——2007. "The Role of Education Quality in Economic Growth".

——2008. Unleashing Potential of Ethiopian Women.

Yamarak, S. and Ghosh S. (2003), "Is Female Education Productive? A Reassessment", Mimeographed: Tufts University, Medford.

Yeshi, Haile Mariam (1994), "Ethiopian Women in the Period of Socialist Transformation, Economic and Political Weekly".

Yeshimebrat, Mersha Kassa (2007). Gender Equality, Higher Education, Transformation and Reform in sub-Saharan Africa: The Ethiopian Experience, Phd Desertation.

Yeshimebrat M., Alemayehu B., Dawit A. and Yismaw Nigussie (2009), "The Study of Policy Intervention on Factors Affecting Female and Causes of Attrition in Higher Learning Institution of Ethiopia", A Study Paper submitted to MoE, Gender office.

Young, A. (1995), "The Tyranny of Numbers: Confronting the Statistical Realities of the East Asian Growth Experience", *Quarterly Journal of Economics*, 110(3): 641-680.

Young, Iris Marion (1990), Justice and the Politics of Difference, Princeton, NJ, Princeton University Press.
ZHENG Yongnian, GUO Xiajuan and Zhao Litao, "Women's Political Participation in China", EAI Background in 2009.
Zenebework, Taddesse (2003). "Gender Policy Dialogue', Forum for Social Studies, Ethiopia, Addis Ababa.
Zenebework, Bisrat (1986), Research Priorities on Women and Employment in Ethiopia, Unpublished paper.

Websites

www.developmentgateway.org
www.worldbank.org/education
www.Unesco.org
www.undp.org/women
www.unifem.org
www.un.org./womenwatch
www.undp.org/policy/docs/undg
www.unmillenniumproject.org
www.mdgender.net
www.worldbank.org/povery/stratagies/chapters/gender.htm
www.gender-budgets.org
www.iaffe.org-the
www.genderaction.org
www.un.org/rights-universal
www.ohchr.org/english/bodies/index.htm
www.iwraw-ap.org
www.whrmet.org
www.un.org/reform/dossier.htm
www.onorg/esa/coordination/ecasoc
www.unfoundation.org/program/index.asp
www.ilo.org/public/english/bureau/gender

Index